AF400901

The Capital of the Superficial

The Capital of the Superficial

Julia Firley

Copyright © 2023 Julia Firley

Julia Firley has asserted her right to be identified
as the author of this work in accordance with
the (UK) Copyright, Designs and Patents Act 1988.

All rights reserved. No portion of this book may be reproduced,
stored in a retrieval system, transmitted, in any form or by any
means, without written permission from the publisher.

Published by Liberty In Print

First edition

ISBN 9788396544650

To my family

Contents

Introduction

Nothing is as it seems. The illusion is a means, and the façade is power.

Humans are first and foremost storytellers, and expatriates tend to have the best stories. The ones in this book have colourful experiences, complex personalities, real struggles, astonishing resilience, and in many cases, a remarkable grasp of reality. There is the German girl who came to hide from her past, the French wife whose husband left her for a younger woman, but she managed to turn it all around and emerge more successful than ever, the Slovak who traded herself for promises that proved to be lies, and the American who made a home in Arabia. Then, there are the locals who stood up to the authority and the countless renowned intellectuals who resigned themselves to servitude and duplicity.

This is a story of how a small, impoverished country was transformed almost overnight into a wealthy, corrupt, powerful welfare state controlled by a few shrewd families. We will observe what happened to the people who found themselves wealthy all of a sudden. We will also see how foreigners flocked from all corners of the world to work there, or to exploit others. A system was created to serve the interests of the few at the expense of many. A society was brainwashed into accepting a deep-rooted, thinly veiled caste system and a Big Brother-style regime. The small country amassed power and influence over superpowers. They used their money and realpolitik to interfere in the affairs of other countries. The façade became the strength, and lies superseded truth.

Alongside true stories, the book presents facts and analysis that should give cause for concern because what happened in the oil rich state is taking place in various countries worldwide.

$$\text{CHAPTER 1}$$

Normal Schizophrenia

'We've had a new patient in the clinic today who hears voices. She says there are strangers in her home; she is convinced the voices are real. She is paranoid,' says one psychiatrist to another with a smile while we are all sitting having our coffee by the marina.

'Ah, schizophrenia then?'

'Yes, finally a textbook case of a "normal" mental disorder. Something I can treat. All of the other cases we've had this week are the usual suppressed people from controlling, conservative families. Or victims of domestic abuse. And how am I supposed to help them? Tell them to cut all family ties? Move to the States?'

'I know what you mean. I feel paralysed listening to all these stories. You'd have to see the case I saw yesterday. She was stunning! I couldn't contain myself. I could fall in love with her instantly. And an educated person, too; she studied in Seattle. She thinks she's depressed but she doesn't meet any of the criteria for depression. Her parents married her off to a man from their circle. She had never seen him before. She was weeping, and I wanted to weep with her. She said she is anxious, she feels like crying all the time, and she can't focus. She asked me if there was any medication that could help her – she just wants to forget about everything and fall asleep.'

'Did you prescribe anything?'

'Like what? I asked her, "What are you going to do with your life?" She said, "What can I do? I can never divorce my husband

and go back to live with my parents. I will give him five or six kids and wait until death separates us." I told her she was going to live an unhappy life. She replied, "Look around you, who's happy?"'

That conversation between my friends took place years ago but it's still stuck in my brain.

~

When I came to Kuwait, I kept making new acquaintances and friends. I was curious to learn about people's stories, and also I could afford the time to listen. I met people from different walks of life: housewives, hairdressers, architects, ambassadors, teachers, house maids, shop assistants. Some of them were Europeans, some were Kuwaitis, Arabs, Filipinos, Americans. One of my friends happened to be a psychiatrist who had studied in Canada, and through her, I met a few of her colleagues.

Strangers in a foreign land, we watched in surprise how our presumptions, analogies, and expectations were crushed one by one, and we struggled to comprehend how things operated behind the curtain. Some of us assumed we knew; some left it at that and focused on their own joys and troubles. And some of us became lay social scientists and investigators, trying to make sense of ourselves, these people, and the country. We went around, talked with the locals, read articles and books. We drew analogies, came up with theories and explanations, only to later discover that our initial conclusions were often wrong.

What we initially agreed on was that this society differed considerably from our own ones. Yet, soon we discovered they are on their way to becoming like the Kuwaiti one.

From infidelity to the Middle East

It was 10th December, afternoon, and heavy dark clouds loomed outside as cold rain seeped down. I was staring blankly at my screen, trying very hard to focus on my work, the sixth cup of tea that day standing on my desk. What excuse could I use? I have to leave this office before I die of boredom. I knocked on my boss's door:

'Evelyn, could I leave a bit early? This weather makes me want to kill myself.'

'I can see what you mean. I have this terrible headache today. Do you have any urgent work?'

'There are a couple of things I'd like to finish. I can do that from home.'

'Fine, fine, go. Just get me some paracetamol before you leave, could you?'

'Sure.' I went to look for the painkillers, a smile appearing on my face.

We had been living in London for five years. I loved that city so full of life, green parks, museums, and beautiful bridges. On weekends, we went for morning jogs and indulged in the fanciest afternoon tea. We would party with a small pack of friends, go to the theatre, make out-of-town trips. Only the dreary weather… oh God, let the winter finish already.

I was going home, in my mind's eye seeing my dear husband half-lying in an unmade bed, with a laptop on his lap, as he did every day for the past month. He would sit there or in the armchair, still in his pyjama, one foot propped against his other knee, vigorously tapping on his keyboard, sending out yet another job application to a university on the other side of the globe. Despite completing a PhD at a reputable university, getting a suitable job was proving to be a nightmare of sorts. Is this what searching for an academic post looked like? A week ago, he was happy because he got an interview at a university in Fiji. I'm not even sure where Fiji is!

Most of his friends from the doctoral programme were not doing much better. A couple of them went back to their previous jobs; one friend became a sheep farmer in New Zealand while searching for a post, another friend works at a nearby wine shop.

The second I opened the front door to our flat, I felt that something was wrong: the floor had been cleared – the piles of books and papers had disappeared, and there was a pleasant scent of perfume mixed with the smell of cooked dinner in the air. Oh no, we only just got married and he's already cheating on me. I didn't utter a word. He ran over to me, hugged and kissed me, and I stood there, frozen, frantically trying to work out who she was and what I was going to do to her. What am I going to do to him? Throw him out in the street? But this is his place, he pays the rent. Leave? But where am I going to go? He began to babble something incoherently, and then he suddenly exclaimed:

'I got a job!'

I jumped for joy but then I noticed his face expression, which was not joyful at all. What did it mean? I couldn't wait to get out of this place, escape this bitter cold and my boss constantly talking about herself, her new diet which would allow her to lose another ten pounds in six days and find a charming man at least ten years younger than her. Living in a small rented flat an hour away from my work was also taking its toll on me. And then he dropped the bomb:

'It is in Kuwait.'

I felt like someone struck me over the head with a sledge-hammer. Kuwait? In that case, give me Fiji or infidelity.

A country profile of myths and facts

As someone who has studied economics, I couldn't resist creating a statistical profile that contained every detail I could find about the country I was about to move to, long before buying my plane ticket. I spent hours poring over charts that presented the demographics, income distribution, crime rate, and political system. The problem is that figures and charts can only go so far in capturing the essence of a place. For one thing, these metrics describe constructs, not people. Average household wealth is not the same as a person's socio-economical status. We can belong to the top one percentile today and fall to the bottom of the ladder a few years later, and crime rates are not always indicative of how safe a given neighbourhood is. Statistical data is nothing without context. In some cases, we may even find that a certain metric was defined inaccurately on purpose. The same politician who got elected on promises to boost the economy would claim that the situation has improved since he took office even if it worsened and he would find statistics to support his claim. In Kuwait, you see this manipulation of facts even without setting a foot in the country. The same government which in 1990 claimed that there were over a million Kuwaitis, in 1991 stated that the number of nationals was 640,000.

Another way to understand a country is by reading its constitution and laws. Unlike North America and most of Europe, the Kuwaiti constitution declares a religion for the state, which is Islam – similarly to fifty other Muslim countries. This means that there is no separation between the church and the state, or, to be precise, the mosque and the state. Penal laws regulate private life as much as the public space. Intimate relationships, dietary and religious practices, attire are the business of the state. In Kuwait, as well as the other fifty countries, consensual sex between two unmarried adults is a serious crime. Homosexuality is a crime punishable by law, not – a private matter. Apostasy is considered a threat to the peace and order, not – a personal choice. Polygamy is legal, and objecting to it on principle is a violation of the law.

My first impressions of Kuwait were: a dingy airport, the conversation with customs officers I had anxiously anticipated, and then, out in the night, the brightly illuminated and wide, black three-lane road leading to my new home. A very modern, smooth, three-lane road with many exits, bridges, and intersections.

During the day, the dark-grey of tarmac is accompanied by a sandy beige in the colour palette of Kuwait's landscape. Sandy-beige ground, beige sky, beige houses stretch as far as the eye can see. And the low hedge running along Kuwaiti roads conceals the fact that there is nothing but sand beyond it.

This beige tint squeezes its way into houses and apartments. You will find a layer of light-orange dust on the sink when washing your face in the morning and on the shelf when reaching for a book. It even lands on crockery inside kitchen cupboards. A German friend of mine would get vexed every time there is a sandstorm: 'For goodness' sake, I live in the most expensive high-rise, not in a cardboard box next to the street!'

Every time I used to imagine the desert, a romantic picture would come to my mind: dunes of golden sand with a wavy pattern painted by the wind, oases with crystal clear water and a thousand and one nights of passion. The reality of Arabia is by no means cinematic. The desert is a mixture of grey and beige, studded with stones and meagre plants but what is ubiquitous are piles of everlasting rubbish left by people who camped there. You can encounter snakes and scorpions and from time to time a lizard, which is considered a delicacy by some of the nomads.

Humankind can tame this ground with the greatest difficulty. Maintaining a patch of green in front of the house costs inconceivable amounts of money and effort. It means watering three times a day throughout most of the year, applying fertiliser. The plants alone are expensive because a big majority of them are imported. A mature palm tree can cost over $1500. Greenery is definitely a luxury good.

Some Kuwaitis do their best to bring the much coveted and desired greenery into their households. My husband and I did, too. First, we bought beautiful small lemon and orange trees but it was a foolish idea and soon the trees withered. After that, we would buy plants more suited to the local climate. We had a small pomegranate tree, a variety of creeping jasmine, lush rosemary shrubs and a cardamom plant. Shopping for them alone was a pleasure. Every time we browsed in the gardening centres, our eyes would light up like a child with a pocket full of coins in a sweet shop. Preferably we'd have half of the stock. It is hard not to notice that many houses and neighbourhoods are devoid of greenery.

                        ~

Velvety black, sticky oil spilling out of wells and into barrels. Dazzling sunshine hitting the eyes and heat pouring down from cloudless skies on the heads of thousands of workers. The horizon embellished with imposing high-rise office towers, grand palaces and family mansions, each one more beautiful than the previous. Streets full of luxury sedans and SUVs, carrying their passengers to never-ending shopping sprees in gigantic malls with a myriad of designer boutiques, fashionable cafés, and high-rated restaurants. One phrase to sum it up: easy money.

But it is a complex and multifaceted place, despite the initial impression.

All kinds of people arrive. Some are drawn by familial ties. Most see it as an opportunity to improve their material stance. 'I will be making much more money than in my homeland. The work is hard and the hours long but I will be getting more than a fair income. I know it is less than the locals get, but the salary is good enough for me. In a couple of years, I will have saved up for my dream.'

We, Westerners, think of the locals as conservative Muslims who pray five times a day after they hear the call booming from the minarets. Their wives wear black and cover their hair. They divorce Western women after they are done with them or keep them and their children hostage. We used to read about that in the papers. After a few months here, we start thinking that many of them are more like us in the West: liberal, tolerant, and fun-loving. There are a few churches and some religious minorities are free to practice their faiths.

Many foreigners complain that Kuwaitis are paid big salaries for nothing. All they do is shop, eat, smoke shisha, and sip tea in *dewaniyas* while they gossip and argue loudly and fervently. They live in grand houses with numerous servants; they have many wives and even more children who go to state-funded schools. They get free healthcare at home and abroad. And they don't pay any taxes. None. We, immigrants, have to put in the work, whether it is here or in our homelands, and count every penny. These people are lucky and they boast about it.

His Highness the Emir runs the state. According to the Kuwaiti constitution, the emir is the head of the executive, judicial, and legislative branches of government. He is also the head of all armed forces. Only a member of a tight circle within al-Sabah family can become an emir. The government controls the oil revenues, which make up nearly the entire budget of the country. The Kuwaiti dinar is the highest-priced currency in the world: one dinar equals roughly three US dollars. World leaders and heads of the most powerful states reckon with the say of these sheikhs. Wherever they go in the world, presidents and prime ministers, kings and queens welcome them with honours and show respect.

In the public arena, they are called generous, charitable; they are called a 'humanitarian leader of our world'. The rulers of the small emirate should not be underestimated. They have outsmarted the West on many occasions. They own the world's oldest sovereign wealth fund worth around $750 billion in assets and significant holdings in major corporations worldwide.

Kuwaiti dignitaries have played mediators in different political disputes in the Middle East. They have hosted international summits and humanitarian aid conferences; they have given millions of dinars to charity. In 2018, Kuwait hosted International Conference for the Reconstruction of Iraq. It is little known that since 1991, Kuwait has collected $52.4 billion from Iraq in reparations, the final payment of $44m having been made on 13th January 2022. Kuwaiti institutions had lodged claims with the UN Compensation Commission for the total of $352.5 billion. Critics argue that it was unjust for the Iraqi nation to bear the financial burden of Saddam Hussein's actions, as they were not responsible for his deeds. It has been also suggested that Kuwait was awarded this significant sum of money through its influence over Western politicians and institutions.

Meanwhile, international media constantly report on infringements on personal freedoms in the country. Human Rights Watch keeps issuing reports about Kuwaiti courts sentencing their own citizens to 5 years imprisonment for offending religion, the state, or the head of state on Twitter. Could these reports be true? Five years in jail for a tweet. They lead readers to believe that the state thwarts any expressions of opinion that carry a hint of criticism against it. They reinforce the notion that the Kuwaiti regime is something to be feared. Kuwaitis must feel suffocated in their homeland. These people are not lucky and they know it.

～

Once a Kuwaiti is born, he or she gets $150 a month from the government until the day they turn 26 or get a job, whichever comes first. The same government gives every family a plot of land and a $230,000 interest-free loan to build a house. Education is free from kindergarten to postgraduate level and thousands of Kuwaitis study in the United States, Canada, Great Britain, and other countries on scholarships awarded by the government. A Kuwaiti student receives $3000 as a monthly allowance while studying abroad or $600 a month if they study inside the country. All Kuwaitis enjoy a free health services cover and every year thousands of them are sent to the best hospitals in North America and Europe to be treated for cancer and other serious diseases at the expense of their government.

Having lived in Kuwait makes one see a different picture. At first sight a country flowing with riches, it has an ailing health-care system, practically no public transport and one of the most dysfunctional and disregarded education systems in the world[1], where the curriculum worsens each year. In the Global Competitiveness Report of 2019, Kuwait stood very low in the category of labour market, innovation, and graduate skill-set.[2] Phrases like 'natural environment' and 'taking care of the planet' exist merely on the pages of children's books – they have been sidelined in the government's agenda. Still, this all has a bearing on the inhabitants' welfare. Kuwaitis, whenever they can afford it, resort to the use of private hospitals and private schools; they leave to distant parts of the world to breathe fresher air, spend time in the nature, enjoy art and culture. A big number of the roads are in a terrible shape and

---

1 In 2003, Kuwait ranked 116. worldwide in public spending on education, estimated at 3.76% of GDP (UNESCO). More recent reliable data is not available.

2 Global Competitiveness Report is issued annually by World Economic Forum. In the category of labour market, Kuwait comes 101st out of 141 countries; in human capital: skills – 77th; in innovation capability – 108th, in the skill-set of secondary school and university graduates – 112th, and in time required to start a business – 125th. It holds 1st place in macroeconomic stability together with 32 other countries. Ranks for year 2019.

trash piles up in many areas. Kuwaiti families have to wait for over 15 years to get the free plot of land and the interest-free loan, and frequently the offered land will be in the middle of nowhere. And the loan is not enough to build a house in that expensive country, where all the materials are imported and monopolised by the few big companies. There is no such thing as a free market here.

A friend of mine, a Canadian Moroccan, kept repeating every time we went for a walk: 'I tried reading about Kuwait before we moved here and the only thing I found was that it's the richest country in the world. Where are the riches? This looks worse than any poor area in Morocco.'

Not all Kuwaitis are rich. They do their best to look rich, and some have the delusion of being rich. The dream about a life in splendour, in a palace laid with marble, surrounded by fountains and servants spending hours on polishing a collection of sports cars does not come true for everyone. It is reserved for the lucky individuals who were born into one of a few special families, or got into the right business at the right time. According to the Housing Ministry, around 80% of Kuwaiti families do not own a place to live and are renting, while the few affluent individuals claimed most of the land as their private property.

Not even all the members of the ruling family are wealthy as there are many important people for the wealth to be distributed among. For instance, Jaber Al-Ahmad Al-Sabah (ruled 1977-2006) had at least fifty children, and now these children have their own families. Each one of his wives and ex-wives – the estimated number being two hundred – got a share of the riches, too, and receives an allowance. In the area where I lived in Kuwait, there was an enormous house, or rather a palace, which that emir had given to one of his wives as a gift. When they were getting married, he was almost eighty, and she was a teenager (some say she wasn't even yet fifteen). A simple girl from a modest family became a multimillionaire (rumour talks of $250 million in cash). But not all the members of this circle are as lucky. What is more, any feuds within the family result in troublesome relatives or those who cross the red lines being cut off from influence and money.

The local perception of wealth and poverty differs from that in other regions of the world. There are no starving or homeless citizens here as Kuwait provides them with a broad range of social support. This includes a guaranteed job in a public institution, which often involves stamping documents in exchange for a salary of $1200-2000 a month, and/or benefits such as unemployment benefit, child benefit, disability benefit, widow's and divorcée's benefits, disabled child carer's allowance etc. For most Kuwaitis, poverty is the inadequate quality of education in public schools and of healthcare in local clinics; it is lack of one's own abode and occupying a cramped space in the in-laws' house; it is a Kia bought with a loan. Many people are in debt. Credit cards are easily given to citizens but harder to pay off. They can have multiple loans and credit cards, and no one will bat an eye, but when the payment deadline comes, the banks show no mercy. The instalments eat up their salary, and they go and borrow money from family or friends with a made-up reason to buy their groceries. In 2016, the Ministry of Justice issued 182 397 orders of travel bans (commonly known as the no-fly list) and arrest warrants, 90% of which were caused by unpaid bills, debt, overdue alimony.[3] Kings of the hill, top of the heap.

What about people who are not eligible for any kind of governmental benefits but whose permanent and only home, whose domicile, is in Kuwait? They are dependent on the charitable nature of the society. Driving to and back from a shopping mall along small side roads, every time I go past the same man sitting

---

3 There were 80,000 travel bans issued against Kuwaitis and expatriates in 2020, and 47,512 from January to end of October in 2021. In 2022, 5,495 travel bans were issued by the Family Court against citizens and residents. (Albayan online, 21 May 2006, in Arabic).

at a roundabout with a box of watermelons. He's there even in July, when the watermelon season has finished and the fruit offered for sale are unripe and tasteless. He covers his face with a *ghutra*, trying to protect it from the scorching sun. Is he a Bidoon? A refugee from one of the war-torn neighbouring countries? If this is not poverty, I don't know what is, I think to myself.

On various buildings all over the country, in every entrance to every public administration department, inside hospitals, in every classroom, courtroom, police station, and so on, big pictures of the ruler and his heir apparent hang. The faces of these old, stern men in their traditional attire and with dyed moustaches watch over their people and everything that goes on in the tiny state. The same pictures are printed on the inside cover of every schoolbook. From kindergarten to university, students are taught to praise the emir and his crown prince. Every official who appears on TV must start his talk by praising Allah, Muhammad, the Emir. Imams end their Friday sermon by asking Allah to protect the Emir and his Assistant and grant them their wishes. The motto of the Armed Forces is: Allah, Kuwait, the Emir. An entire department with 2000 workers and a 9 billion USD budget, the Amiri Diwan, is responsible for looking after the Emir and the ruling family. The one singular person – the emir – is head of the state, chief of the armed forces, head of the legislative authority, head of the executive branch, head of the oil council, and the head of judiciary. This one person appoints judges, ministers, army, and police personnel, has the right to dissolve the parliament, grant citizenship and revoke it. He is the source of all power, according to the constitution. The current Emir is the brother of the past two emirs who ruled from 1977 to 2020. Their father ruled from 1920 to 1950. Their grandfathers ruled before that. Criticising the emir is punishable by law with 10 years in prison and can be considered treason, which carries the penalty of capital punishment.

Most Kuwaitis still choose to see their country as democratic. It is common to attend a talk where the academic speaker who has a PhD from an American or British university viciously criticises the lack of democracy in the USA, Europe, Iran, Israel, or Syria. By the end of the talk, the fierce pro-democracy speaker would praise the Emir and the Kuwaiti constitution.

The hundred and fifty dollars a month, the interest-free loan, the various other benefits and handouts – are they an adequate pay for duplicity?

It seems that all these people have decided not to notice certain things, as this is more convenient. But like in every society, alongside the opportunistic, complacent, and narrow-minded individuals, as well as superstitious religious fundamentalists loudly promulgating their aspirations, you will find a group of open-minded, enlightened, and concerned citizens. Those who look beyond their back yard, who keep up to date with current politics, and care about the future, not just here and now. I've heard stories about people and of people, some quite young, who do not accept the existing reality and struggle like fish caught in a net. Often having studied abroad, they compare the life 'here' and 'there', not knowing whether to leave permanently or take up the Sisyphean task of fighting the system. By posting their opinions on Twitter, Instagram, or YouTube, they risk getting a prison sentence, losing their job, and at the very least being booked in for a night and unpleasant court proceedings. Finally, there are people desperately searching for a meaning for their lives between Starbucks and sushi, Gucci and Burberry, Porsche and Mercedes on the one side, and on the other side those who engage with enthusiasm in social discussions and charity projects. Nevertheless, we, foreigners, want to paint them with the same brush called 'oil, money, Islam' by force of habit.

CHAPTER 2

Ramadan. 'So many people are going to die'

June 2016 brought my first ever Ramadan in a Muslim country. For weeks before the holy month started, the interior ministry carried out a media campaign to warn people against disregarding its regulations.

To be clear, all residents of Kuwait, Muslim or not, are obliged not to drink, eat or smoke whether in public or at any place where others could see them, as stipulated by Law no. 44/1968. Breaking this law is punishable by up to one month in jail and a $300 fine, also for any persons who force or facilitate such behaviour for others. Any venue which enables eating or drinking would be closed down for two months. Many expatriates get detained, jailed, and deported for drinking water. All other Muslim countries have similar laws. Every year, people get arrested for eating or drinking or smoking in public, whether it is in Morocco, Egypt, Jordan, Iran.

A Kuwaiti professor who was a cancer patient told me that all the water fountains have been removed from hospitals, including the one where she goes for her treatment. Patients waiting for chemotherapy are not allowed to drink or eat because it is against the law, she told me in despair. 'Can you imagine that we were forced to hide bottles of water in our bags and go to the toilet to have a few sips? They also closed the canteens to prevent us from getting anything to eat. I am sixty-five years old but still not free to eat or drink when I please.'

Private cars, shops, workplaces, classrooms are classified as open spaces that fall under this law – others can see what is going on inside it. I have seen mothers driving around with blankets in the car, which they use to cover their elder children whenever they want to drink some water while on the road. A few years ago, a renowned novelist was arrested by the police and charged with breaching this law. She was at a hairdresser's when a couple of policemen stormed in to find her holding a cigarette. The story was covered in newspapers.

One day around noon, as my husband and I were coming home, we found a furniture delivery van parked in front of our house, searching for another address. The temperature outside was just under 50 degrees Celsius, and the workers in the van looked exhausted, to say the least. We asked them if they needed some water or food and they hesitantly accepted. We invited them inside our home to rest and cool off in the air conditioning. After they drunk some water and sat down, they seemed like entirely different people. Since dawn they hadn't touched any food or drink for fear of the harsh repercussions they might face. There were five young men in total, four of whom were Hindus. The fifth was a 22-year-old Egyptian who had come to Kuwait two years prior, as he told us. He had tears in his eyes as he shared his story while sipping his coffee. 'I am drained, starving, thirsty, and I have a terrible headache. Work starts at 6 a.m., which means that I must wake up around 5. I came to Kuwait so I could send money to my poor family in Egypt. I have five sisters who don't work and my father's pension is very small, so they are all dependent on me. I work ten hours a day, six days a week in this heat. I need coffee and food. I cannot fast, and I can't even say that to anyone.'

The Islamic calendar differs from the Gregorian calendar in that it follows the moon rather than the sun. Its year is 11 days shorter, hence, Ramadan keeps moving each solar year. During the time I lived in Kuwait, Ramadan fell in July, then slowly moved to June and finally May. These months are within the period of the biggest heat in the Middle East.

Before and during every Ramadan, numerous medical doctors appear on television to give their recommendations regarding fasting. They all affirm with a shocking level of confidence that indeed, it is healthy for all people to go all day without water and without food, even for those who take medication for chronic diseases such as hypertension, diabetes, epilepsy, and heart conditions. They assure that these patients should fast and take their medication only at night.

In many cases, these are the same physicians who are on TV all year round, in the remaining months explaining the importance of taking plenty of fluids, especially in the summer, as failure to do so might result in dehydration and kidney failure. They recommend that people should eat small quantities of food frequently.

The biggest stars in Ramadan are the imams who fill the airwaves with all kinds of talk shows for staggering pay checks. Some imams have TV or radio shows in which they preach, while others explain the Quran or the hadith. Some recite the Quran in a smooth, melodious voice, and some speak about the Prophet and glorify his life. The most popular shows are the ones in which imams answer callers' questions. Every year the same questions are repeated but the answers may vary from one imam to another. Many people watch these shows to learn about the rules, others for entertainment. Some even record calls they find hilarious and share them on social media. There are callers with chronic illness who are angry because their doctors told them not to fast and they want the imam to confirm it is perfectly safe and healthy to fast. There are people who ask if brushing one's teeth, showering, pretending to be sick to skip work is halal or not. In one phone call, an outraged man told an imam that he was in a crisis as he forgot it was Ramadan and made himself a heavy meal which he had just finished eating and which he described in detail. As the man was speaking, the imam's face said that he didn't believe a word of the tall tale but nonetheless he rushed to say that this was 'a gift from Allah; you need to continue fasting and thank Allah'. 'The meal was so heavy and salty, didn't you hear what I just said, I am so thirsty right now', the caller said indignantly. After thinking for some time, the imam told him to take his car and intend to travel. Once he has driven away from the city, he can break his fasting, as Allah permitted travellers to eat and drink. 'Remember, you will need to fast an extra day later to make up for this one,' the imam advised. The most interesting questions usually relate to sex. 'I am not sure if it was still night or not when my husband did something with me', a woman asks in a sensual voice. 'Can you elaborate? What did he do, what did he do?', the curious imam replies in one of these widely shared clips. Another caller asks if kissing her husband is permissible or not and if so, what should she do as she cannot help herself. A newlywed complains that her husband is not interested, 'all what he wants is to eat, sleep, and smoke'.

Some Kuwaitis are excited about the upcoming Ramadan. It's true that from the dawn prayer until the dusk prayer they won't be able to eat, drink, have sex, smoke but every evening and night is a festivity. It's as if you celebrated Christmas twenty-eight days in a row.

In Ramadan, the working day is shortened for the privileged minority of people so that those fasting – or from another perspective, those celebrating – have more time to rest. Kuwaitis anxiously await the announcement that dictates their working hours. Regardless of whether they will be told to come in at 8:30 or 10 in the morning (instead of 7:30), no one is going to reproach them for being a little late beyond that time, and then leaving early, while at noon taking a longer prayer break. Management will be doing the same. It is common knowledge that during that month no cases are going to move in ministry departments.

Meanwhile, the construction workers, delivery men – a big proportion of whom are not Muslims – work long hours in the heat, not allowed to have a sip of water. The injustice they experience in this region every year in this month attests to the different standards to which people are held. The divide between two societies living next to each other in this country cannot be clearer than during Ramadan. There are the natives who mainly work for the government. They sleep, they eat, they hardly go to work. 'Come tomorrow, the staff are not here.' Those who don't work usually sleep until afternoon. They wake up, go to mosques to pray and recite the Quran. After that, they sit in front of the TV, waiting for their meal. On the other side are the foreigners, Muslim and non-Muslim, who have to cook and deliver the food, stock and man the supermarkets, keep the oil plants running, produce all the pastries and cakes for the night feasts of the upper class, and tailor all their new gowns. Their working hours triple. For them, it's a month of suffering.

The children cannot wait. I had been wondering if children also fasted and whether I would allow my children not to eat or drink the entire day. If they were Muslims, I would probably have no choice – even worse, they might have wanted to fast. The Islamic clergy recommend that children older than 7 years should refrain from eating and drinking during sunlight and so, from this age parents encourage fasting. In the majority of conservative households once children turn ten, they would be forced to fast. Children want to imitate the adults in the family, like them participate in the observances, and above all be praised; they keep comparing themselves with peers at school who are already fasting the whole day. In addition to that, children can be more conscientious at following rules than grown-ups. One teacher swallowed a fly at the school playground and while she was chocking and sputtering, a third grader (an eight-year-old) approached her and pointed out that she had just broken fast and if she did that on purpose, she needed to fast additional 60 days to compensate for it.

After sunset, it's time for the much-awaited *iftar*, which means breakfast, the first meal of the day. *Iftar* is not just about satisfying the basic needs of your body – it is a social event, celebrated with family and friends. Slightly later, another heavy meal called *ghabka* is served, and before dawn, people have a third meal called *suhoor*. Essentially, every night of Ramadan becomes a marathon of overeating.

Ramadan has become a commercialized event all over the Middle East. People spend much more on food and entertainment during this month than any other time of the year. They also tend to spend most of their time watching TV. Most of the soap operas have their premieres during Ramadan.

A few brave voices have tried hinting that Ramadan has a detrimental effect on the economy, and more importantly, on the population's health. During the day, there are numerous cases of people fainting or collapsing due to excessive fasting. While driving through residential neighbourhoods, one can often spot ambulances waiting in front of houses.

My husband recalls a case from his workplace when a young woman collapsed. 'I remember her vividly: tall, pretty, she had big eyes and a childlike face. No one knew what had happened. She was taken away in an ambulance. Her brother came later, bringing her medical leave for a week but she didn't return after that. I saw her a few months later and I didn't recognise her. She was very pale, had bad skin and dark circles under her eyes. She was missing teeth. She said she lost her kidneys and was going to go to dialysis every day. The day it happened, she hadn't had water for more than 20 hours, and she hadn't been drinking enough water the whole week beforehand. She was twenty-two. The doctors told her she can't have children.'[4]

Last Ramadan, he attended four funerals. 'So many people are going to die again,' he says to me this year.

Such incidents occur frequently during this month but they are overlooked or not publicised. Whenever they are reported, the media and doctors insist that the death or illness had nothing to do with fasting. More so, people who are personally touched by the tragedy, such as the parents of a child with chronic kidney damage, will claim it, too. Instead, they blame the victims for not drinking enough water at night, rather than questioning the society that pressures people to accept such harmful practices.

One of my friends claims that Ramadan fasting improves her skin and that scientific publications confirm the health benefits of observing the fast. She forgets, however, that they refer to refraining from eating, not from drinking.

Why do Muslims fast? To get closer to God, as well as to walk a mile in the shoes of the less fortunate, to experience hunger and need like them. What about the many millions of destitute Muslims around the world who are already hungry? Why are they supposed to be fasting?

The lives of those coming from big, multi-generational families are not easy during this period due to reasons quite contrary to abstention. They run from one feast to the next: *iftar* at another uncle's, *ghabka* out with friends, *suhoor* at brother-in-law's. All

4 There are general guidelines regarding adequate fluid intake for optimal kidney and overall body function, with urine output serving as an indication of hydration. For adults, the urine output should be above 0,5ml per kg of body weight per hour (above 1 ml/kg/h for children) to prevent acute kidney injury. If a person is not drinking for a prolonged time, the production of urine decreases which could lead to acute renal failure and even permanent kidney damage. Chronic kidney disease might in some cases reduce fertility in both women and men, and for women, increase the risk of complications during pregnancy, which affect the health of the mother and the foetus. Sometimes, the risk is too high to consider getting pregnant.

invitations need to be honoured and reciprocated, every night. Children, who accompany the rest of the family, the next day are carried into the kindergarten sleeping in the arms of their parents. Thank goodness for private kindergartens with cot beds.

On the third Saturday of Ramadan, I drive with my family to dinner at a friends' house. On the way, we stop at the biggest confectionery in the area to get dessert. Its small car park and driveway are swarmed with cars. Someone is just leaving and we take their spot but a moment later, a queue forms of people coming in from the main road who are less fortunate than us as there is no space for them. Inside the shop, bare shelves reflect light. Clients are fighting over the last of the dry biscuits, at which they wouldn't even glance in normal circumstances. There is a *kunafa* pastry shop just next door and there, the situation looks similar. We get in and out with a previously ordered box of pastries, pleased with ourselves, drive out of the car park and breathe a sigh of relief, leaving the whole commotion behind. We brace ourselves for what further awaits us.

A moment before clock hits zero hour, it's chaos in the streets. Everybody is in a hurry to reach home for the supper-breakfast, and each one is hungrier than the other. People are driving onto the pavement to bypass traffic or to turn around and find a better route. We wait patiently in the line of cars until the traffic lights change. Later, we let all those speeding at 160 km per hour in the highway pass us. Slightly nervous, I imagine how rude it must be to be late for *iftar* at someone else's home and make them wait before they can begin the first meal of the day. Too bad; better this than risking an accident.

In this month, drivers become even more out of control. Many people are hungry, extremely irritable, and their reaction time is slower. There are many tragic traffic accidents. And the Kuwaiti police, who are after all public servants, don't seem to be working during Ramadan. Most police stations are empty, almost deserted. You have to be lucky to spot a police car before *iftar* – they are long at home, thinking of all the food they are about to eat.

～

Around halfway through Ramadan, *Garge'an* (or *Girgian*) is celebrated. Children dress in festive outfits made specially for this occasion and they go from house to house singing, collecting sweets in exchange. You might not see that everywhere but in the old city neighbourhoods, people keep this custom alive. This tradition is meant to commemorate the birth of the Prophet's grandchild, when according to some accounts, townspeople appeared at his home to congratulate him and were offered sweet treats.

Women go to tailors and get *darrae* made – these are elegant, embellished long dresses – in order to look festive in the evening. Some ladies get a few pieces made each season and they follow the latest trends. There are women who wear their *darrae* the whole day long, whether at home or out shopping. One of my European friends got such a dress made, too.

'They told me I would need one if we were invited to a Kuwaiti house for *iftar*,' she explains.

'And have you worn it?'

'No, it's been in my closet for two years now. No one has invited me.'

～

It is easy to guess who is fasting and who is not. In Ramadan dry, chapped lips are not something to be ashamed of – quite the contrary. When sticking to our routine we go for a walk along the Avenues on a weekend morning, we pass many smiling, rested, and evidently well hydrated faces. Every few metres, lonely figures sitting in empty outdoor seating areas of closed cafés catch the

eye, mostly of elderly men in white *dishdashas*, reading a newspaper or lost in their thoughts – as if they did not want to break
their habit of coming daily to the same place for a morning cup
of coffee. But the tops of their tables, like all other ones, are bare.

In public administration, schools, private offices, if you enter
without knocking on the door, you might find a person eating.
A woman could always make an excuse that she is on her period
but what about a man?

My colleague's grandfather, a person with vast life experience and a secularised world view, would travel abroad every
year the day before the beginning of Ramadan. While the locals
there were fasting, he would sit on the porch in the morning
with a newspaper and a cigarette in his hands, and then relish
every bite of his breakfast. He took advantage of the directive that
fasting is not obligatory when you're travelling. In theory, every
day without fast has to be made up for at a later time, however,
that is a different matter.

Those who observe the fast wait impatiently for the clock to
strike for *maghrib*.[5] (The Shiites calculate it a few minutes later
than the Sunni.) They have one dilemma: what to do first – have
a smoke, a cup of coffee, or sink their teeth into something tasty.

After the lunar month of Ramadan, lasting 29 or 30 days,
comes the Islamic holiday of *Eid Al-Fitr*, literally the Festival of
Breaking the Fast, when Muslims celebrate that Ramadan ended.
Its exact date is announced a day or two beforehand, based on
observation of the moon; sometimes according to the Shiites it
falls a day later than the Sunni but formally, Kuwait follows the
Sunni announcement. Kuwaitis get three days off work – in rare
instances the government grants more than three days for the
public sector – which they spend with their close and distant
relatives. There is a feast, of course, phone calls and wishes over

---

5 Maghrib – the fourth prayer of Muslims in the day, recited after dusk.

WhatsApp to family and friends (*Eid Mubarak!* - Happy Eid), there is a special prayer and a sermon at the mosque. Everyone puts on their best clothes. Children get *eidiya* from grown-ups which is a gift of money. Many people take the option of spending the holidays abroad and changing the climate. Prices of airline tickets during the time, as on other local holidays, go through the roof, and still the country empties out.

~

Another significant religious holiday for Muslims, *Eid Al-Adha*, commemorates Ibrahim's willingness to offer his son Ishmael in sacrifice to Allah. It is an important tradition and a highly recommended practice in Islam to slaughter an animal, usually a lamb: shepherds choose and sacrifice the best specimen from the herd, and city folk buy a live animal from the market and hire a butcher who carries out the deed in their house's front yard. Some even do it in the street. I've been told that because of this, the Festival of Sacrifice is not a favourite holiday among Kuwaiti families as many don't like seeing the blood.

The Sunnis believe that no other holiday beyond these two should be observed. Despite that, the Prophet's birthday, Islamic New Year, *Isra and Miraj* (the night of the Prophet's ascension to heaven) along with the exuberantly celebrated National and Liberation Days of 25th and 26th February are all public holidays in Kuwait. The latter, patriotic holidays, are particularly beloved in the country; foreigners join in the revelry, too. Houses and streets are decorated with flags and billions of lights in green, white, red and black; schools organise 'Kuwaiti days'. The authorities declare additional days of rest, and again, many people leave the state. The ones who stayed gather along the main coastal road, armed in water pistols – adults and children alike. They spray the cars driving slowly past them in a massive parade, particularly eagerly when they notice any open windows. If on one of these days you go anywhere near Gulf Street, you are going to get wet of your own accord. The festivities of independence days last in practice the whole month, from the beginning till the end of February. I cannot imagine that these holidays could ever be banned.

In the eyes of most Arabs, we are all Christians or infidels if we look and sound like Westerners. They just differentiate between what they think of as important people, such as the English and Americans, and those they perceive as poor, which are Eastern Europeans. In contrast, a Kuwaiti may not consider himself an Arab. In fact, many Lebanese, Syrians, Egyptians, Moroccans are neither Muslims nor Arabs, although they speak a dialect of Arabic. Since Arabic is a language of many dialects and accents, a person from Morocco would find it difficult to understand a Saudi or a Yemeni, and vice versa.

Amongst the Arabic-speaking population in the country, the native Kuwaitis are a minority. Scores of Egyptians, Syrians, Lebanese, Jordanians, and Bidoon also reside here, who at first glance, together with the natives, might appear as one Arab nation to the inexperienced eye. Putting them all into one pot, however, is like telling a Pole that he is Russian, or a Scot that he is English. Each of these peoples has their own identity. If you look closely, you will notice differences in their appearance, behaviour, manners. A simple example: women tie their headscarves in a different way that reflects their specific group. Syrian women prefer white or light-coloured headscarves, while Egyptians like bright colours and patterns, and Kuwaiti women typically wear neutral colours and sparkly details. Men from Persian Gulf countries like wearing their national outfits: characteristic floor-length white or cream robes, in Kuwait called *dishdashas,* and headdresses on their heads, while Egyptian and Jordanian men tend to wear trousers and a shirt. A keen observer will identify a visiting Qatari by the tassels hanging from his *iqal*[6], which the Kuwaiti headwear does not have; or a Saudi man by a winged collar instead of a band collar on his *dishdasha*. You can spot an Omani man from a distance by the turban-like style in which he ties his *ghutra*. A man wandering about in the company of women thoroughly enveloped in black is likely a local Bedouin or a Saudi on holiday with his wives and daughters.

Kuwaitis are not a homogeneous group. They can trace their roots to Iraq, Persia, Najd, Yemen, Egypt, India, Palestine. Since the beginnings of Kuwait, there has been a clear distinction amongst the native people between city-dwellers, those living within the walls of the city – *haadar* or *hadhar* – and desert-dwellers – Bedouins. The former were mostly seafarers, craftsmen and merchants, the latter – shepherds and warriors. Some differences remain sharp, impossible to miss.

The Bedouin, or Bedu in short (should not be confused with Bidoon – a social group of stateless people about whom I will speak later) originate from nomadic desert tribes who came to the territory of Kuwait from all directions – Saudi Arabia, Iraq, Syria, Yemen. Some of them have been naturalised, others weren't. Until 1960s, they moved between the outskirts of different cities. For a long time, their access to education or civilisation in general was limited, therefore stereotypically they are perceived as a primitive and uncouth people.

Currently, they constitute the majority of the nation.[7] Amongst Kuwaitis they can be told apart by their characteristic accents when they speak and their last names which are tribal names rather than family ones. Women who wear black robes and cover their faces are usually Bedouins. City women either cover just their hair with hijab or don't even do that.

---

6 An iqal is a black, thick cord holding a ghutra – headdress – on a man's head.

7 For the past forty years, the Bedouin have been slowly naturalised, increasing the number of citizens. For example, in 1981 citizenship was granted to 200 000 Bedouin – at that time roughly 30% of nationals.

The Bedouin stay faithful to blood connections and tradition. They marry within clans: marriages between first-degree cousins are legal and extremely common. Even within the same tribe, they differentiate between different branches of the clan. Some tribes don't marry between each other, and they would rather kill their daughter or son than allow them to marry from a clan considered below theirs. Their tribal identity is stronger than their affiliation to nation or state. Some Bedouins like to emphasize their separateness. That's why their loyalty – to anyone – is often considered questionable. In Sinai Peninsula, some Bedouin clans had joined ISIS against the Egyptian army; the Bedouin serve as volunteers in the army and police in Israel. In the Gulf states, they are also mostly employed as soldiers and policemen for a good pay, so that there is someone to defend the regime in case of social unrest.

Every tribe and a branch of the tribe has a leader called a sheikh who is in charge of his group's affairs. Gulf governments as well as Iraq, Jordan, and Syria tend to empower Bedouin sheikhs to a different extent. Tribes function as social institutions, equipped with various regulations and mechanisms to maintain the unity and solidarity among its members and differentiate them from others. Amongst their social mechanisms they have jail, a form of exile from the tribe, and blood money, which is given as compensation to the relatives of a person killed. They also employ methods such as vengeance, honour killing, ostracising dissidents as means to maintain order and peace within the community. They prefer to rely on their own code of honour rather than the state law, whenever they can. When a child is born, it is customary for the family to slaughter a goat or a lamb; during a wedding feast camel meat is served to a jubilant crowd of many invited guests. The Bedouin are very religious; they are also superstitious: they believe in demons (*jinni*) and the power of talismans. At the same time, their traditions and their clan come before the religion.

Invasion is another important part of the Bedouin identity. They teach their children about the incursions which they had carried out before they were settled in the 1950s. Attacking other tribes or invading cities and looting properties as well as kidnapping girls is considered an honourable act. To this day, they name their sons Ghazi (invader), Salab (robber), and their daughters Anfal (spoils), and Ghazwah (invasion). They adore the wolf because it is shrewd and lives in packs. Handiwork as well as farming are looked down upon, and tribe members who practice them are considered inferior to the warriors and cattle owners.

On the other hand, famous is Bedouin hospitality, which stems from the tradition of harsh nomad life that no traveller should be turned away – Bedouins know first-hand how harsh the land and conditions can be. Whether it is applied to every and any guest, I cannot say.

In the winter season, large camps emerge across the desert landscapes of Arabia, not just in Kuwait. Every year some force drives Bedouins to pack their bags and relocate for a while to the vast empty land. Some of them camp for months. A while ago the government introduced paid licences as a requirement for setting up camp in the desert. Modern nomads surround themselves with big fences, inside of which they install electricity generators, off-road vehicles, quads, TV-sets. As a mark of their presence, they leave behind heaps of rubbish that scatter in all directions each time the wind blows.

There is one particular character trait of Kuwaitis that does not win them many friends: the conviction that they are superior and entitled to everything. It can be observed in public offices, where they jump the queue; on the roads; in their treatment of immigrants. When a Kuwaiti is walking down a corridor, cleaners hastily move aside to make way for them. Shopping assistants bend over backwards to please them. Kuwaitis are often impolite and blunt as customers. They have been known for their brazen behaviour when spending holidays abroad. Their grandiosity is perceptible also during discussions, where a Kuwaiti man or woman speaks from the position of infallibility and absolute self-righteousness, expressing an expert opinion regardless of the subject.

After many years spent here, I've come to think that perhaps there are reasons for their attitude. Kuwaitis constitute by far a minority in their own country and they want to assert their distinctiveness and protect their identity.

There are around 4,7 million people living in Kuwait, with nationals making up about 30% of that number.[8] The vast majority of the population are aliens – citizens of foreign countries, with Indians constituting around 1 million, followed by Egyptians (600 thousand), Filipinos (250 thousand), Bengalis, Syrians, Pakistanis, Sri Lankans, and other nationalities. The entire country's area is just under 18 thousand km2, making it almost the same size as Wales or the state of New Jersey, but a quick glance at the map reveals that the vast majority of Kuwait's land is desert, leaving its inhabitants squeezed into a handful of cities along the coast. The capital governorate and its surroundings alone are estimated to house 75-80% of the population, with another 15% residing in Ahmadi.

It's easy to see how Kuwaitis may feel overwhelmed by the foreign presence. Many express their frustration in private and on social media: 'Foreigners are taking up apartments, jobs, parking spaces. They congest the streets so badly that my commute to and from work takes an hour instead of 15 minutes.' While polls in the United States show that many Americans often feel like strangers in their own country, no such polls are conducted in Kuwait. Here no one gives a damn about the opinion of the average citizen.

---

8 Exact up-to-date numbers are not available. Last national census was carried out in 2005. Central Statistical Bureau estimates the population of Kuwait on 01.01.2019 at 4,420,110 people: 1,335,712 Kuwaitis and 3,084,398 non-Kuwaitis.

The majority of migrants, whether low- or high-skilled, view their stay here as temporary. They cannot acquire citizenship, therefore they are not interested in building a better country, a better future for everyone. My obstetrician, an elegant Syrian who was educated in the USA, once shared her honest thoughts with me. When I asked her: 'Do you like Kuwait?', she didn't hesitate for a second. 'No. I'm here just for the money.'

Many of Kuwaitis have noble qualities. They are generous and hospitable. They love hosting family and friends, providing food and drink to guests. For them such gestures indicate prestige and influence: historically, the crowds listened to whoever fed them. Kuwaitis remember the times when food in the country was scarce and so they provide food to others on different occasions such as funerals, or religious seasons such as Ramadan. Many put fridges in front of their homes, which contain water and snacks, so that the poor workers in the streets, who are often underpaid and exploited by the few rich company owners, would find something to eat. When they go out, they make sure to have small banknotes in their pocket which they then hand out to cleaners, parking attendants, shop assistants, restaurant staff. In fact, their tips are the basis of sustenance for a number of workers whose wages are so low that they would otherwise starve.

Kuwaitis can be selfless and kind not only amongst themselves but also towards foreigners. Like the one who stopped to help when he saw a crashed car at the side of a road and the European faces of its owners, still bewildered, speaking to the police. Those faces belonged to a friend of mine and her husband, who were glad that the Kuwaiti man joined in and accompanied them in the discussion. He also interpreted for them what the other party, the driver and his passengers, were talking about: those teenagers drove into their car and were trying to deny it. After that, he helped the couple fill out forms at the hospital where their daughter was taken for observation. While waiting for the child's test results, the Kuwaiti man phoned his wife and she came to the mother and the child to keep them company.

I also witnessed such a scene. A woman dressed in 'Western' clothes: a t-shirt and a knee-length skirt, was shopping at the old *souk*. At one point two young men started following her and shouting insults. An older man in a traditional dress noticed this, thought it to be unacceptable, in one second took off his *iqal* and began hitting them with it. Many others came to support him and the two men had to run.

This story, in turn, happened to Sebastian. One day he and a large group of friends decided to spend a day out at a farm in the faraway area of Wafra. He and his husband were driving ahead; they stopped their car at the gate to the farm to wait for the rest of the cavalcade. There was a house near the gate and a man walked out of it, he started chatting them up in a friendly manner. He invited them inside – he didn't want to hear otherwise – and entertained them until the rest of the group showed up.

'Every time we eat at the *souk* – you know, in one of those fish restaurants, where you dine on an oilcloth, but the food is fresh and delicious – someone would chat to us,' says Sebastian.

'Kuwaitis?'

'Yes, in their traditional white clothes. Older men. They join us at our table and ask all kinds of questions. If you say you're from Poland, they reply: "Oh, yes, amber and Wałęsa". They crave information and it's so genuine. No hidden agenda, just genuine curiosity.'

The Bidoon: One thousand lies

On 3rd December 2020, the speaker of parliament, Marzouq al-Ghanim, made a seemingly outrageous statement in a speech aired by all national television channels : 'Being a Bidoon in Kuwait is better than being a citizen of any country in this world.'

The Bidoon (Bidoon – short for *Bidoon jinsiya*, which means without citizenship) are stateless people who are considered illegal immigrants by the Kuwaiti government. This state of affairs goes back to 1961, when Kuwait became independent from Great Britain. Based on a conducted census, most people in the area were declared citizens, while others were left suspended, without an official homeland. Not all of the wandering nomad tribes applied to be naturalised, and some voices say that a portion of the nomads might not have been aware of the census happening, despite it having lasted for a number of years. Some groups of people didn't see the importance of registering or even opposed it. Others were simply denied citizenship as they were citizens of other countries.

As oil revenues flowed in, the country developed rapidly, but this growth was hindered by a severe shortage of manpower. There simply weren't enough citizens to fill all the posts being created. In the newly founded country, there was a particularly acute shortfall of military and police recruits. To solve this problem, in the 1960s-80s the government began recruiting from the Bidoon population; they were neither citizens nor expatriates. In return, the Bidoon families were granted free healthcare and education on par with the Kuwaitis. During that time, people from Iraq, Syria, Jordan also came to work in Kuwait, and for some of these migrants, claiming they were Bidoon made the application process easier. The initial Bidoon and contract soldiers were then joined by new economic migrants who quickly grasped that declaring yourself an undocumented person in Kuwait could confer many benefits.[9] The majority of these migrants together with their families permanently settled in the country, boosting the number of the Bidoon. They had not foreseen that, eventually, the government would start curtailing the Bidoons' rights until one day declaring them illegal residents.

Thus, there is a group of Bidoon who have been stateless for generations, whose fathers and grandfathers lived in this land – de facto Kuwaitis; there are also those who took up residence thirty-forty years ago and claim to be Bidoon.

The process of naturalization is governed by stringent conditions, including the requirement that the candidate must speak Arabic and have been a Muslim for at least 5 years. The right to vote only applies after 30 years of being naturalised, and the right to stand for election – never (article 6.).

The rules concerning nationality are complex and keep evolving since the moment of issue. Although certain pathways to citizenship are outlined, they are rarely implemented, since the final decision of the authorities is always arbitrary. Above that, Kuwait does not recognize dual or multiple citizenship. If an adult Kuwaiti was discovered to have a passport of another country, they could lose the Kuwaiti one. In practice, there are many known instances of Kuwaitis holding the US or other citizenship[10] without any implications.

It is worth mentioning that there are different classes or tiers of citizenship, corresponding to consecutive articles of the Nationality Law of 1959. (Other Gulf countries apply a similar rule.) Each adult Kuwaiti person holds a nationality document,

---

9 Human Rights Watch (13 Jun 2011). Prisoners of the Past, Kuwaiti Bidun and the Burden of Statelessness.
10 Habib Toumi (3 Nov 2014). 28 Kuwaitis renounce US citizenship. Gulf News.

separate to the identity document and the birth certificate, that indicates the article according to which he or she has the right to nationality. This document has to be presented when for example one is voting in National Assembly elections. The strongest is the 'original' or article 1. citizenship – it is boasted by generations of people whose ancestors settled in Kuwait before year 1920. Article 3. of Nationality Law says that children of unknown parents will be considered Kuwaitis; and article 5. asserts the possibility of granting citizenship for outstanding services to the country. Citizenship acquired by naturalization, granted by Emir's decree (grace), is considered weaker as it can be more easily revoked than the original one. The government uses this prerogative as a means of controlling individuals seen as disloyal.[11]

The number of Bidoons in Kuwait is estimated at around 100 thousand people, although some organizations have suggested higher figures. The majority of them consider themselves Kuwaiti and don't intend to leave the country which, as they say, is their homeland. Their status and living conditions vary greatly depending on factors such as how long they have been in the country, where they came from, where and for whom they work, whether they are perceived as genuine candidates for naturalisation or frauds. There are those who are treated as citizens or second-class citizens, covered by state education and healthcare, issued passports. They are employed in the army, police, or public sector as nurses, teachers, school guards, on salaries often lower than those of Kuwaitis but in many cases higher than those of expatriates. Then, there are those who are worse off, living in shanties and taking up arbitrary jobs to make a living. Some Bidoons complain that they are being denied their rights: they are not being issued birth, marriage, or death certificates; state education and healthcare do not cover them. Without any official documents, they are unable

---

11 Jane Kinnimont (2013). Citizenship in the Gulf, in: Ana Echagüe (red.), The Gulf States and the Arab Uprisings, Madrid: FRIDE, p. 47.

to cross the border. Some feel they have no other choice but to bring a folding chair and take a spot by a street selling seasonal fruit and roasted seeds. Bidoon children can also be seen walking among cars at traffic lights, offering plastic toys for a couple of dollars. Their income constitutes an addition to a slim family budget.

When my husband was collecting our daughter's birth certificate at the hospital, the man issuing it noticed that the mother and the father came from two different countries. He struck up a conversation: '*Ammi, ammi*[12], can your daughter have two passports?' 'She can', my husband replied, to which the man responded: '*Ammi*, I am Bidoon, I don't even have an ID. I don't have a driving licence, nothing at all.'

There are opinions that the Bidoon are mostly people who migrated to this territory relatively recently from neighbouring countries and who have destroyed or hidden their actual documents in order to fraudulently apply for the local citizenship and partake in the present prosperity. (Until a certain time it was also technically possible to falsify one's origin whereby e.g. Saudis, Iraqis, or Syrians paid Kuwaitis to register their child as one of their own.) This argument is being repeated by the Kuwaiti government as the reason for refusing to naturalise all of the Bidoon. In some cases, they are not being issued any documents in order to force them to disclose their presumed original papers. Many Bidoon left Kuwait in the face of the 1990 invasion; some were forcibly displaced to Iraq after the war, in accordance with the claim that they had sneaked into Kuwait with the Iraqi army or that they had fought on the enemy's side. While some Bidoon had been granted citizenships before the invasion, thereafter it became a precedent.

____

12 *Ammi* means 'uncle' and expresses respect for the addressee.

On one hand, the Kuwaiti population would rather avoid a hundred thousand people suddenly joining their group. This would diminish the benefits, allocation of houses and land, which have already been slowly shaved down by the state. On the other hand, it has been said for years now that at least thirty thousand Bidoon have a legitimate claim to citizenship, and many Kuwaitis empathise with them. In recent years, the number of Bidoon naturalised annually has been low.

In 1996, the Executive Committee for Illegal Residents' Affairs (ECIR), popularly called the Bidoon Committee, was created to deal with their matters. One of the ways it is attempting to solve the problem is pressuring Bidoon to admit their original nationality and investigating their cases. In October 2022, the Committee issued a report about the number of Bidoon who disclosed their citizenship, or had it revealed, in the previous 11 years. It stated that 18427 Bidoon had either already possessed other citizenships or were in the process of obtaining them based on their ancestry. This process is sometimes straightforward, while a portion of people have to start from scratch. According to the Committee, there were 12901 Saudis, 1835 Iraqis, 1137 Syrian, 318 Iranians, 116 Jordanians, and other nationals who had been previously registered as stateless.

The work of the Bidoon Committee also involves issuing different kinds of documents for the Bidoon, helping them obtain their original documents, and if they are eligible, it assists in their application. According to the committee, in 2021 the Bidoon received $50 million in the form of financial aid from the public Islamic charity Zakat House. It also said in 2022 that 33000 Bidoon ware enrolled in the Kuwaiti educational system.

One significant barrier to naturalization is having a criminal record. If all Bidoons were to be naturalised, it would have also applied to Mohsen al-Fadhli, a senior member of al-Qaeda who was born and lived in Kuwait. There are some conservative

Kuwaiti groups that campaign against the naturalisation of Bidoons on the grounds that they have a different national identity and many of them have criminal history.

There are communities of Kuwaiti Bidoons all over the world, in countries such as Britain, Australia, New Zealand, Canada, the USA, Sweden, and Finland. A few months after I moved to Kuwait, I went to visit a friend who was living in Stockholm. She asked me to stop by her work to pick her up. She was excited to introduce me to one of her colleagues who, she said, was a Kuwaiti. Once the man learned I was living in Kuwait, he seemed shaken and he quickly corrected her saying that he had been born in Kuwait and lived there all his life before emigrating to Sweden, but he was a Bidoon, not a Kuwaiti. Over the years, thousands of Bidoon have emigrated legally and illegally to Europe, North America, and Australia.

At the same time, there are many ex-Bidoon who have settled back in Kuwait after obtaining Western citizenship. I've met a man who was born and grew up in a stateless family in Kuwait but later emigrated to Finland and was naturalized there. After a few years, he returned with his family to his country of birth. He explained that, like many others, he had moved to Finland to obtain a powerful passport that would allow him to travel anywhere and ensure a good future for his children with access to free education and social support from the Finnish government, but left Finland for religious and cultural reasons and preferred to live in Kuwait.

Stateless people exist in all the Gulf States, and other parts of the world for that matter, but their plight often goes unnoticed and unreported. In contrast, it is a vivid issue in Kuwait due to the historical and economic context. It is undoubtedly a highly charged issue there, especially during elections; many feel personally touched by it. It can be true for some of the undocumented that living in their original homelands would make them worse off than being a Bidoon in Kuwait.

The man with many faces
and a myriad of stories

One of the first people I met in Kuwait was Mahdi. He is a family friend. When we leave for a long holiday, he is the one who checks on the house, waters the plants, and turns the cars on so that the batteries don't die. You'd want to say: a man with a heart of gold to which all his actions are subjected. And it's upsetting to watch how life does not reward his kindness. That is, until you get a closer look.

A heavily built man. When he's out of the house, he usually wears a *dishdasha* and a less-than-neat *ghutra*. At home, he puts on stretched t-shirts and old, pilling tracksuit bottoms. When I see him during social occasions, he's always jovial and smiling; when he telephones my husband, it's most often to complain about something or ask for a favour. Aside from being a self-proclaimed expert on all subjects, he likes to boast about his barbecuing skills and the unparalleled taste of the meat he prepares.

Mahdi[13] with his wife and four children lives in a house he bought twenty years ago, at the age of twenty-something, with money he inherited from his parents, and a low-percentage governmental loan. Until recently, his elderly mother, whom none of his siblings were keen on taking care of, also lived there, but she died. Currently, they are renting one floor out to a British

---

13 Mahdi is an important figure in the doctrine of Shia Islam. It is the name of the Twelfth Imam who stays in hiding and is expected to come before the Final Judgement to conquer evil – a kind of a Messiah. Any man who bears that name comes almost certainly from a Shiite family, as do Jaffar, Musa, Hasan, Hussain and Raza. On the other hand, Abu Bakr, Omar, Othman and Aisha are names given predominantly to Sunni children. For all intents and purposes, by naming their son Mahdi, parents map out his entire life.

family. The house is big but in desperate need of renovation. Still, it seems that relatively little work would be required to live in more pleasant surroundings: scrubbing the floor tiles clean, putting a fresh coat of paint on the walls, burying the wires that meander through every wall of the main room underneath plaster. The neatest space in the house is a room, or rather a hall, assigned for a Muslim Shia worship place (*hussainiya*). Shiny carpets in vivid green hues cover the floor, a tapestry with a quote from the Quran hangs on one wall, there are cushions for guests to sit on and an armchair for an imam.

The children are not required to help at home. Their task is to focus on studying and relaxing. All house chores have been given over to two young maids, who by the way also have mobile phones with contracts and a very manageable workload.

When it comes to disciplining his children, Mahdi fluctuates between being very harsh and extremely indulgent. Sometimes he would beat them up for missing one of the five daily prayers or the girls for using make-up, and other times he pretends he cannot see the misbehaviour. Whenever things are not going well for him personally, he compensates for it by indulging the children with new gadgets or Starbucks trips. In the face of problems, he turns to Allah for help. A few times a year he goes on religious pilgrimages as a crew member of an Islamic travel agency and comes back spiritually renewed. He calls my husband on the phone and proclaims: 'I feel great. I prayed to Allah, he answered all my pleas.' But in fact, nothing changes. There is no improvement of his health, nor any prospects for an overdue promotion at work or a pay rise, and the children are close to failing at school. If there are changes, they are for the worse. Usually, a couple of days after the first phone call, another one comes: 'I can't take it. Everyone is against me.' Mahdi says the manager at work is against him, his family, his neighbours, the clerks, too, and above all, the government which discriminates against him. 'Why do they want me to go to work?

No one works,' and 'The government is against me because I'm a good Shia. They are corrupt and hate decent, honest people,' he often repeats. But he also sees some good sides to his situation: '*Alhamdulillah*[14], I'm not a junkie or a criminal or homeless.'

His pilgrimages to Karbala, Mashhad, Mecca, and other similar places usually last a week or two, sometimes longer. When he goes to Saudi Arabia as a supervisor with a travel office to help pilgrims in Hajj, he can be away from home for over a month, without his family. He tells us that he enjoys these trips as he can pray, meditate, and assist first-time pilgrims. Most importantly, no one tells him what to do: he sleeps whenever and wakes up whenever. He is very critical of other members of the crew and the customers as well. Most of them go on these excursions to have sex, not to worship, he says. The way they do it is through temporary marriage. This form of marriage, legal among Shia but banned among Sunnis, consist of a verbal agreement between a man and a woman to marry for a specific time in exchange for a dowry paid by the man. The duration of the marriage could be an hour or even less and after the agreed time, they part. Many of his co-workers, says Mahdi, as well as many guests go on these trips to hook up and avoid their strict homes. There is a man in the crew who offers good money for any girl who would agree to such a marriage. During one of the trips, the man had eight different women over the course of six days.

The nature of Mahdi's job and the leniency of his superior, who also travels a lot, are the reasons he is able to make these trips without taking formal leave from work. The job itself is in one of the less significant, marginalised ministries and by no means demanding – unless all the employees are on holiday, in which case Mahdi covers a few posts at the same time, including the managerial ones. But even then, he's not straining himself. After so many years in

---

14 *Alhamdulillah* means 'praise be to God' or 'thank God'.

one place he knows the processes and procedures inside out. The monotony of the daily routine weighs upon him greatly. Before fingerprint scanners were installed at ministries to monitor employees coming in and out, he could sleep in and leave work early on a regular basis; that's if he showed up at all. If you phoned Mahdi before 10 o'clock on a working day, most often he wouldn't pick up; he'd still be asleep. He would call back later from a restaurant where he was having breakfast. When the boss was sent into early retirement, Mahdi, due to his experience and seniority, was supposed to get that post, however, it was decided that a cousin or sister-in-law of some important man's chauffeur had to be given priority instead. In Mahdi's opinion, she is incompetent and incapable of managing the department efficiently. He, in turn, has completely lost his motivation to work because they have treated him so unfairly. Every morning he looks for a reason to call in sick, ignoring the fact that further absences will be deducted from his pay.

Mahdi's eldest daughter recently turned 18. Despite thousands of dollars spent on private tutors, she finished high school with grades too low to get into a good university. She used to boast about her skills in French language and that she was going to become a translator of French. It seems, though, that Hind has had other things on her mind than pursuing career plans. She's been spending most of her time browsing on Instagram and Snapchat, retouching selfies she would post there, and messaging with friends. Her mother discovered a string of messages on her phone that she was exchanging with a secret boyfriend. With her final grades, Hind has barely been accepted into a teacher's college, a type of higher education that is considered to be of last resort. She is to train as a music teacher there, which would at least give her a guaranteed job in the public sector.

Aware of Hind's inclination towards romance, her mother asks a cousin's daughter, who attends the same college as Hind, to keep an eye on her. After a couple of weeks, that girl declares she wants nothing to do with Hind nor does she want to be associated with her. She says that during breaks between lectures, Hind does not join other girls chatting in the cafeteria but she sits away talking or messaging on her phone. On some mornings, she gets picked up by a young man from a car park near the university and dropped off before the end of the last lecture, so that the father, who comes to get her, wouldn't know. What a scandal!

For Muslim parents such a daughter is a real headache. She brings dishonour to her house. If word about her behaviour got out – and the Kuwaiti world is very small – any proposals of marriage from respectable parties will bypass her and her sisters, too. Her whole family could be ostracised and even shunned by relatives. Moreover, honour killing is common all over the Islamic world, and Kuwait is not an exception.

The girl seems to be immune to any efforts at introducing discipline. Talking to her or taking away her phone brings no results, neither does grounding or taking away her cosmetics – and her parents have lost hope for a bright future for her. Her younger sisters have started to follow suit, and the parents don't know what to do. Not long ago, they were feeling proud of having done a great job in this one arena: raising children. Mahdi prepares for another pilgrimage. His knee might flare up again and he will suffer from back pain but he is certain that this time he is going to win God's graces for his daughters' education and good marriage.

Every Arab couple desires a son. After having three daughters, Mahdi and Fatma didn't want to take any more risk and entrusted the next conception to professional hands. That's how Muhammad was born. The one boy amongst girls, he is given special care and attention. He's been sent to a private school where all classes are in English. He speaks English better than any of his older sisters. His dad takes him to men's meetings, even late at night. The son gets all the treats he wants, including fries and pizza at late-night hours. He is a cheerful, happy child and a bit of a clever-clogs. At the age of eight, he is morbidly obese.

The son's name was an obvious choice. Mahdi declares: 'In every house, there has to be a Muhammad. If you name your son Muhammad, nothing bad can happen in your home. I love the Prophet so much, I named my son after him.'

In his house, Mahdi runs a *hussainiya*. It's a place of religious meetings for Shia where they commemorate and contemplate the events leading to the killing of Imam Hussein, the grandson of Prophet Muhammad. *Hussainiyas* normally operate for two months every year. During this time, the host organises the meetings, prepares food for the guests, and hires an imam to preach to the audience. The role of a host bears a certain social status. In return, guests leave a donation. The more enterprising hosts are able to make good money from a *hussainiya*; after paying off the expenses, the whole income will be passed on to a religious purpose.

Whenever we visited them, Fatma, Mahdi's wife, would find ways to entertain me despite the language barrier between us. She would talk about her children, show me hundreds of their pictures on her phone, and if she struggled to explain something, she would find a suitable image online. In reply to my concerns about my daughter's health or eating habits, she would reassure me that this also happened to her children and would pass. Her words were quickly supported by another dozen or so pictures of her children. Over time I was considered trustworthy enough to land Fatma's wedding album in my hands (I finally saw what her hair looked like) and to hear about their recent trip to Thailand, during which she could kiss her husband at a romantic dinner, hold hands with him, and even take her headscarf off.

In pictures taken at her wedding and prior to it, one can see a charming young woman. As she got older, she acquired a second chin and quite a bit of extra flesh. She tells me how during one of family events her graceful moves caught the eye of her future mother-in-law. She was a teenager when she got married, about to start community college. Her husband didn't want her to stay in the college or to work, for different reasons. Partially, he was convinced that he was doing her a favour. Also, his mother suggested to him that a non-working wife would have less sway. At first glance, Fatma's everyday activities look typical: she takes care of the children, oversees cooking and cleaning, shops at the Avenues, dines out with her husband. Once you get to know her better, you find out she likes sleeping until late morning and habitually watches soap-operas while much of the cooking is done by her two maids. She spends a great deal of time out of the house, either at her mum's place, shopping with her daughters, or having coffee and shisha with her female friends or sisters. Mahdi would usually watch TV on his own, anyway. He has a separate room in the basement where he sometimes sleeps. In the past, he used to beat her up for going out too often or when she got on his nerves in another way – he wouldn't even feel very guilty because the Quran approves of that.[15] He doesn't do it anymore.

As a rule, Fatma puts on a lot of make-up. She likes wearing clothes with loud colours and bold patterns and tries to follow the street trends. She spends a lot of time and effort on improving her looks – within the available budget. She had a nose surgery done in a pop-up clinic, the consequences of which she has been experiencing until this day. There are nights when she cannot sleep due to pain.

---

15 Quran 4:34.

As if this wasn't enough, a while ago Fatma talked her husband into going to Turkey with her where she would undergo a liposuction. A few months earlier the four of us were sitting in a restaurant and Mahdi was telling us how hard it was for him to lose weight and that he was thinking about a gastric sleeve, to which Fatma replied that under no circumstances was he to do it, that it was dangerous and she would divorce him. Her recovery after liposuction took three weeks. During the first three or four days he sat at her bed, assisting her but eventually he grew tired of it, so he would go sightseeing instead.

I saw her a couple of months later. With full make-up, blue contact lenses, she could be mistaken for her own daughter. She looked very slim, just a trace of her second chin remained. Although she was still sore then, she declared that 'it was worth it'.

～

We constantly hear about Fatma and Mahdi's worries regarding their children: low grades, laziness, arrogance towards the parents. Mahdi tries to talk to his daughters about their behaviour and grades, but their responses are dismissive and disrespectful. They criticise him for constantly taking sick leave without a good reason and they admit they have no intention of having jobs in the future since their mother never had one.

One day, Mahdi calls saying that he and his wife want to see us urgently and that they are in front of our home. Their eldest daughter, Hind, has run away and she won't answer her phone. Mahdi says he will go to the police and report her, after all, this is a Muslim country and a girl cannot leave her father's house without permission. My husband tries to calm him down; when he phones the girl, she picks up and tells him that she has been driving aimlessly for few hours and that she doesn't have spare clothes or money. He promises that if she comes to our home, he will try to mediate between her and her father and she can even stay at our place for the time being.

She comes and she and her father start arguing.

'You ungrateful, lazy kid!' Mahdi screams, 'You won't do any work. You should be ashamed of yourself.'

'You don't do anything either, you are always away, travelling with your friends or going out. You leave us for months on end,' Hind replies. 'Even when you are at home, you are staring at the TV or sleeping. You vote for whoever gives you money and constantly lie to people about everything. You fake being sick all the time. I know you've had many mistresses! One of them is my friend's mother; my friend saw you with her in their house and she told me you had a temporary marriage!'

Hind wouldn't stop: 'My mother is no better than you. All she cares about is herself. She is either out with friends or watching TV. She goes to all these mosques to meet her friends, so they sit and gossip, drink tea and eat.'

It shocks me how they are very cold to each other, and then they just leave together.

Months before we leave Kuwait, Mahdi calls a mutual friend we happened to be dinning with, asking if he knows a doctor who could give him a sick note. 'Are you okay?' the friend asks him. Yes, Mahdi is fine but just doesn't want to work, and by the way, two or three weeks off would be great. The mutual friend doesn't know such a doctor. Besides, due to a new law, doctors cannot issue very long notes without the need of hospitalisation. Still, it is not difficult to find a doctor who would provide a two-week sick note. Tomorrow Mahdi is leaving for Karbala. There is no doubt that this time Allah will hear all his prayers.

Navigating hypocrisy: Omar

Amongst ordinary citizens, Omar is probably on the other end of the scale compared to Mahdi. He leads a comfortable life, has a big house of his own, drives a Porsche, and has a million or two in the bank. He travels frequently for business and pleasure. Religion is of little or no importance to him; he doesn't even visit the mosque to keep up appearances. Instead, he prefers to read – he reads a lot. He does sports on a regular basis and takes part in expeditions, one of which has been to the North Pole. To unwind after a long day, he enjoys a drink of good whisky, which his supplier sells to him at a small discount from the black-market price. Spanish tapas being some of his favourite foods, he always relishes the cured ham and pork sausages he receives as gifts from abroad.

He comes from a Sunni family: his father was an MP, and his mother belongs to one of the few oldest merchant families in Kuwait. With a degree in business from the United States, Omar now works at a company owned by a senior member of the ruling family. The company's CEO comes from one of the powerful merchant families, too. Omar is third in the firm, which means he is exactly where he should be: he doesn't pose a threat to anyone, nor will he get any higher. He's not part of the corrupt elite; he keeps his head down. Are there any people envious of his job who are waiting to backstab him? Naturally, he has experienced trials and tribulations in his life, lost jobs, but he has always got back on his feet. What helps is that he's extremely dedicated and professional at his work. As a rule, he tries not to rely on *wasta* (connections) as he knows there is always a possibility it could backfire, like the time he asked his big connection to help with getting his son a good job. They did help – by sending the son to a post at a remote location. If he had applied to the same company through the normal route, he probably would have got something central.

His wife comes from money: her father owns a retail company with branches all over the country, and that's where she works. In fact, she paid for their house, and also tastefully decorated it. She does not cover her hair. After Omar and Dalal met, they dated for a while before deciding to get married. Inside the house, they live as modern a life as possible, openly discussing various subjects with their two sons and daughter; nothing is taboo or *haram*. They can have an alcoholic drink in front of their children, which is unimaginable in traditional Muslim households.

At the core of Omar's actions lies his desire to provide a good life for himself and his family. Although his children are grown-up now, he has always tried to insulate them from that part of the society whose influence he considered harmful: the corrupt, the idle and lethargic, the pious. To achieve this, he keeps the conservative part of his extended family at a distance so that his wife and children would not have to put up with constant criticism of their life choices, their liberal clothing and so on. Omar loathes the hypocrisy of many of his relatives and friends and enjoys recounting a story about one of his extremely religious relatives to highlight their duplicity. One time, the pious and wealthy married man came to visit Omar in Madrid, where he was working. To Omar's astonishment, the man came to his flat accompanied by his mistress. They then joined Omar in a tapas bar. Initially, they pretended that they did not drink but later ordered alcoholic drinks. Everything was fine until the bartender brought some Iberico ham, which Omar had ordered. The couple suddenly became histrionic, shouting at Omar not to touch the pork as it was *haram*. 'So, adultery, drinking alcohol, lying are all fine with you but pork is off-limits?' he told them.

Omar's three children live and work in Kuwait, holding good jobs in the private sector, mainly with European expatriates.

However, they often feel that they don't fit in. They struggle to understand the mentality of their Kuwaiti peers and some of the things happening in the country. Others perceive them as 'the posh people who don't belong'.

It's not easy for Omar, either. He is stuck in a daily struggle between what he believes in and what the society expects of him. He is aware that if he pretended to be religious, if he tweeted a few times in praise of the rulers, it would be enough to make his life cushier. He knows the dark side of Kuwait very well but he doesn't want to accept it or fight it. Instead, he's resolved to stay happy.

CHAPTER 3

Intimacy under regulation

A worried father brings his daughter to a mental health clinic where an old friend of his works as a psychologist. 'My daughter is engaged to be married, we have signed the [marriage] contract, and she has been spending time with him, but lately she has been behaving in an odd way. She says she doesn't want the marriage. She's determined. How can I talk sense into her?' he asks. It is clear from his further talk that he is looking for a quick solution, ideally a trick that would allow him to manipulate or convince the daughter his way. His friend suggests one of his senior colleagues. 'She is a competent psychologist, and she will talk to her.'

The girl is 19. She is petite and looks like she is about to drown in the folds of her black abaya. She tells the psychologist that her parents threaten to take her car and phone away and pull her out of university if she doesn't follow their plan. Halfway through the session, the girl breaks down and bitter sorrow pours out of her. Her fiancé, 22 years old and her first cousin, treats her like a slave: she has to cook for him, wash his clothes, wait on him, and follow his orders. He is violent and abusive toward her, forcing her to do different things, things which are difficult to speak about to anyone, let alone her parents. (Sometimes a couple has intimate relations once the contract has been signed, even though the wedding ceremony has not yet taken place.) After two hours of conversation with the psychologist, the girl calms down. At the end, she states: 'If this is marriage, I never want to have a husband.'

The psychologist asks the girl to wait in the office and goes straight to the waiting room where the father is sitting. 'Why are you marrying her off at this age?' she asks. 'Besides, she is very petite and sensitive.'

'We marry children at an early age to keep them chaste. The Prophet, peace be upon Him, instructed us that girls should marry at an early age.'

The old, stubborn psychologist ends the conversation with these words: 'If you go through with this wedding, after a few months she will either come back to you divorced and pregnant or she will be cheating on that idiot. And this will be on you.'

In the end, the young woman got the divorce paper and she is currently pursuing her higher education. I wonder, for one brave girl, how many are there such who swallow their tears and accept what is forced upon them by an ignorant society and timid parents?

Although Kuwait's political system is referred to as constitutional monarchy, the second article of the constitution declares sharia (Islamic jurisprudence) as a main source of legislation in the country. Sharia regulates all aspects of people's lives, even the smallest matters. Many of these rules concern relations between a man and a woman. Not all rules of sharia are applied in practice. There is no cutting off thieves' hands, and bank loans have interest rates. Premarital and extramarital sex are crimes but not punishable by stoning to death. According to the criminal law, two unmarried adults who engage in a consensual sexual relationship face from 3 months to 5 years in prison and a fine. In case of foreigners, there are also deportations.

A Kuwaiti cannot rent a hotel room in his homeland unless he comes with his wife, submits a marriage certificate and two IDs:

his own and his spouse's. Hotels must keep copies of these documents to make them available to the police if required. And if the wife is not there with him, the man won't get a room. This rule is applied more or less strictly also in many other Muslim countries.

A pregnant woman stepping inside a hospital to give birth has to have a marriage certificate with her. If the calculated conception date falls before the date of marriage, the new parents face a serious predicament: the hospital will not issue them the child's birth certificate and would report them to the police to charge them with adultery. This fate nearly befell Susanna and Andreas who married half a year before their son was born. Susanna recollects: 'My husband begged this *niqabi* clerk to turn a blind eye and in the end, she gave us the certificate. He kept coming and asking until he got it. Afterwards, we bought her an expensive set of perfumes; she was very pleased.' Children born out of wedlock to women from poor countries such as India, Philippines, or Ethiopia who live here are automatically taken away by the authorities and put into an orphanage. The father usually cannot be identified, and the mother gets deported to her home country.

Sager, a young Kuwaiti man, shared his thoughts on the popular approach surrounding marriage: 'The idea of children is not about having a child and raising a child. It's not how it works here. Here, you get married to have sex. You don't get married to start a serious relationship or build a family or build an empire but to satisfy your sexual needs.'

~

Women in this part of the world are on the losing side for many reasons, most of which have a religious basis.[16] Many of the sharia

---

16 Quran 4:34: 'Men are in control of women by the advantage of what Allah has given one over the others and by what they spent from their money so righteous women are devoutly obedient, guarding what Allah asked them to guard, as for those from

laws reduce women to the property of the man. The testimony of a male witness equals that of two females.[17] Siblings are not equal when it comes to inheriting as a daughter gets half of what a son receives.[18] A woman cannot be a witness in a marriage. The wife in the Quran is presented as a sexual object whose purpose is to satisfy her husband's needs, 'a farmland' or 'place of cultivation'.[19] Through the words and deeds of Muhammad, as written down in the hadith, the religion establishes women as the inferior creature: they are called deficient and spiritually poor[20]; they are compared to animals such as a dog and a donkey[21]; on many occasions, it is argued that women should categorically submit to men. In sharia court trials, males who kill a female relative are either acquitted or receive a very light sentence.

In accordance with sharia, a man can marry a Muslim, Christian, or Jewish woman, while a woman – only a Muslim man. A Kuwaiti girl-friend of mine married an American; they lived in Kuwait for a few years before moving to the USA. How was it possible? The man had to convert to Islam, otherwise she would be charged with adultery – and adultery of the worst kind: with a *kafir*. In case of marriages of mixed faiths (non-Muslim mother), children always have to be raised in the 'more honourable of the two religions' which is Islam. Children are registered as Muslims at birth, and any attempts to change this can lead to charges of apostasy, which is punishable by death in many

---

whom you fear stray – advise them, forsake them in bed and strike them but if they obey you, seek no means against them. Indeed, Allah is all exalted and great.' (See and compare the translation of Saheeh and/or Murdoch.)

17 Quran 2:282.

18 Quran 4:11.

19 Quran 2:223. 'Your wives are a place of sowing of seed for you, so come to your place of cultivation however you wish and put forth [righteousness] for yourselves.'

20 Sahih al-Bukhari 2:541: 'O women! [...] I have not seen anyone more deficient in intelligence and religion than you.'

21 According to Sahih al-Bukhari (1:490), Prophet Muhammad said that dogs, donkeys, and/or women passing in front of praying people invalidate their prayer.

countries. Although in Kuwait and some other Muslim-majority countries there is no specific law against apostasy or deserting Islam, other laws are employed to punish such people.

As in most Muslim countries, in Kuwait citizenship is passed to children only by the father. Women from wealthy Gulf states who decide to wed a foreigner are deemed foolish and reckless as any children they might have lose all privileges given to citizens.

In Islam, to get a divorce a woman has to prove that her husband was severely harming her or that he is not a practising Muslim anymore. This involves a strenuous court proceeding that can take a few years, especially if she is not connected. A man, on the other hand, can divorce his wife or take another wife at any time without providing a reason, with an immediate effect.

Long-term expatriates, especially women, who are well-versed in the local laws and practices, offer sincere advice to Western women who decide to marry a Muslim and move to a Muslim-majority country: convert to Islam. In the event of a divorce or the husband's death, a Christian or Jew has no rights to their children or the assets. In line with the Quranic provision, even a Muslim wife doesn't take the entire inheritance but a small portion of it: if the deceased left no children, his widow gets one-fourth of the assets while the remainder goes to his parents, brothers, uncles, and other relatives, and if he had children, the wife gets just one-eighth of the assets while the rest is distributed among his children, with sons inheriting twice as much as daughters.[22]

Polygamy is legal for men – but a crime for women. A man is allowed to have up to four wives at any given time. He is expected to treat them fairly financially as well as in terms of physical contact. Although Allah declared that it is impossible for a man to be completely fair towards his wives if he has multiple ones, he should not desert any of them.[23] If he does, Allah is forgiving.

22 Quran 4:12. 'And for them [the wives] is one fourth if you leave no child. But if you leave a child, then for them is an eighth of what you leave (…)'.

In spite of what new converts from the West are often told, a husband does not require the first wife's permission to take another wife. Many times, a woman would find out after her husband's death, during the division of his estate, that he had another family. In Gulf states, polygamy is still very common, especially among the rich, tribal, and uneducated. Since the influx of Syrians to the Gulf, many men have taken Syrian girls as second or third wives. Countless young girls have married Saudi and Kuwaiti men who are old enough to be their fathers, if not grandfathers, out of need and to obtain residency.

Fewer and fewer educated men are interested in having more than one wife – at least not on a permanent basis – because of the obligations that come with it. If they feel the need to have a relationship with someone other than the spouse, they prefer to use the institution of temporary or travel marriage, or yet another way.

---

23 Quran 4:129.

An older neighbour was happy to explain that by marrying off his young daughter to a wealthy, connected sheikh twenty years her senior, he had hit the jackpot. At the time, the groom already had two other wives but that didn't bother my neighbour. He became a father-in-law to a sheikh and grandfather of young sheikhs. 'My daughter was young and attractive. But do you think that she would have looked the same at the age of forty or fifty? Now she lives in a palace and spends summer holidays relaxing in Switzerland and shopping in New York. She owns properties in the States and Europe. If she had married an average guy her age, she would have either been a divorcee or struggling to make ends meet. But I secured her future, her kids' future, and the future of all my other kids and grandkids. We travel first class and stay in five-star hotels. We have real connections and can get things done with a phone call. And then, when the sheikh is dead, my daughter and her children will get millions of dollars.'

Of course, his daughter was lucky as in most cases the old men would divorce these girls after they got bored with them or they found someone new, leaving them with nothing but the dowry and a few gifts – if they didn't take them back.

Most, if not all, sheikhs in the Gulf have many wives and children. Ibn Saud, the founder of Saudi Arabia and its first king, who died in 1953, had 72 children with at least 22 wives. His eldest son Saud, who ruled from 1953 to 1964, had 108 children with numerous women. His half-brother Abdullah, who effectively ruled from 1996 to 2015, had more than 30 wives and 36 children. The current King Salman has 3 wives and 13 children. In Kuwait, people estimate that Jaber Al-Sabah, who ruled from 1977 to 2006, had more than 200 wives. He had 50 children, many of whom are holding key positions in the government. Most of Qatari, Bahraini, and Emirati sheikhs have multiple wives and throngs of children. Each and every child born to a member of one of the six ruling families in the Gulf receives a stipend from the day he or she is born until the last day of their lives. The same applies to the Jordanian and Moroccan royal families as well as rulers of the Arab republics. They also get lands, money in the form of handouts, commissions, tenders, or contracts, all from the public budget. Moreover, all the senior positions in the Gulf governments are reserved for the sheikhs.

During the time I lived in this region, I discovered that there are many women who wouldn't mind being a second, a third, or even a fourth wife even if the man is not wealthy or prominent, like some singles past their youth, girls from poor families, some of the expatriates. Many young girls who are oppressed in their parents' homes would do anything to get away. They rationalise being one of several wives as not that bad. They think they could be like sisters, or at least not enemies. In many cases, instead of putting up with their controlling father, mother, and brothers they would find themselves in a much worse situation.

One summer morning, Michelle and I are sitting in a stylish café by the sea, with upholstered armchairs, mirrors in golden frames, and ornate cages with live parakeets. It's definitely too expensive: 2.5 dinar ($10) for a small cup of coffee with very little foam.

'Do you know anyone with two wives?' she asks me out of the blue.

'I do.'

'Kuwaiti?'

'Yes. A friendly guy in his thirties. His story is not typical, though. He comes from a working-class family, and he got married for the first time when he was very young. It was an arranged marriage, with a cousin, actually. The girl was beautiful, she still is, but her character leaves much to be desired. Their families pushed them both into this relationship. It didn't work out and they got divorced shortly after their first child was born. Then he fell in love with a work colleague and married her. It's possible that he first fell in love with the workmate and then divorced his first wife, or perhaps he never divorced at all. He would not admit it. You know, being a divorcee in Kuwait is hard. When his first wife realised that she'd probably end up lonely, she told him that if he wanted to see his daughter, he had to get back with her. She thought that she can make him divorce the other woman but that didn't happen. And now he's got two wives. I have no idea how he convinced the other one to let him remarry the first one. She must love him very much. Or she didn't have a choice.'

'And they live all together?' Michelle asks.

'Noooo, no,' I attempt to convey with the tone of my voice how unfeasible it would be in their case. 'The wives hate each other. They have separate apartments, a few kilometres from each other. According to the timetable agreed upon by the three parties, he has to move to the other home every day at 7 p.m. So every day he is in charge of taking care of one of the two families. He's got one day, Saturday or Friday, for himself.'

'But there is nothing more than formality between him and the first one, right?'

'Well… I'm just going to tell you that last year they had another baby. He has the same duties toward both wives. Guess how many children he's got,' I add.

'Tell me.'

'Four and four. Eight. When one wife gets pregnant, the other one immediately wants another baby, too.'

'And how does he provide for them all?'

'In his case, both wives have good jobs. One is an engineer, the other – a teacher. Plus his salary. But that's barely enough for them, anyway. And he is stretched thin. Every time he calls my husband, we can hear supermarket announcements in the background. He's either getting the groceries or taking the kids to a tutor or taking one of his wives out to dinner.

One day my husband and I went out with some friends to Texas Roadhouse. He was sitting there with his second wife, the favourite one. She was so happy with the outing and the food that she posted some pictures of it on Instagram. But remember, he has to be in the other home at 7 p.m. So, they finished quickly and he dropped her off. When he was parking his car by the second house, he found his other wife all dressed up, with full make-up, ready and waiting outside. She was raging. He said "hi" and she said: "This is my night! If you wanted to take her for supper, you should have waited until tomorrow." "Ok, love, let's go out." "You're going to take me to the exact same restaurant!", she demanded. He said, "Sure." To our amazement, we saw him coming in again with his first wife, who insisted on saying hi and chatting with us, telling us the story in detail while he kept smiling. They sat next to our table and we heard their conversation. She ordered two huge steaks with all available sides and extra-large cokes. When he was taking his time, chewing slowly or drinking Pepsi, she would screech: "What, is my face killing your appetite? Does food taste better with her?" She took many pictures and posted them online, tagging the second wife and me.'

Being a woman in the Middle East

Beata moved to Kuwait in 1988. She has two grown-up children. The younger one is a deputy head teacher in one of the renowned schools; the elder one works in administration of a big petro-chemical company. Neither has started a family of their own, yet.

She met her husband in a disco; he came on holiday to then communist Poland. That was in the late 80s. Beata is a blonde with eyes so big and so blue, you could drown in them. On top of that, her figure is petite and slender. I can imagine how bewitched this man must have been and how hard he must have tried to charm her. He presented himself as rich and successful, a sheikh from the capital of oil. She moved for him to a completely foreign country and an unfamiliar culture, despite her family and friends' warnings, somewhat against her better judgement. When she looks back, she says: 'Of course, I was infatuated with Fahad. But I was also curious. My adventure streak took over: I was convinced that I could make it and wanted to prove it to myself and everyone else.'

She told me that before they got married, Fahad had three conditions: she would not take a job, she would not drive a car or wear trousers[24] – she agreed. Soon, she found out that in this hot country with virtually no public transport and no pedestrian walkways, the inability to drive was like being in prison. So she came up with a plan and during a month-long holiday in Poland, she completed a driving course. She had to pass at the first attempt, and she did. Once she had the license, slowly but steadily as dripping water wears away a stone, she began convincing her husband to let her drive. And finally, she could leave the house

---

24 Sharia sanctions such a demand: a man has the right to order his wife not to work, study, or leave the house without his prior permission.

whenever she wanted. She had some independence, could take her toddlers to the clinic, get to know the city. After a while, she realised she needed a job, and she found one as a teacher's assistant in a kindergarten.

It was a similar story with the clothes restrictions. She got rid of them gradually, following fashion trends: she first started wearing skirt-like wide pants, then culottes, then bell-bottomed jeans, and so her trousers became slimmer and slimmer until they turned into jeans. Now when I meet her, she usually wears a t-shirt and figure-hugging skinny jeans. Except, she has also been divorced three times, twice with the same man. The first one was a result of the husband's boredom with the wife, a.k.a. infidelity.

Family courts in Kuwait are governed by Islamic law known as sharia. This legal system is incredibly complicated and self-contradicting. There are several Islamic legal schools which have different rulings based on the particular school's understanding (jurisprudence) of the ancient Islamic books. Thus, different judges, and sometimes the same judge, can issue a different sentence depending on the legal school and the interpretation he accepts as valid. Women are not allowed to be judges according to sharia and they don't even work as clerks or secretaries inside the courts.

The rules for dissolving a marriage in all of the different schools favour the husband. In practice, it is enough for the man to state the word *talaq* in any form, even through a text message or WhatsApp, to end his marriage. According to sharia, the man has the right to resume the marriage within three months if he wishes, and the woman should stay at his home unless he told her to leave. She does not have the right to marry anyone else during this time, and some jurist would say she does not have the right to leave the home. If the man did not resume the relationship within the three months, he has to re-do the contract and pay a new dowry if he wants the wife back. Otherwise, the divorce is complete and the woman can marry someone else.

If the man said *talaq* thrice to his wife, this results in irrevocable dissolution of the marriage and is called triple *talaq* (triple, or final, divorce). There is a verse in the Quran that says that after such a divorce, the man cannot remarry the same woman unless she became someone else's wife first and got divorced or became widowed. Most importantly, that second marriage has to be consummated.[25]

After divorcing her second husband (who is not important for the story), Beata remarried Fahad. She wanted his help in executing a certain plan: this time after getting married, she immediately applied for Kuwaiti citizenship. After waiting the required amount of time, she was naturalised, and from then on, she no longer had to worry about visas and sponsors to stay close to her children.

Despite divorce rates among Kuwaiti couples being among the highest in the world (around 3.7 per every 1000 citizens), the life of a divorcée is very difficult. There is a huge stigma in the patriarchal society against spinsters and divorcées. A divorcée still needs her ex-husband's permission for mundane transactions concerning her children, such as medical procedures or moving schools, obtaining a passport, or even an ID card. Her chances of remarrying are slim to none unless she agreed to be the second or third or fourth wife.[26] And even then, men prefer a short affair on the side. Men from the Gulf, regardless of their age, looks, and intellect, are only interested in the newest goods, wrapped in shiny clear cellophane, with a bow and a logo of a well-known

---

25 Quran 2:230. This rule was most probably meant to deter Muslims from countless divorces and marriages.

26 In 2017, 8824 new marriages of Kuwaitis were registered. Among these men, 764 were still married to another wife, 62 married a third wife, and 13 married a fourth wife. The number of concluded divorces between Kuwaitis was 4839. In 2021, 11322 new marriages of Kuwaiti bride and Kuwaiti groom were recorded, and 5144 divorces between Kuwaitis concluded. Source: Central Statistical Bureau, Annual Bulletin For Vital Statistics, Marriage And Divorce 2018 & 2021.

brand on top. She has to be a young, pretty virgin, from a good family with money; he – is a man.

In case of a divorce, a woman does not receive alimony for herself but only for her children, even if she has no income of her own. A Kuwaiti woman usually returns to live with her parents, while a foreigner is often left only with her substitute family: friends. If she has not been naturalised and her visa or residency was awarded through her husband, she will have to find a new sponsor: this could be an employer, whether fake or real, or her child. Finally, her social status after divorce plunges. If her family and friends are traditionalists or care about what people say, they will likely avoid the company of a divorcée as conventionally, it is the woman who takes the blame for the separation, and the reasons for it (factual and alleged) weigh heavily on her reputation.

Women must defend themselves against the bias, shaming, and harsh comments, and often build a whole melodrama around their failed marriage and divorce, portraying the ex-husband as the devil incarnate. It is a common practice throughout the Middle East for women to accuse their husbands of having affairs, being homosexuals, dealing drugs, to obtain a divorce or custody of the children after their divorce, or to strip the ex-husband of visiting hours. In contrast, some men falsely accuse their wives of infidelity to avoid paying the dowry or to take the children away from them. Newspapers regularly report stories of courts annulling marriages due to women having undergone plastic surgery, a gastric sleeve, or liposuction before marriage and not informing the prospective husband. Judges would rule that these actions constitute fraud under sharia, thus the women must pay back the dowry.

The legal system in Kuwait and the social values turn divorced couples into enemies competing against each other and blocking the other side from having a normal relationship with their children. In many cases, one of the parents would not get to see the offspring for long periods of time. A friend of our family was always complaining that his son, who permanently lived with his mother, didn't want to see him, and if and when the boy agreed to meet and would get into his father's car, his face was always sour. The dad couldn't understand why. He tried his best to be on good terms with his ex-wife and to spend time together with his son, taking the boy out to eat at his favourite restaurants, to ride bikes, to the cinema, to trips abroad. When the son grew older, it became clear during a conversation where this attitude had its source.

'You are a loser. You couldn't be with us and now you cannot even keep a new relationship with any woman,' the teenage son accused his father in anger.

'I don't want to get married again because I don't want to have more children. I don't want to repeat the mistake I made with you. I keep kicking myself that I wasn't close to you, that I couldn't be a hands-on father.'

'Really? My mother said that you're so miserable no one wants to be with you. She said many other things, too. I always thought you were really bad. And she always warned me not to tell you what's going on in our lives because you could use it against us. That if you knew she got another husband you would take me away from her and I would never see my siblings. Are you going to take me away?'

Some women in the Middle East endure ill treatment and their husband's indiscretions in order to avoid divorce. Sarah and her husband, both Kuwaitis, have lived in emotional separation for years. They have teenage children. In their case, she works and provides for the house while he spends his days on the sofa playing PlayStation, occasionally leaving the house to meet with friends. In fact, Sarah often doesn't know where her husband goes. Despite feeling very lonely and taking antidepressants, she refuses to file for divorce. 'Who would want me after that?", she says. "I don't want to go back to my parents' house. And at least in front of people I'm married and I have my home.'

Another woman has just had her fifth baby after everyone in her family was certain she and her husband were done having children. She took the decision about conceiving again on her own, without consulting her spouse. Once she confessed: 'I know I'm not good enough for him. I wanted to bear him many children so that he wouldn't leave me.'

In contrast to that, Beata is contented with her life. She has found a landlord who rented her a small apartment where she lives with her daughter. She doesn't answer to anyone. She has insulated herself from this society. (Although she does help her ex-husband; after all, he is the father of her children. He is old and infirm, and has been abandoned by his other ex-wives.) She regularly meets her girlfriends, who are mainly European, for coffee or at boozy house parties, maintaining a strong social circle. Officially she does not work – she receives a monthly divorcée benefit to which she adds extra money by driving her friends' children to school. Every year or two, she flies to Poland to visit her father, and at least once a year, she goes on holiday with friends to some exotic location abroad. This time, they are going to Thailand. She has made peace with all that has happened, she says.

CHAPTER 4

Rewritten history

National history is a crucial subject for any country and society as it functions as the basis of our identity, culture, and heritage, and shapes interactions within and between nations. While it can be a powerful tool for fostering unity and patriotism, it is susceptible to manipulation and distortion to serve political ends, such as controlling the population, legitimising the power of a certain group, and justifying their actions. This applies not only to authoritarian regimes but also to democratic nations. Throughout the ages, national history has been a means used to advance specific agendas of those in power as well as the opposition and other interest groups. It is often a sensitive and dangerous matter.

Egyptians, Moroccans, Syrians, Iraqis, Iranians are taught that Arab armies liberated their ancestors from cruel, godless, and unjust national rulers, and that they all share a common Arab identity. However, this narrative ignores the rich diversity and complexity of the Middle East, which is home to diverse people with unique cultural and historical backgrounds. There are countless struggles and conflicts among these different groups as they compete for control over land, resources, and political power. Competing narratives are created about who are the rightful native inhabitants of a particular region, what their identity is, and who has the right to rule.

Therefore, it is not surprising that governments seek to create a unifying version of history, which itself lends credibility to the status quo. They may strive to control tradition and the content of history education through censorship, propaganda, and the suppression of alternative narratives.

Kuwaiti schools teach the history of Kuwait in three simple stages. As a result, all children believe that before the year 2006, which is when the recently passed Sabah al-Ahmad al-Sabah became an emir, there was very little there in Kuwait. The adults reckon that before the ancestors of emir al-Sabah moved to this land, Kuwait was an empty piece of desert, uninhabited and disconnected from the rest of the world. And all of the Muslim countries share the conviction that the history of humanity began with the arrival of Prophet Muhammad and his companions. Not a word is mentioned about any of the ancient civilisations of whose territories this land was a part, let alone any other civilisations.

Writing the history of this region in a truthful manner is an impossible task, and dangerous at that. The available accounts of events are full of discrepancies, contradictions, and fabrications. The wandering Bedouin tribes left no written records, and the records of the old civilisations have either been destroyed, censored, or disregarded. Even the Islamic texts, often taken as factual, were written centuries after the events they describe, by people who were foreign to the language and region.[27] To reconstruct many events, we can only rely on later narratives and accounts of travellers from the West and North.

A part of a larger whole

It is taught that in the mid-18th century CE, a group of tribes seeking respite from a drought in the heart of the Arabian desert: Najd, came to the area of present-day Kuwait. Together, they were

---

27 Patricia Crone & Michael Cook (1977). Hagarism: The Making of the Islamic World.

known as Bani Utub, and among them was also the clan of al-Sabah. Narratives about the Utub electing Sabah bin Jaber as the first emir of Kuwait in 1756, and Kuwait flourishing and becoming a hub of trade and commerce under the rule of al-Sabah family, have been heavily emphasised in the region. It should come as no surprise that nowadays few members of society want to remember events prior to 1756, nor do international politicians and decision makers. This date is often used to legitimise the status of Kuwait as an independent state as well as its rulers' claim to power, land, and any goods this land yields, and their assertion that it is to them that Kuwaitis owe their prosperity. Moreover, they emphasise the notion that they rose to power through the consensus of the people and in accordance with Islamic teachings.

Archaeological finds throughout the country confirm an almost continuous existence of a settlement since 13,000 BCE. This indicates that the Kuwaiti state was not born in isolation from the rest of the world but for centuries was part of other lands, states and nations, and has had numerous ties with other regions. Different remnants from, amongst others, proto-Hellenistic and Hellenistic times have been found in Kuwait, mainly on the island of Failaka, known as Ikaros by the Greeks. In its time, the area could have been a part of Alexander the Great's empire. Archaeological excavations provide evidence that as early as the sixth century CE, it was inhabited by Christians, as shown by countless remains of churches, monasteries, figures of crosses, and gravestones. In 1756, Kuwait was part of the Ottoman Caliphate, as were Iraq and the rest of Arabia, which is another fact Kuwaitis choose to ignore.

Where al-Sabah came from and the establishment of the state is one of the most sensitive and politically charged topics. Their history indicates that they were always connected mainly to the sea, not the desert, as previously to settling in Kuwait they lived on the coasts of Qatar and Bahrain as well as on the

Persian side of the Gulf. This is what makes their opponents argue that they are neither Arabs nor nomads. In response, they have assured that they are originally from the Arab tribe Anazzah, which inhabits the northern part of Iraq and Syria and exists in some parts of Saudi Arabia.

Located on land and marine trade routes between the Levant, Mesopotamia, India, Najd, and the Horn of Africa, Kuwait for centuries participated in the trade of pottery, textiles, spices, wood, dates, horses, pearls, and slaves. Moreover, as Kuwait lay at the intersection of several grazing tracks, the various Bedouin tribes that roamed these tracks also traded there. Over the ages, its inhabitants held such professions as fishermen, merchants, sailors, caravan guards, city guards, pearlers, shipwrights, farmers, pirates, and smugglers.[28,29,30]

As for the land, its history is quite complex. Some argue that up until 1905, Kuwait together with the surrounding areas nominally belonged to the Ottoman Caliphate, although it was managed by local sheikhs from al-Sabah family, who were recognised by the Ottoman headquarters for the region in Basra. Historical and political sources of that time, the most important being the British archives, confirm that Kuwait was indeed a very small semi-autonomous part of the Ottoman Empire. John Gordon Lorimer, a British historian and the officiating British Resident in the Persian Gulf at Bushire (Bushehr, Iran), wrote: 'In 1775 Kuwait was regarded as a dependency of Basra.'[31] Husain Khalaf al-Shaikh

---

28 The British Resident in the Persian Gulf to the Government of Bombay, Bushire, 21st November 1889, IOR: R/15/1/200 5/65 I, as quoted in Jerzy Zdanowski (2008), Slavery in the Gulf in the First Half of the 20th Century. A study based on records from the British Archives. Warsaw.
29 Husain Khalaf al-Shaikh Khazal (1962-1970). Tarikh al-Kuwayt al-Siyasi (The Political History of Kuwait), vol.1. Beirut: Matabu Dar al-Kutub, p.41-42.
30 Alfred De Witt Mason & Frederick J. Barny (1926). History of the Arabian Mission, 1855–1923. New York: Board of Foreign Missions, Reformed Church in America.
31 John Gordon Lorimer (1915). Gazetteer of the Persian Gulf. Vol I. Historical. Part IA & IB, p. 1002 (1157/1782).

Khazal, the son of one of the most important lords of the region, wrote that during Abdullah II Al-Sabah's reign, the Ottoman minister of Iraq, Medhat Pasha, recognised the Kuwaiti sheikhs.[32] In contrast to that, in 1793, the British Bank moved from Basra to Kuwait for two years. Kuwait also provided refuge for merchants from Basra who were fleeing exploitation by the Ottoman, which demonstrates that the country was separate from the Ottoman administration of Iraq. Before World War I, the Germans wanted the Berlin-Baghdad railway to end in Kuwait, not just Basra, but the Kuwaiti sheikh supported by the British foiled that attempt. It appears that the sheikh was wary of the idea that the Ottoman soldiers could easily move into his country at any time. Despite having been at times under the protection of different powers, Kuwait maintained control over its internal affairs. This applies to many cities and regions within the Arab world.

The situation of Kuwait is by no means unique. Many regions in this world are seen differently by different people. For instance, some may argue that Gibraltar, with its distinct British influence, is essentially a British territory, while others insist it should be recognized as part of Spain, or Morocco. The identity of various countries is indeed a fascinating subject for serious historians to examine.

Dramatic changes occurred in the region when the local sheikh Muhammad al-Sabah, who had been acknowledged as the representative of the Ottoman Basra government and as the legitimate leader by the people of Kuwait, was killed along with his brother. One Kuwaiti historian describes how Mubarak al-Sabah killed his half-brothers, Sheikhs Muhammad and Jarrah, to seize power. The following morning, he gathered the senior people of the country to declare himself the ruler. The historian wrote: 'He came wiping tears from his eyes, and we don't know:

---

32 Husain Khalaf al-Shaikh Khazal (1962-1970). Tarikh al-Kuwayt al-Siyasi (The Political History of Kuwait), vol.1. Beirut: Matabu Dar al-Kutub, p.38.

were they tears of happiness and joy or tears of sorrow and sadness. Maybe happiness has tears similar to sorrow.'[33] Mubarak then attempted to secure the support of the Ottoman Caliphate for himself as a vasal.

Other historians do not corroborate this version of the assassination story. Moreover, Sheikh Mubarak is widely regarded as one of the greatest statesmen in the history of the region. He was the founder of modern Kuwait and the mentor of King Abdulaziz, the founder of Saudi Arabia, who lived in Kuwait for many years. Due to his success in defeating much larger countries and stronger armies, he earned the title of 'The Lion of the Arabian Peninsula'. He held deep animosity toward the Ottomans, whom he saw as cruel and corrupt occupiers. Kuwait's population grew under the Sheikh, as people were drawn in by what they referred to in Arabic as *nadhaam* , which means a rule of law, instituted by him. Mubarak invited the British and Americans to establish Western education and healthcare in his country, saying that the locals suffered from diseases and ignorance, and he pledged to support their efforts. The American missionaries described the Kuwaiti society as orderly, fair, and tolerant, and its ruler as approachable and open to suggestions.[34] When one of the American doctors suggested building a fence to protect Kuwait from invasions, Mubarak famously replied: 'I am its fence'.

Brits enter the scene

How did the British come into the picture and why are they so revered in Kuwait to this day? In late 19th century, the British Empire controlled large parts of India, from where they sourced

---

33 Abdul Aziz al-Rasheed (1978). History of Kuwait. Beirut, Lebanon: Al-Hayat Publications, p.148 (in Arabic).
34 Sandra Shinn (1996). American Mission Hospital: Kuwait, UNESCO Report.

goods otherwise unavailable on the British Isles; one of their trade and transport routes led through the Middle East, and notably, Kuwait. Mubarak realised that the Ottoman days were numbered, thus, he sought military protection from Britain in an attempt to separate from the north and gain more control over this small port town. He bet on the winning horse, prioritising the good of his country over loyalty to the imperial force. In 1899, he signed a secret protection agreement with a representative of the British government in India, and Kuwait became a British protectorate. He was the first to wage an attack against the Ottoman army in Basra at the beginning of World War I in cooperation with the British. Kuwaitis, similarly to all other Arabs, were anxious to be freed from Ottoman rule and its cruelty. Furthermore, Mubarak consistently sought to expand his territory and waged several failed expeditions into the heart of current-day Saudi Arabia. These ventures were also preventative measures to ward off potential attacks on Kuwait by other tribes and sheikhdoms.

Due to an annual stipend from the British and their protection, the country thrived. Within a short time, formal Western education was established. Up until 1912, there had been no schools in Kuwait, and the rich would send their children to study in India or Iraq. The middle class would learn how to read and write and memorise some passages from the Quran in religious *madrasas* run by imams, who were the teachers, judges, and government propaganda officers all in one. The vast majority of the population worked in labour-intensive jobs and lacked basic literacy skills.

The American Mission hospital, established in 1909, was the first hospital in Kuwait. This institution, run by nuns and missionaries, saved countless lives. It introduced vaccination and combated contagious diseases rampant in the region. Many contemporary Kuwaitis ruminate about how the country was ungrateful for shutting down this hospital and erasing its contribution from its history. Many would say that the staff saved their lives from tuberculosis, bubonic plague, cholera, or smallpox, and they still remember the free food that was given to them by the people who were declared unwanted infidels once there was no need for them. Nowadays, the buildings, which stand by the sea in Kuwait City, host the Amricani Cultural Centre, rich with artefacts from many regions and eras.

Since gaining independence, Kuwait has banned missionary work in the country.

The British Empire also played a key role in the formation of other countries in the region: Saudi Arabia, Bahrain, Qatar, the United Arab Emirates, Egypt, and so on. Many times the British drew straight lines on maps without much regard for territorial interdependencies of local peoples or clans.[35] Many times they established, or helped establish, rulers who were most aligned with their goals, and other times those who muscled their way to the top or deceived them. The effects of their multi-faceted and erratic politics in the Middle East are still evident up until this day. On the other hand, many Arabs argue that if it were not for the British, these would have been lawless, ungovernable lands. They seem to long for certain aspects of the British rule. One widely-known anecdote in the region tells of an Iraqi Kurd who was appointed an attaché in London in the early seventies, less than 20 years after the British withdrew from Iraq. Upon arriving at Heathrow and seeing the flag, he burst out screaming: 'Evil occupation, unjust occupation, why did you desert us?'

After WWII, a weakened Great Britain slowly withdrew from the Middle East, to be replaced by local rulers and traditional entities. The USA's influence in the region – both in politics and business – was steadily growing. It became the protector without interfering in domestic policies or demanding a share of the wealth.

---

35 See: Sykes-Picot Agreement of 1916; Uqair Protocol of 1922.

Foreign adventurers poured into Kuwait when news spread about the existence of significant oil reserves in the areas surrounding the Persian Gulf. The prospect of big gains drew in enterprising individuals from abroad. In the 1930s, Sheikh Ahmad al-Jaber al-Sabah signed a concession to a joint American-British partnership named the Kuwait Oil Company (KOC) to explore, extract and sell oil from what was considered the territory of Kuwait. In 1938, KOC struck the first commercial quantity of oil, and in 1946, after the end of World War II, the first export load left the country.

At that time, the majority of Kuwaitis lived in abject poverty. The enforced laws were unjust as they favoured the rich families at the expense of the rest of the population. For instance, the diving law stipulated that if a diver died, his debt to the owner of the ship would be transferred to his children. The judges in the court presiding over the issues of diving and sailing were made up exclusively of ship owners, and their sentences could not be appealed. Alan Villiers, the Australian adventurer and writer who sailed with Kuwaitis in 1938 and spent a few months in Kuwait, observed that the vast majority of people were the poor, who took loans from ship owners before they sailed in order to keep their households. The small ship owners were all indebted to the few rich merchants, who were themselves indebted to the Sheikh, who collected taxes from every ship and all goods that entered or left the ports. Villiers described how the rich of the society had several wives, big houses, an abundance of food, while the rest of the population suffered and lived miserable lives.[36]

Earlier in the same year that Villiers resided in Kuwait, a group of merchants demanded that Sheikh Ahmad al-Sabah

---

36 Alan Villiers, The Sons of Sindbad, 1940, London, Hodder & Stoughton Limited.

share power and wealth with them. Initially, the Sheikh agreed and an election for a council was held that year. The right to vote was limited to the upper class, who could select representatives from around a dozen merchant families. Once elected, the council members demanded that Al-Sabah relinquish a portion of his income to them and share his power. They also began deporting residents of Iranian descent and established relations with the Iraqi government. In response, Ahmad dissolved the council, and his men suppressed the ensuing revolt, killing two people and arresting others. Five members of the council were jailed in harsh conditions, and others fled to Iraq. One of the demands of the opposition at that time was for Kuwait to be united with Iraq, as Iraq had a parliament and an elected government representing the upper class.

The golden era

In 1950, Ahmad died and his cousin, who sympathised with the opposition, became the ruler despite the objection of many of al-Sabah. It was the beginning of an era of economic prosperity. Roads, ports, an airport, public offices were built, as well as a seawater distillation plant. Further oil concessions were given and further oil wells gushed. The Kuwaitis grew self-assured and took matters into their own hands: on 19th June 1961, they signed an agreement with Great Britain to become independent, becoming the first sheikhdom in the Persian Gulf to do so. At the same time, Sheikh Abdullah al-Salim al-Sabah declared himself the first Emir of Kuwait.[37] Iraq objected to Kuwait's independence, and the Soviet Union prevented Kuwait from becoming

---

37 The anniversary of the signing of the Declaration of Independence falls in the month of June, however, due to the hot summer weather, the National Day is celebrated on 25th February, which marks the day that the first emir was crowned.

a member of the United Nations. Iraq claimed that Kuwait was part of Basra, and the people living there were originally Iraqi. They also claimed that Kuwait as a sheikhdom was a small town surrounded by a wall, therefore the land near Basra, where most of the oil was spilling, belonged to Iraq, not to Kuwait. In 1963, the Iraqi president was toppled by a military coup and executed. Many have claimed that Kuwait played a part in that coup and this is why the new leadership accepted Kuwait's independence. Many Iraqis accused the Kuwaitis of bribing the new president, who recognized Kuwait as independent from Iraq.

By 1976, the Kuwaiti government took over control of KOC while giving the prior owners the right to purchase oil at a discount.

All these oil wells rose in an uninhabited desert, a no-man's-land. The oil fields were discovered by Western engineers, and the wells were drilled by low-paid local and expatriate workers. All the same, the entire revenue that was generated flowed to the ruling families, making them some of the wealthiest families in the world without much effort or contribution on their part.

Kuwait's golden era, which began under the British protectorate, continued throughout the 1960s and 1970s. During these years, the country's national institutions were formed: the constitution and the National Assembly. Journalists, poets, musicians, and actors enjoyed relative political freedom. Al-Arabi magazine, established in 1958, held a prominent position as the leading Arabic-language magazine worldwide. In 1966 Kuwait University was founded. Women, rather than covering their heads with the hijab, showed off their legs in skirts that were knee-length or shorter. People would spend their free time going to concerts, theatres, bars, or cinemas . The inauguration of the Sultan Gallery in 1969 marked the region's first contemporary art gallery, hosting exhibitions of renowned artists. Looking at Kuwait's current state of affairs, it is hard to believe that the country was once a pioneer of progress and modernity in the region.

Alas, this process comes to a halt in the following years. The unofficial stock market Souk Al-Manakh, which had been created by a few well connected and powerful individuals as parallel to the national Bursa, crashed in 1982. It had operated in stocks of hundreds of fake, non-existent, or overvalued companies registered in other Gulf states and used post-dated cheques as the main financial instrument. At the shutdown, the outstanding cheques from thousands of big and small investors who had trusted the market were valued at $94 billion. This, along with a substantial decline in oil prices, prompted tightening of the rule of an iron fist. In 1976, the emir suspended the Parliament for the first time (an unconstitutional move) and dissolved all the political parties and societies except for the Muslim Brotherhood.

Shrewdness in their blood

Kuwait's rulers have always been shrewd. Many times, they have interfered in the affairs of other countries without taking responsibility for it. The Palestinian Liberation Organization was created in Kuwait, and its leader Yasser Arafat lived in Kuwait and worked for its government. The current leader of Hamas also spent the first part of his life in Kuwait, studied at Kuwait University, and worked as a teacher in a local middle school. The Jordanian queen Rania was born in Kuwait and lived there until she was 20 years old. During the Lebanese war, Kuwait supported different sides (as Lebanon was divided into many factions) and was an influential player. When Khomeini was ordered to leave Iraq in 1978, he sought to relocate to Kuwait, however, was denied entry at the border and subsequently moved to France. In 1979, after Khomeini, with the help of Western media, managed to topple the Shah – a friend and ally of Kuwait – Kuwaiti officials were among the first to congratulate him and show their cautious support to his

Islamic regime. In the Iran-Iraq war that lasted for eight years, the Kuwaitis supported Saddam Hussain financially (sources report a sum of $14 or $16 billion) and fuelled his fervour. At the same time, they kept their diplomatic relationship with Iran open, and many have suggested that they actually did provide the Iranians with funds, especially in the early stages of the war.

After the conclusion of the war, Hussain demanded that the Kuwaiti money and interest be written off as a gift rather than a loan. (The Gulf countries loaned Iraq a total of $39 billion – other sources mention $60-65 billion – and the Paris Club a further $40 billion.) At the same time, Iraqis were accusing Kuwait of selling more oil internationally than the agreed-upon quota as well as of stealing Iraqi oil through slant drilling into their fields near the border. Iraq was bleeding financially, deep in foreign debt, and its currency plummeted from $3.3 to less than 20 cents. Saddam lashed out in July of 1990, accusing Kuwait of duplicity and of waging a covert war to destroy his country.

Yet, it was Iraq's own internal policies that served as the primary catalyst for its decline. Saddam's regime conscripted over a million Iraqi civilians, forcing them to fight against Iran. All males between the ages of 18 and 60 had to serve in the army for an indefinite period; some ended up serving for more than 8 years. By withdrawing tens of thousands of farmers and factory workers from their jobs, the Iraqi regime turned some of the most fertile lands into deserts and ruined industries. Iraq, once the world's largest exporter of dates with over 30 million palm trees in the 1970s, saw 90% of these palms vanish by 1990 and had to start importing dates. Additionally, billions of dollars were spent on ammunition, weapons, and army provisions. By the end of Iraq-Iran war, the Iraqi budget was heavily dependent on oil revenues and foreign aid.

Several Arab leaders intervened to contain the disagreement between Iraq and Kuwait, but the Kuwaitis were adamant in

refusing to yield to Saddam's demands. The Jordanian prime minister stated in a documentary produced by the Saudi TV channel
MBC that he had warned Sabah Al-Ahmad that Saddam was serious, and had pressed him 'to solve the issue; he [the emir] replied:
what is he [Saddam] going to do? if he wants to occupy Kuwait,
let him do it, and the Americans would get in and remove him.'

The war

On 2nd August 1990, Iraq invaded and after a short fight annexed
Kuwait. Iraq claimed that there was a military coup by Kuwaitis
who wanted to be united with Iraq, as it had always been a part
of Iraq, 'a province lost' only temporarily due to Great Britain's
colonial activities. There were also the charges of Kuwait's slant
drilling and purposefully dumping oil prices through overpro-
duction. Emir Jaber al-Ahmad al-Sabah, the government, and
the majority of the ruling family, including the then Minister of
Defence Nawaf al-Ahmad, fled the country within hours of the
invasion, leaving the majority of citizens on the ground. International negotiations proved ineffective, and on 26th February
1991, a joint coalition force consisting of 35 countries led by the
United States moved into action and liberated Kuwait from occupation. At Saddam's behest, the retreating Iraqi army set Kuwaiti
oil fields on fire. Over the following months, an estimated four
million barrels of oil leaked into the sea and land until the spill
was contained, and the last burning oil field extinguished on 6th
November 1991, with the anniversary being remembered and
celebrated in Kuwait.

Nowadays, the Americans appear to be the guarantors of
peace in the region, both by means of their foreign policy as well
as more tangibly, with around 15 thousand of their troops stationed at military land and air bases in Kuwait, at the expense of

the American taxpayer. The most well-known one, Camp Arifjan, is located in the south of the country and looks like a small city. The presence of the soldiers becomes particularly visible to the public when they walk around the city on their pass days. But the Americans, like the rest of the non-Kuwaiti population, are treated as labourers. They are not permitted to express their opinions or practice their religion in public.

CHAPTER 5

Freedom of expression:
Countries with two gods

The current emir is regarded as a mere continuation of his shrewd and feared half-brother Sabah al-Ahmad al-Sabah. In fact, many Kuwaitis think that Emir Sabah nominated Nawaf as his crown prince because the latter was known for his loyalty. During his rule, Sabah al-Ahmad run the country as a puppeteer with various tools and tricks. He surrounded himself with a small group of assistants on whom he kept a constant watch; he trusted no one. It was known that whenever he praised someone in public, it meant this person's days were numbered. One famous example is that of his nephew Mohammad al-Khalid al-Sabah: he appointed him as the minister of interior and entrusted him with crushing the opposition. After he succeeded in his mission, Sabah al-Ahmad met with him while inaugurating the new ministry headquarters. In front of cameras and the senior officers and administrators, he stated that Mohammad al-Khalid was the best minister for that department and he fully trusted him. A few months later, he had him removed from the post on accusations of corruption, and the general attorney investigated al-Khalid along with the other officials.

An elderly Kuwaiti, a vice-minister in Emir Sabah al-Ahmad al-Sabah's government, recalls his former job: 'I'll tell you now, the entire country is ruled by one person. One person and his closest group. Within this small group, they make state-level decisions based on their experience or whatever comes to their minds at that moment. Every time I had an issue and went to the minister, he would tell me to wait until he consulted the big boss. Sometimes, when one of the ministers would make a decision and publicly announce it, he had to revoke it later because the Emir had a different view. For example, Minister So-and-so' – he gives the name here – 'scheduled a conference and announced it in the media. An 'advisor' from the Emir's circle must have read about it, as the next day the Emir summoned the minister and asked: 'What conference? What conference are you calling? There's no conference.' It doesn't matter if the government seats are filled with the Emir's nephews or cousins, as in practice, even the government has no power. This is true for all the Arab states. None of the rulers shares power.'

Saying that the current Emir Nawaf al-Ahmad and his Crown Prince Mishal al-Ahmad have been in power since they were born is only a slight exaggeration. Their father Ahmad al-Sabah ruled from 1920 to 1950 and was succeeded by his cousin and brother-in-law Abdullah al-Sabah, who ruled until 1965. Both Nawaf and Mishal were given key governmental positions in their twenties and have remained in power ever since. During their elder brother Jaber's rule between 1978 and 2006, the two were part of a small group that ran the country. When their half-brother Sabah became emir and 'the source of all authorities', according to the Kuwaiti constitution, the two brothers were his right-hand men. When Sabah al-Ahmad died in September 2020, posters with his likeness were promptly taken down and replaced with those of the new emir, Nawaf, smiling on them.

The Lord Above and the Lord on Earth:
Two Figures of Reverence

In the Middle East, the head of the state is treated like a god. The level of veneration toward him surpasses that of even medieval European kings. In Muslim countries, every ruler is considered to be a caliph, which means successor, of the Prophet Mohammad. The Quran contains a verse which explicitly states that it is Allah who grants authority to rulers and takes it away from them. Muslim kings and emirs often highlight this verse and other texts which instruct Muslims to be obedient to their leaders. For 1400 years, Islamic Caliphates were centred around the ruling families, not around the land or the population. They were called after the dynasties, such as the Umayyad, the Abbasid, the Fatimid, the Ottoman.

It appears that the leader of the nation deserves only reverence and praise. In public buildings, hospitals, schools, in offices, restaurants, workshops, pharmacies, and shisha shops – wherever you look, there are portraits of the Emir and his half-brother, the Crown Prince. Not just in the main halls but in each single hospital room, each single office. There are so many of them everywhere that eventually, the brain stops registering them. A person sightseeing the city might initially be shocked with the number of pictures of their Royal Highnesses looking at them from building walls, posters, banners – sometimes so big that Mao Tse-Tung would have been envious. After driving around the city, a friend from England who was visiting me quipped: 'Propaganda is strong here.'

I was surprised to find the same signs of reverence for the rulers in every Middle Eastern country I visited, whether they were republics, such as Egypt, Iran, Syria, or monarchies; secular or religious.

School children begin the academic year with a ceremonial thank-you to the emir. Public television and newspapers are filled with endless praise and gratitude for His Highness. International guests flatter him during speeches. Fearful citizens make a point to hail him even in private conversations.

The leader of the nation allows only reverence and praise, and any form of criticism is strictly prohibited. A minister once cautioned journalists and newspaper editors: 'We do not accept press infringement on the regime. This is your country and doing any harm to the ruling family will eventually hurt the country.'[38]

These limits apply to individuals, too. Expressing opinions is risky as potentially anything can be deemed offensive. Disrespecting the state or head of state is punishable with up to five years imprisonment.[39] There are also harsh laws in place that deal with blasphemy. Comments insulting Islam in any way are officially classified as a form of hatred, sedition, or discrimination, and prosecuted under the National Unity Act, carrying a penalty of up to seven years imprisonment and a fine of $30,000 to $660,000.[40] A relatively new cybercrime law lays down punishment of up to ten years in prison for using the internet to overthrow the regime by force or 'to change the social and economic system that exists in the country'.[41] These laws are worded in broad terms, leaving prosecutors with significant discretion in their interpretation and application. There is no statute of limitations on them, and lawsuits

---

38 Agence France Presse (08 Feb 2000). Kuwait's FM Warns Newspapers Off Criticizing Ruling Family, as cited in Human Rights Watch (01 Oct 2000), Kuwait: Promises Betrayed: Denial of Rights of Bidun, Women, and Freedom of Expression.
39 Article 25. of the Penal Code of 1970 imposes punishment for 'anyone who challenges the rights or the authority of the Emir, commits lèse majesty, or disrespects the Emir'.
40 Article 19. of 2012 about National Unity. Before that, Article 111. of the Penal Code 16/1960 was in use which imposes up to one year in prison and/or a fine of up to 1000 KD on 'anyone who distributes (…) opinions that include sarcasm, contempt, or belittling of a religion or a religious school of thought, whether by defamation of its belief system or its traditions or its rituals or its instructions.'
41 Article 7. of Cybercrimes Law of 2015.

can be filed years after the alleged event. Numerous laws regulate the substance and manner of public speech. A single statement may be punished multiple times for each inappropriate comment or phrase separately, as well as under various laws. Anyone who finds a statement offensive can file criminal charges against its author, and it is often private individuals who sue others for blasphemy, defamation, insulting groups or public figures, disturbing the peace. The state avoids being directly involved whenever possible.

Different laws are enforced with similar fervency for the genuine pursuit of justice as they are to intimidate, harass, or silence political opponents or members of certain groups, and to achieve other desired outcomes. Regimes prioritize stability and order above individual liberties. However, this approach can also lead to the unjust persecution of innocent individuals, as autocrats may use the guise of fighting terrorism as a pretext for suppressing legitimate dissent.

The outbreak of the Arab Spring revealed that most of the Arab states are powerful entities and enjoy considerable support among their populations. Meanwhile, many of the activists turned out to lack realistic prospects or plans for the day-after, and in some cases, they proved to be more corrupt and autocratic than the regimes they opposed. These events also made the presence of undercover police more conspicuous. There are people who keep an eye on the situation on the ground, as well as those employed to watch footage from countless cameras located in public authority offices, public buildings, shopping malls, streets, university lecture halls. Other workers are combing through Twitter and Instagram for suspicious posts, listening to phone conversations.[42,43] Their job is to monitor the mood of the people and pick up on any behaviours that could be considered dangerous .

---

42 Twitter @TheGulfPortal (20 Aug 2020).

43 The Arab Weekly (16 Sep 2020). Kuwaiti crown prince's son named head of key security agency.

Police General and an Underminister of the Interior Masen al-Sabah said in a popular TV interview that the government knows everything. 'We have a file on everyone', he declared and suggested that people who keep quiet and do not cause trouble are safe, but trouble-makers could have their files disclosed.

Criticising the judiciary, legislative bodies, armed forces, police, politicians, or members of parliament, can potentially lead to legal charges being filed by the general prosecutor. Despite that, the Kuwaiti people have shown courage – or is it recklessness? – many times. They are most outspoken in private gatherings and on Twitter, a platform they are particularly fond of, after blogging lost popularity. A young teacher named Sara Al-Drees wrote in 2013 about the emir Sabah al-Ahmad: 'a great actor before cameras and a tyrant behind the scenes'.[44] For her four tweets, she was sentenced to a total of 20 months of prison with labour. Ultimately, the Emir pardoned her and her mother went to thank him. In 2015, Al-Drees was prosecuted again for a tweet deemed offensive to Prophet Muhammad.

Since 2012, many people have been indicted and sentenced for written or spoken words. Common charges include blasphemy against the Prophet, his wife, and his companions, mocking Islam (but never other religions), provoking religious tensions, jeopardising national security, inciting rebellion against the regime, painting a negative image of Kuwait abroad, insulting the judiciary, insulting the emir, insulting the rulers of Saudi Arabia, Bahrain, UAE, Qatar, Iran, or other countries with strong ties to Kuwait. For instance, from 2012 to 2015 over 106 people were accused of insulting or opposing the legitimacy of the emir, and some of them were sentenced to prison terms.[45] Between

---

44 Human Rights Watch, 20.07.2013. Kuwait: Teacher Faces Jail over Twitter Comments.
45 The Human Line Organization, Social Workers Society and Musawah Group's Parallel Report to the State of Kuwait's Report Submitted to the Human Rights Committee, August 2015, Kuwait.

February 2016 and December 2019, courts ruled on 589 cases involving Twitter users, resulting in 37 prison sentences. The vast majority were acquitted.[46]

Dr Fatima Al-Matar, professor of law at the University of Kuwait, was accused of blasphemy over a joke she posted on Twitter. The joke depicted a dialogue in which she asked God for either a Ferrari or women's rights and gender equality, to which God replied: what colour do you want the Ferrari to be? Dr Al-Matar is a human rights activist who has written in defence of freedom of speech and protested against the censorship of books. A few years prior to this, she had been indicted for insulting the emir and questioning his authority. We don't know how the last case would have ended, as she did not stand trial: before it began, she fled to the United States with her daughter, where they were granted asylum.[47]

The Kuwaiti court sentenced Georgette Abu Murad, a Lebanese Christian TV presenter, to a year of imprisonment and a fine of 5000 Kuwaiti dinars for saying in her programme that 'God doesn't have time to answer the prayers of each and every one of us'. She also told a joke in which a man asked God for a win in the lottery to which God replied that the man should first buy a ticket. She was acquitted by the court of appeal.

In a more serious instance, a former MP was charged for offending the Egyptian president right before his visit to Kuwait, accusing the Egyptian people of taking Kuwaiti money, and threatening the government and the regime if they continue providing financial aid to Egypt. Another person was indicted for recording and publishing a video in which he burned his Kuwaiti passport. A lawyer and Shia activist was prosecuted after expressing support for Houthi 'martyrdom bombers' against Saudi

---

46 Country Reports on Human Rights Practices for 2019, United States Department of State, Bureau of Democracy, Human Rights and Labour.
47 Kuwait Times (16 Jan 2019). Kuwait prof flees to US, claims asylum.

Arabia and other countries, and on another occasion insulting Sunnis during Ramadan. These are the same Houthi rebels who have imposed Shia Islamic law in the territories they control in Yemen, and one of their main ideas is *khums*, a religious tax on people and local government to be divided among the descendants of Prophet Mohammed.

When reviewing various cases of people sentenced to lengthy prison terms for tweets, one notices that many of them are not political activists fighting for equality or human rights but rather extremists calling for toppling of the regime, inciting sectarian violence or civil unrest, threatening national security. These are the ones receiving the harshest sentences. For instance, Sagar al-Hashash was sentenced to a total of 92 years incarceration. He had been using Twitter to call for toppling the regime. In one of his posts, he posted a picture with instructions on how to make Molotov cocktails. In many cases, the accused belonged to extremist groups and had been under surveillance for months if not years. Hamad al-Naqi received a sentence of 10 years in prison for posting a series of tweets insulting the rulers of Saudi Arabia and Bahrain as well as Prophet Muhammad, and supporting the Shia uprising against the regime in Bahrain.[48] Musab Shamsah was sentenced to 5 years in prison for a tweet which said that Hassan and Hussein, the sons of Muhammad's cousin, Ali, were superior to their grandfather Muhammad himself.[49] Shamsah, a conservative Shia, publicly expressed an opinion that was deeply provocative not only to Sunnis, who constitute the majority of the population, but also to Shia who don't agree with such a statement. Another person tweeted that he 'hoped Kuwait would be the 32th province of the Islamic republic of Iran.' Such radical

---

48 Human Rights First (05 Nov 2013). Kuwaiti Appeals Court upholds Blogger's 10-year Prison Sentence.
49 Alice Kirkland (21 Nov 2013). Kuwait: Twitter user imprisoned for five years for 'insulting' Muhammad. Index on Censorship.

individuals vilify the Kuwaiti government for not imposing sharia in the country, which requires stoning people and cutting off hands for crimes, forcing women to wear the hijab.

The portrayal of free-speech restrictions in Kuwait and other Gulf countries in Western media often misrepresents them as lawless states that arbitrarily throw thousands of people in jail for private tweets or innocent talk. It bemoans the 'grave erosion' of free expression in the region. The writers of these articles tend to be foreign to the language and the culture, which may cause them to overlook crucial contextual details. In some cases, they might be part of opposition groups that seeks to topple the regimes. Furthermore, while Western independent media report on instances of accusations being raised against human rights activists, they rarely follow up on the cases to show they were dismissed or the accused acquitted, leaving readers with a distorted view of the situation.

An article that described a young Kuwaiti being arrested for his tweets 'criticising the Gulf monarchs' club' failed to fully acknowledge their significance. This Twitter user employed derisive language, calling the rulers of neighbouring Saudi Arabia and Bahrain 'impure' (*najas*), a term which in Arabic denotes something that has to be cleansed and purged, and 'bathroom slippers', which are regarded as the dirtiest and lowest object in any house. 'Interchangeable pairs of bathroom slippers' is an old slang expression, referring to a time when the left and right shoe were made of a piece of wood with a ribbon for the toes and were indistinguishable, which most likely was meant to imply that Bahrain was merely a part of Saudi Arabia.

Many media outlets covered the story of a Kuwaiti academic who was summoned by the prosecutor, based on viewers' complaints, after she stated in a TV interview that the country's constitution supersedes the Quran and Islamic law. It is, however, considerably more difficult to find information about the case having been dismissed. The public prosecutor stated that Sheikha Al-Jassem had the right to express her opinion, there was no ground for charging her, and that 'freedom of speech cannot be curtailed and not every discussion on religious matters is blasphemy'.

The frequent news reports detailing cases of freedom of speech suppression and violations create the impression that the Gulf rulers are ruthless, irrational, and severe in their enforcement of the law. But it is important to look beyond the superficial statistics. There aren't many cases that result in imprisonment. Many individuals are granted pardons, acquitted by a higher court, or released early. Some are allowed to flee abroad. The intention of the authorities is to keep people in line by instilling fear without provoking them to rebel or causing a public outrage.

Kuwaiti ruling class also strives to keep a subtle balance, all with the aim of staying in power and avoiding a civil war. This applies to all the Gulf states. It is a self-preservation instinct.

While it is possible in Kuwait to criticise the government's policies, members and decisions – depending who you are – attacking the Emir is considered absolutely off-limits. Neither does the regime tolerate calls for violence or unrest. It's not difficult to see how various laws can be used to silence dissent and stifle opposition, however, for many people this kind of suppression is preferable to a civil war.

Similarly, the opposition is to some degree tolerated in Kuwait. If it starts to present a serious threat to the regime, they deal with it in a covert way. One method of silencing opponents is by discrediting or disgracing them: by orchestrating a leak of an embarrassing piece of information, for instance about an MP being found in a compromising situation with a strange woman; by repeatedly broadcasting a politician's one awkward speech, or by making one clumsy sentence or unflattering picture of an adversary a trend on Twitter. Sending a woman to seduce an individual who got in the way or thinks himself an independent thinker and a rebel is neither new nor uncommon in this region. In a country where a person's public image is crucial, it's difficult to regain credibility.

The biggest deterrent in dealing with people who are considered a threat to national security is stripping them of their citizenship.[50] In such an instance, children and grandchildren also lose their citizenship as well as the right to public education, healthcare, benefits, and the ability to travel abroad. They become stateless, which is a fate that some people consider worse than death.

By law, the minister of interior and the prime minister have the right to withdraw or cancel a person's citizenship in certain situations, without having to give a specific justification[51], and at the same time, courts do not have jurisdiction over issues related to the sovereignty of the state and citizenship.[52] Unlike in Britain, illegal immigrants in Kuwait don't have the right to seek legal recourse in court.

In the past decade, citizenship was revoked, among others, from Ahmad Jaber Al-Shammari, owner of Al-Youm newspaper and a TV station under the same name, who published articles and broadcast programmes which stood in opposition to the government, as well as transmitted coverage of the 2011-2012 anti-government protests and published information about an alleged plot to overthrow the government in 2014. Officially, he was charged with posing a threat to national security. It was leaked that he had acquired Kuwaiti citizenship through forgery. One former MP asserted that 'Ahmad Jaber Al-Shammari' was a fictitious,

---

50 See e.g.: The Economist, British issue (26 Nov 2016). Protest and lose your passport. To silence dissidents, Gulf states are revoking their citizenship.
51 Nationality Law (decree 15/1959). In line with e.g. Article No. 13(5), an individual who 'disseminated opinions which may tend seriously to undermine the economic or social structure of the state or is a member of a political association of a foreign state' can be stripped of their citizenship.
52 Article 1. and 2. of the Legislative Decree No. 23/1990 regulating the judiciary.

made-up name. There was another big question that concerned the public: the source of Al-Shammari's money, since he had come from a poor background and had started as a small reporter. It had been alleged that he was acting on someone else's orders.

The case of Abdullah al-Barghash, a former MP and vocal supporter of radical Islamist movements, is one of the well-known examples of citizenship revocation in the country. It was revealed that decades earlier, he and his elder brothers had acquired citizenship through fraud, claiming that their ancestors had been living in the country before 1920. His brothers and their children were also denaturalised, affecting 59 people in total. For many years, Al-Barghash had been tolerated while he vilified the regime and the society, called for sharia to be the law of the land, and interfered in Kuwait's international relations. He crossed all the red lines, and ultimately, the government decided to take action based on the strong case they built against him.

A similar fate befell journalist and spokesman for the opposition Popular Action Movement, Saad Al-Ajmi. His Kuwaiti citizenship was revoked as the prosecution proved he had another citizenship. Three years later, the Emir issued a decision to restore Al-Barghash and Al-Ajmi's citizenships, but not before Al-Ajmi renounced other nationalities and submitted a written apology to the Emir. They both received second degree nationality which does not allow them to run for parliamentary elections. Al-Shammari remains stateless.

In the context of the fight for freedom of speech, it is worth mentioning the numerous academics, journalists, and writers who have been courageously diagnosing social problems and issues in Kuwaiti society, paying the price for offending those in power. On the other hand, there are political commentators and members of parliament who decry and highlight some instances of corruption, speak critically of the government, other MPs, and high-ranking people, while at other times, at opportune moments, they might direct their fire towards the opposition. For that reason, some people don't consider these voices to be truly liberal but rather view them as a safety valve for the regime.

Even the harshest measures find support from a segment of the general public. Kuwaiti society is diverse, with various competing groups, factions, and ideologies. Therefore, a strong government that can keep consensus and unity amongst its citizens is desired by the vast majority. At the same time, people long to express their opinions and ideas and evaluate the country's institutions without fear of retribution or persecution.

One thousand and one books

The only Arab Nobel laureate in literature is Naguib Mahfouz, and his most famous books were banned for decades throughout the Middle East, including in his homeland of Egypt. Censorship of books in this region goes back for centuries and has been shaped by religious, political, economic, social factors. Throughout history, there have been long periods of time when books and ideas were considered dangerous. Many thinkers and poets in this region lost their lives because of their written words long before the Middle Ages. The printing press technology was suppressed in the vast Ottoman Empire and the rest of the Muslim world for nearly 300 years. There is a deep-rooted fear of books in the psyche of some people. And the list of banned books keeps growing.

Every year in November, the Kuwait International Book Fair held at the Mishref fairgrounds attracts throngs of visitors. And every year, a small group of people would protest against censorship of books. Activists would stand in front of the National Assembly building, holding signs with slogans such as: 'We choose what we read' and 'Don't decide for me'. The number of books banned in Kuwait is astounding. In 2018, the media reported that 4390 titles had been outlawed in the previous five years – nearly a thousand that particular year.[53] Photos of the censorship committee reports leaked trough a Twitter account. Twelve censors – six Arabic and six English readers – must have worked fervently to have classified 948 books as unsuitable for Kuwaiti readers. Many books were rejected because of individual words, taken out

---

53 Kuwait Times (16 Apr 2018). 4390 books banned in five years.; Rod Nordland (01 Oct 2018). From Orwell to 'Little Mermaid', Kuwait Steps Up Book Banning. The New York Times.

of context, such as: angels, Satan, Adam, Eve, which were deemed to have crossed the line of decency, just in case. The censors felt that in many instances even words like 'breast' or 'thigh' were also dangerous to people's minds.

Principles on which Kuwaiti censorship is based are complicated. The Little Mermaid shows too much cleavage. An encyclopaedia with the picture of David by Michelangelo also reveals too much. One of the books was banned because its author 'falsely accused her father of molesting her'. Another publication included a scene of rape which took place in Mecca and there were fears about worsening the relations with Saudi Arabia, despite the book being permitted there. In the censors' opinion, some texts were too sexual, others 'favour atheism', and still others propagate religious sectarianism. The Divine comedy, The Brothers Karamazov, The Hunchback of Notre-Damme could not escape the censors' ire.

But there are many books for which it's difficult to see a reason for censorship. One year, a particular novel might be acceptable, and the next year it would be banned. The easiest way to explain it is to say that banning a book is much easier than releasing it. If one Arab-language country prohibited certain books, others would follow suit. One of the censors in Kuwait said: 'Blacklisting a book is really straightforward, but if I allow it, I have to answer numerous questions about it. There is a list of topics and expressions that are forbidden which we must adhere to. Another colleague who worked with me banned many books for no good reason. It's almost impossible to reverse it.'

In the Arab-speaking world, forbidden books are available on the black market, such as from under the counter in certain shops. Even some sellers in large bookstores would chat up visitors and ask: 'Are you looking for an outlawed book?', then point to a semi-hidden shelf or an upper floor filled with 'contraband'. 'A Banquet for Seaweed' by the Syrian writer Haidar Haidar was first published in 1983, but was banned in the year 2000 after

Al-Azhar, the main Islamic institution in Egypt, orchestrated a massive protest calling for the blacklisting of this novel, which many people had never heard of before. Ironically, this led to its sales skyrocketing. 'It was banned, so I got it. I started reading it but it was so boring that I couldn't pass the third chapter', one Kuwaiti told me. Oftentimes, a publisher would seek to provoke a controversy around a book to boost its sales.

The number of classics banned in the Middle East testifies to the governments' lack of appreciation for literature. It seems that they have left decisions about censorship to lower-level officials, pressured by radical movements, which altogether results in arbitrary, random outcomes. There are many radical factions in Kuwait who seem to disagree on all subjects except banning of all literature that is non-Islamic.

In 2000, Kuwaiti writer Leila al-Othman was sentenced to two months of prison for indecent language used in her collection of short stories called 'The Departure', which had been approved by censors sixteen years earlier. The court did not specify which expressions exactly breached the law; the defence lawyers thought it might be the word 'lustful' in the description of sea waves as well as one of the male characters saying to his roommates in an act of desperation that they could rape him. A couple of months later, a higher court overturned the penalty, however, it upheld the ruling that the book was immoral.

During that same hearing, the court found poet Aliya Shu'ayb, associate professor of philosophy at Kuwait University, guilty of blasphemy and 'publishing opinions that ridicule religion' in her tome of poetry published 1993. As her lawyer said, the only mention of God in the book is the phrase 'God's secret map'. Dr Shu'ayb thought that the charges against her were part of a long-term persecution from fundamentalist groups in the country for the statements she made about lesbianism occurring among students at the university.

There is a small yet vocal body of book lovers and advocates for free speech who protest the censorship of literature in Kuwait. Armed with posters, they take to the streets. On social media, they show off contraband within their private collections with the caption 'I have drugs in my house'. One year a further frenzy was caused by an artist who installed a 'Cemetery of Banned Books' in a plot of land near the fairgrounds during the Book Fair: over two hundred symbolic headstones with titles of some of the books barred from Kuwait. The installation was visible to the public for a mere couple of hours before the authorities removed it, yet it succeeded in becoming a Twitter sensation.

'There are already very few meaningful books in Arabic. There is no free flow of information in Arab countries,' I heard from friends. 'That's why Kuwaitis want so badly for their kids to learn English. Do you think people here are stupid?'

Radicalisation

In 2020, a social media storm erupted when an account published videos and pictures of Kuwaiti girls sunbathing in their swimsuits at a public beach. Someone called the police who showed up very quickly. Parts of the confrontation between the girls and the policemen who came to disperse them were leaked through social media.

'You have no right to remove people,' the girls objected. 'This is a public beach; we want to bathe. Where is the law that says we cannot?'

'We have instructions directly from the ministry,' the policemen's reply was definitive.

All the girls were taken to the police station, where they were forced to sign a letter stating that they wouldn't do it again, before they were released. Such behaviour can result in a charge of disturbing the peace.

Many people are continually frustrated by the suffocating restrictions of rights but time and again they find themselves helpless. The intermingling of males and females is regulated and restricted. The cultural and entertainment options available for the public are limited, especially taking into account the sizeable population of the country, which makes finding engaging activities or experiences to enjoy a challenge. There are no theatre plays being staged, and live music concerts are few and far between. Public art galleries are non-existent. There is not a single place that sells alcohol. There is not one disco or night club. And sports clubs are an arena reserved for the rich to compete for ownership, fame and power, not for the youth to self-actualise. Non-Muslims are not allowed to practice their religions in public. For over a million Christians living in Kuwait, there are five churches which are filled to the brim during all services. The hundreds of thousands of Hindus and Buddhists have no temples. Shia Muslims have been trying for years to obtain permission to build more mosques. Although Jews lived in this land for many decades, there is not one synagogue, and the old Jewish graveyard has been sealed off and no one can get inside it. The main force behind this suppression of freedoms are Islamic fundamentalist organizations, the same ones that collect money to build mosques and Islamic schools in the West.

After five years of working at the same institution, a Kuwaiti friend discovers that a few of his colleagues are talented musicians. Among them, one plays the violin splendidly – he might have been a professional musician – another plays the piano, a third plays the keyboard, and the third man's sons sing beautifully. Yet another colleague plays the oud. They enjoy playing music for themselves and their friends, but none of them admitted to it for a long time. Why?

In Kuwait and in all Islamic countries, music and art carry a stigma of immorality. Until now, musicians are viewed as morally corrupt, while female singers and dancers being stigmatised as sinful and depraved. In Kuwait, measures aimed at radicalising the society were gradually carried out after the death of the moderate ruler Abdullah III in 1965, followed by a period of intensified efforts called *Sahwah islamiya*, 'the Islamic revival', in the 1980s. Muslim Brotherhood sympathisers at the helm of the country were flexing their muscles. Older Kuwaitis remember how booths with megaphones appeared near markets in the city centre, with long-bearded men broadcasting through them: 'Sister, put the hijab on! If you don't want your father to burn in hellfire, cover your hair! Brother! Leave a donation for your brothers in Afghanistan! They are fighting for the souls of all of us!' The authorities also made every effort to associate alcohol with promiscuity or immorality by fabricating stories in newspapers, such as: 'Man raped his friend's wife after they both got drunk' or 'Man invited his friends for a glass of alcohol and then offered him a night with his wife'.

During this time, religious education, which had been considered by both students and teachers as trivial, began gradually replacing music and arts classes in schools. Religious education was divided into two separate subjects: Islamiyah and Quran, and soon expanded from one hour class in a weekly schedule to a few hours a week. Moreover, official sources disseminated views that music was the voice of the devil and it drew people away from Allah. Music was 'an invitation to adultery'. Furthermore, it was forbidden to paint anything that possessed a soul, and because the prevailing belief was that animals had souls, this ban applied to almost everything that could inspire artists. Even a photographer in studios did not do pretty family portraits. Watching television was banned since it also was said to divert attention away from religion. One of the biggest chains of shops selling electronic appliances in Kuwait, whose owner was one of the Muslim Brotherhood leaders in the world, until now does not sell TV sets.

There is a photograph that is famous around the world: three smiling women in miniskirts walking down a street of Kabul, the capital of Afghanistan, in 1972. It is said to have swayed President Donald Trump's decision to continue the United States' military presence in Afghanistan. Less well-known is the speech given by Egyptian President Gamal Abdel Nasser in 1958, during which he and his audience laughed at the demands of the head of the Muslim Brotherhood to legally require women in Egypt to wear hijab. Nowadays, it is extremely rare to see a girl there who is not wearing a hijab; many Christian girls wear it out of fear, not just from the government but the society, too. Hardly a week passes without a report of *niqabi* women attacking uncovered females in public areas or at work.

Kuwaitis also remember a time when they could enjoy plays regularly put on in local theatres, fasting during Ramadan was a choice, and smiling women in short skirts and short-sleeved blouses freely walked down the streets. I have spoken with Kuwaitis aged 60-70 years who claim that they can't recall any of their senior relatives praying five times a day, when they were children. 'When my father prayed on a special occasion, my siblings and I would watch with curiosity', says one of them. A few decades ago, whisky and wine were served in restaurants and houses, which is reflected in the lyrics of a song by the most famous Kuwaiti singer of the 1920s to 1950s, Abdullah Fadalah: 'two glasses of whiskey and beer is my favourite drink.'

Now, to drink a glass of wine, many Kuwaitis travel to Dubai or Bahrain on weekends. Some point out that the majority of Muslim countries allow alcohol despite it being considered *haram*. In fact, you could count on your fingers the countries in the world where alcohol is illegal for both Muslims and non-Muslims. Saudi Arabia, Bangladesh, Brunei, Iran, Libya, Kuwait, Yemen, Sharja (one of the seven United Arab Emirates) are the only countries where consuming alcohol is a crime punishable by law. In practice, alcohol is not unavailable there but rather it is fairly difficult to obtain. If someone really wants it, they could get anything. In Kuwait, a bottle of red Johnny Walker costs around $300 on the black market. Many people brew their own alcohol for private consumption while keeping it well under wraps, as producing alcohol is a major crime punishable by up to ten years in jail. Police occasionally discover small or large factories in apartments, garage, or farms with labelled bottles ready to be distributed. Every year, there are cases of people dying or losing their sight after they have consumed homemade or counterfeit alcohol containing methanol.

A widespread rumour has it that original alcohol comes into Kuwait through the powerful people who are also responsible for upholding the law. To illustrate the irony, Kuwaitis tell a story of an Iraqi man who arrived in Kuwait in the 1950s. He inquired in the main market if there was a place that sold alcohol. He was told that alcohol was *haram*, and the society was conservative, but if he desired it, he needed to go to a sheikh's house, as he was selling. So, the man proceeded and got what he was looking for. However, on his way back, he was stopped by the militia and taken to the sheikh responsible for security. The sheikh ordered his men to confiscate the alcohol and lash the man in public. Once the man was released, he screamed: 'What kind of country is this? A sheikh is selling and a sheikh is punishing!'

Psychoactive substances are much easier to obtain than a can of beer. Lyrica as well as benzodiazepines are popular. Since these are prescription drugs, those who use them often feel safe, invincible. They would think (and say): 'I don't have anything illegal on me' and 'this is doctor-prescribed.' Drug abuse has become an epidemic in Kuwait, and the true scope of the crisis remains unknown.

A young Kuwaiti, approximately 25 years old, confesses to obtaining his prescription for psychoactive drugs from a neurologist (sic!), paying 60 dinars ($190) for each visit, and another 20 dinars at a special, Lyrica-stocked pharmacy. This supply lasts him for two months. At first glance, he appears to be an average Kuwaiti youth, with wavy hair styled with gel like Ross from Friends, dressed in a polo top, track pants, and white sneakers. But his blurry eyes, fidgeting, and inability to maintain eye contact suggest otherwise. He justifies his drug use to himself and others by saying: 'I took some hashish only. Everyone does it. It's just for fun.' And then: 'Okay, I'm not going to lie, I did all kinds of drugs, some Capti, Lyrica. I know what I'm doing is wrong. My friend died, he crashed his car – he was only 38. I don't want to end up like him.' His strong resolve to quit lasts five days. After that, he gives in to addiction.

Illegal Captagon, a drug that contains fenethylline – a pro-drug of amphetamine – is smuggled into the country in millions of pills, making it readily accessible.[54,55] Local youth perceive them as little more than candy. In response to this crisis, the government launched media campaigns focusing on Islamic teachings. One of the popular slogans plastered country-wide during the campaigns was 'My belief protects me from addiction.' Whenever a new minister of interior is appointed, they typically also begin their job by cracking down on addiction. There is only one public addiction treatment centre operating in Kuwait, which grapples with an acute shortage of professionals and thus struggles to keep up with the increasing number of patients.

Hardly a week would pass without news of a major drug bust or about young people who overdosed. A physiotherapist friend confirms the prevalence of hard drugs in Kuwait, stating, 'I've had many patients coming in after overdosing. Young boys and girls… Having strokes secondary to an overdose. The use of drugs is as common here as in any other country, it's just not something widely admitted.'

Over the years, education systems throughout the Middle East have been subject to systematic radicalisation. Ahmed's wife returned to Kuwait after completing her postgraduate studies in Germany, which took her seven years. During that time, their son attended a German school, spoke German, and took ethics classes instead of religion. The parents are now concerned about how well their son will adjust back in his homeland, which he only knows and remembers from his annual summer holiday. They decide to enrol him in a private school that teaches in English and where he will also continue studying the German language. As bad luck has

---

54 Khitam Al Amir (20 Dec 2020). Kuwait: 2 million Captagon pills, guns and liquor bottles seized. Gulf News.
55 Arab Times (24 Aug 2019). Recently seized 4 mln captagon drug pills carry street value of KD 20 million.

it, optional German class coincides with the mandatory Islamiyah, and the boy has no choice but to attend the latter, since all Kuwaiti children are required to take Islamic education lessons. Furthermore, Ahmed notices that his son's beautiful science and history coursebooks, which the school procures from abroad, have pages torn out. He initially gets angry at him but the boy explains that the coursebooks of his classmates look the same. Ahmed discovers that entire sections on evolution theory and parts critical of the Nazis have been removed from the books.

Kuwaitis my age remember being taught at schools and mosques thirty years ago that Christians were evil people who renounced their own children, ate rotten food, and had horns on their heads (with particular 'facts' tailored to each age group). They were told that masturbation weakened the body, caused conditions such as anaemia, tuberculosis, and seizures, and also led to mental health problems, memory loss, extreme shyness, and potentially suicide. The blame for children masturbating was placed on parents who would allow them to listen to music or watch satellite TV. One lustful look at a woman was considered adultery, leading to eternal damnation in hell, with the only way to avoid it being repentance. In addition to that, children were taught – they still are – that there are two angels sitting on every person's right and left shoulder, writing down their every good and bad deed, hence nothing could be hidden from Allah. Such teachings may lead to various anxieties, such as fear of going to the toilet, in case a *jinni* was sitting there. In this process, their inner compass was to be drowned out with a swarm of formulas regulating every aspect of life, breaking them into the role of a docile follower of the regime.

The ministry of education endorses the memorisation of the Quran – not its comprehension, and reciting it – not reading.[56]

---

56 National and international Quran recitation competitions take place regularly. See for example: Kuwait News Agency (27 Dec 2015). Kuwaiti charity graduates Quran memorizers in Tanzania.

It's commendable when the faithful can recite a few appropriate verses from memory at various occasions. Instead of investigating the meanings on their own, they should rely on their religious authorities for interpretation.

The rise of radicalisation has had far-reaching effects on society, influencing not only culture and education but also laws and restrictions related to citizenship. Since 1982, every person applying for Kuwaiti citizenship has to be a Muslim. If a Muslim who has been naturalised 'expressly renounces Islam or if he behaves in such a manner as clearly indicates his intention to abandon Islam', he or she will have lost the citizenship.[57] Apostates from Islam are deprived of various rights: they are not allowed to get married, whether to a Muslim or a non-Muslim, and lose the right to inherit.[58] A marriage of a non-Muslim man to a Muslim woman is automatically considered void. Followers of religions other than Islam are prohibited from employment in the judiciary, military, or police.

It's been suggested that religion and oil wealth constitute one of the means of maintaining dynastic rule and control over societies in the Gulf monarchies. Some scholars have argued that the rise of Islamic fundamentalism in 1970s and 80s was spurred by the fortunes generated by the oil industry, postulating the concept of petro-Islam. Many claim that the influence of the religious movement started growing after the oil embargo in 1973 and strengthened in the 1980s, when the West and certain Islamic regimes collaborated to support the Afghani *mujahedin* against the Soviet Union. Not only did these regimes fortify their power in their lands but they have also taken the offensive toward the West, where they are building more and more mosques, funding Islamic schools, enlisting new followers. In countries like Kuwait,

---

57 Article 4 (5). of Nationality Law, 1959.
58 Articles 18. and 294. respectively of the Kuwaiti Personal status law (Code of personal status) 51/1984.

Saudi Arabia, Yemen, Libya, and Pakistan, there are laws which require public and closed joint-stock companies to pay *zakat*, an Islamic tax.[59]

There is a clear alliance between the Kuwaiti government and radical movements. The Muslim Brotherhood has been represented in every government formed in the past four decades. With control of key governmental institutions, they have been able to advance their agenda and exert influence over other aspects of society. The education system, civil society organizations, media, and unions have been under their sway for years, often with the complicity of the establishment. This pattern is not unique to Kuwait, but reflects a broader trend across the Middle East, where governments seem to have ceded control of education and civil society to Islamic movements in exchange for the latter not intervening in politics.

The argument about radicalisation may seem presumptuous until you have personally experienced its effects. In the Christmas season some shops and supermarkets put up Christmas decorations, like Christmas trees, and certainly not everyone is pleased with it – the idea of officially banning it comes up every year and has been debated in Parliament. Once, when I was out shopping with a friend, she heard a little girl, perhaps 5 years old, say to her mother: 'Why do they allow these *kafirs*[60] to have Christmas trees?'

Currently, some slow and shaky changes are occurring in the opposite direction, however, the old stigmas are still entrenched in the minds of older generations. This is why music enthusiasts keep their passion a secret and practice it in secret, sometimes even hiding from their own families. The previously mentioned

---

59 Law No. 46 of 2006 by the Ministry of Finance (MOF), which came into force on 10th December 2007, imposes zakat on companies at 1% of the annual net profit (less than the traditionally accepted 2.5%).

60 Kafir – infidel, non-believer, therefore: non-Muslim.

man who plays the keyboard cannot do it in his own home as his wife still believes music is *haram*. Meanwhile, the sale and consumption of alcohol has been legalised in the United Arab Emirates (with the exception of Sharjah), and unmarried couples cohabitating and pregnancies outside of marriage are no longer considered a crime there.

The Muslim schism

After half a year of living in the Middle East, I still come across many things that are new and perplexing to me. One day, when looking out the window, I notice that a big green tent, open from one side, was put up in our street, and there is a tight line of people formed in front of it. Behind a counter inside the tent, a few people are packing something for the crowd, comprised mainly, as it seems, of modestly attired workers-immigrants. There are some steel cabinets behind the packers. They're rotisserie ovens! Inside them, rows of chickens are cooked before being given away to the slowly moving centipede of people in front of the tent. Because today is Ashura, the most important celebration for Shiites.

Shiite children take a day off school. Some of the Sunni children also skip school, since they know there will be no proper classes or teaching. Although many news articles attempt to portray Ashura as a holiday shared by both Sunni and Shia Muslims, very few Sunnis observe it, and if they do, it is for different reasons than Shiites.

On the evening of Ashura, tables and stands pop up in the streets and neighbourhoods, from which the Shiites hand out food to anyone passing by as a way of commemorating the death of Imam Hussain – the most important figure in Shia Islam, seen as a symbol of righteousness, honour, justice, and sacrifice. Hussain was murdered by the precursors of Sunni Islam in the Battle of Karbala, which ensued as a result of the power struggle that started right after the death of Mohammad and hasn't ended yet. The Shia have a saying: 'Every day is Ashura and every land is Karbala', reminding them to live their lives in devotion to God and others, like Hussain did on Ashura. Occasionally, children sit behind these tables in front of their houses, and it's considered polite to stop and accept a glass of juice or a snack if you're driving by. The sight of people sharing food, goodwill, and a sense of community is truly moving and speaks to the unity of the Shia. However, some Sunnis view this tradition with suspicion and jealousy, spreading rumours that it is not generosity but a Shiite plot to wipe out their enemies with poison.

During that time, Shiites gather in *husainiyas* to remember the martyrdom of their hero; they beat their chests and cry. Huge halls are erected or rented for that purpose, and large rooms assigned in private houses, often the biggest and best ones, become *husainiyas*. Some *husainiyas* operate only during the Muharram season, while others hold meetings weekly throughout the year. Women can also attend, but they have separate areas from men. After the religious part of the meeting, you can expect a meal. Guests leave an envelope with a donation for the hosts or buy, for instance, a cooked half-lamb, which is later served to all. Every self-respecting Shiite man has his regular *husainiya* that he attends, where he also drops off his signed cooking pots to be filled with rice and meat later. The bigger the donation, the bigger the pot.

In the context of Ashura, I started realising how deeply rooted and far reaching is the Shia-Sunni 'discord'. Unlike the historical conflict between Catholics and Protestants, this one is very much alive and streaked with passion. It started almost 1400 years ago. At the moment of Muhammad's death, Arab tribes united under his command were left without a leader as firstly, he didn't have a son, and secondly, he didn't name his successor. Sunnis, in favour of tradition, believed that the caliph[61] should be chosen from among Muhammad's closest companions; for Shiites, blood ties were key – they thought Ali, Muhammad's cousin and son-in-law in one person, to be the rightful leader.

---

61 From Arabic: khalifa – successor.

Ultimately, Abu Bakr, a cousin of Mohammad and his father-in-law, was named the first caliph by a small but powerful group of Mohammad's companions. Ali became the fourth caliph in the history of the state, and after him, the Umayyad dynasty took over the rule. The Shia, however, saw Hussain, the grandson of Muhammad, son of Ali and Fatma, as the legitimate successor of his father. Hussain orchestrated an armed revolution against the ruling caliph and his Islamic state, therefore in the eyes of the Sunni his assassination was in a way justified. Here lies the crux of the rift between Shiites and Sunnis.

Fighting for succession and power has been the main theme throughout Islamic history, and it continues to this day. The rift between different Islamic factions often serves as a pretext for attacks and wars, as is the case in countries like Syria and Yemen. Both Shiites and Sunnis are divided into various factions and armed groups, which perpetuate the cycle of violence. While Islam places a strong emphasis on unity between religion and state, this unity has often been interpreted and implemented in different ways, leading to bloody sectarian conflicts.

Muslims tend to argue about their numbers. While some boast that there are 2 billion Muslims worldwide, others contest this number. More conservative individuals contend that the figure should not include Shiites, who number over 150 million, as well as followers of other sects deemed heretical by Sunnis, which could amount to more than half the Muslim population They also highlight that many Muslims who belong to the 'right' sects should not be counted among the real believers as they are not committed and don't abide by Islamic laws. Some point to the Quranic verse which says that very few people are true believers.

In Kuwait, and across the Persian Gulf region, there are several Sunni mosques for every Shia mosque. Shiites are estimated to constitute 30% of Kuwait's Muslim population, the other part being Sunni. They are not being given permissions to build new places of worship, while access to existing ones is hindered, for instance, by adapting a mosque's car park for other purposes, or erecting other buildings around a pre-existing Shia mosque. Sunni charities are wealthier and more influential because, unlike Shia ones, they receive funding and support from their governments. The Bidoon who want to benefit from their help must prove that they belong to the Sunni creed.[62]

The lives of Shiites in this country, and generally of people belonging to faiths other than Sunni Islam, are marked by a sense of frustration. They are typically excluded from high-ranking positions in companies, and although some talented and ambitious individuals are able to move up the ladder to a certain level, once that person becomes too important or knowledgeable, or due another promotion, they are cut off like dead weight. Those who refuse to participate in corrupt schemes may not get far in their jobs, either.

When a Sunni neighbour accuses a Shiite of insulting him, the accused can expect to spend a lot of time in police stations and courtrooms over the following few months. If the situation is reversed, though, the investigation is likely to progress drowsily, if at all, and the case file might even disappear. Trivial lawsuits are often filed not so much in pursuit of justice as with the aim of causing trouble and grief to the defendant. He or she is forced to hire a lawyer, take time off work, arrive early in the morning, and wait for the judge, who will inevitably show up two hours late, only to declare for this and many other cases that day: 'adjourned until next week!'

In Islam, there are numerous minority sects. They all uniformly suffer persecution by fundamentalists such as Sunnis and Salafis or Wahhabis. The media tend to downplay and not

---

62 Claire Beaugrand (2010). Statelessness and Transnationalism in Northern Arabi: Bidoons and State Building in Kuwait, 1959-2009 (doctoral thesis). London: London School of Economics, p. 198; 168.

highlight the fact that not only non-Muslims but also the Shia, Sufis, the Ahmadiyya, and others are being attacked by Islamic terrorists. Although Kuwait is for the most part safe and free from terrorist attacks, an exception occurred in 2015 when a suicide bomber blew himself up among a crowd gathered in an old Shia mosque of Imam Sadiq in the centre of the city. He killed 27 people from the crowd that was praying there that Friday morning.

CHAPTER 6

The Pursuit of a Comfortable Life: Duchess Michelle

Someone told me that living in Kuwait feels like living in an airport lounge waiting for a delayed flight: a never-ending stream of arrivals and departures. Then at one point, you are the one who is leaving. I think this can be true about living anywhere. In the end, we are here for some time. It's sad that we tend to forget to make the most out of what we have. I have learned that what makes life much more satisfying is surrounding yourself with cheerful, genuine people, and aiming to be that kind of person for others. A place may be beautiful, it is but a delight that quickly fades with familiarity. However, the company of captivating individuals is a perpetual source of wonder, no matter how much time passes.

Michelle is one of these upbeat people who radiate an infectious energy. When I met her, I knew we would be friends. I love her sense of humour and how she can say anything that comes to her mind. In many situations, she would state frankly what many would be afraid even to think. Once, we were talking about a woman who was soon travelling on the same flight as me.

'Where is she flying to?' I asked.

'To Holland. That's where she's from.'

'There are so many Dutch people here!'

'Dutch people are greedy, so they're probably here for the money,' she replied nonchalantly. 'Unlike us!' she added, bursting into laughter.

What is it that draws people to Kuwait? Is it majestic mountains and lakes? The freedom to live life on your own terms? Perhaps the advanced educational system or the solid judicial system? The thing is, after we have moved to a new place, we might find that that our hopes were just illusions and wishful thinking. It's easy to believe that the grass is greener on the other side, but what if there's no grass at all?

'We live here as if we were never leaving,' Michelle once told me about her family. And it is easy to see what she means. She and her husband rent an apartment in a prestigious high-rise in Salmiya with a breathtaking view of the Gulf and all the amenities – swimming pool, gym, and sauna. Michelle hires a part-time nanny and a part-time cleaner. And she hosts magnificent parties, with waiters carrying trays heaving under the weight of drinks just so they could immediately collect your glass when it turns empty, and with catered food waiting in shiny chafing dishes. She and her husband are French, they have been living in Kuwait for a year. It is clear Michelle enjoys entertaining guests. What impresses me the most is how relaxed she seems even when things don't go as planned. She just deals with it and moves on. When one party is finished, she already has an idea for the next one, as if it was her way to deal with Kuwait, and to help people find some entertainment. I later learn that the parties are to a large extent sponsored by her husband's employer as a means of networking. He was the only one on his team willing to take on this task.

I first meet Michelle in the winter of 2014. She strikes me as a complex yet practical person. She posts a casual notice on the Expat Mums Facebook group, inviting mothers with small children to meet at a playground in one of the parks at a specific time: 'all are welcome'. At the time, the Facebook group has around five hundred members; now, it's nearly 15 thousand. This is the first meeting I attend and meet several other mums with children. Everyone has a great time and wants to be sociable and helpful. Since then, I start going to these meetings almost every week. Although the group is diverse in terms of nationality, we share common experiences and challenges, since we all left our countries in search of a better future.

This group, along with the many other friends I made, allowed me to see this country and the human struggle from various perspectives.

Michelle is in a way the leader of our 'crew', and Kaitlyn and Corrina are two other permanent members. Kaitlyn is a lovely American from the Midwest. It is remarkable how she always has something nice to say to people. Kaitlyn moved to Kuwait when her husband got a job offer in the petrochemical industry. During their scouting trip to the country, they were afraid to try any of the local food, so it was McDonald's, Applebee's, or TGI Friday's for ten straight days. After they moved here, they felt very lonely, and the thing that helped in the beginning was the familiar American restaurants and shops selling American brands. Kaitlyn now laughs about how her old aunt imagined Kuwait to be a vast desert where the main means of transport were camels. She once called Kaitlyn to ask if they had camel parking spaces.

Corrina is very down-to-earth, well organised, and reliable. She knows all there is to know about children, schools, doctors, and all things Kuwait. She's also American (her application for Kuwaiti citizenship is pending). Her husband is Kuwaiti from his father's side and American from his mother's; he was born and raised in the States, speaks Arabic but cannot read or write it very well. Corrina is among the very few foreigners I know who intend to stay in this country for good. The whole family receives decent healthcare here which they believe can be challenging in the US, and both parents are making enough money to cover private school tuition for their children, which they consider a priority. They have calculated they can afford private education for two, that's one of the reasons they are planning not to have more children.

Many people have been envious of Corrie's job. She works in a prestigious research institute specialising in studying and treating diabetes. She is in charge of the administrative side of research, which includes writing reports, dealing with grant applications and ethical review reports. Every now and then, a big project comes along and then she has to stay at the office after hours to do her and others' work. Corrie laughs at me when I highlight that her job is very important: 'The grass is always greener on the other side.' As our friendship develops, I find out she is bullied by a mean, two-faced, conniving boss who is obsessed with power. A couple of years later she confesses that she's had enough of the mobbing and is considering quitting.

Submitting a citizenship application is something Corrina did very early on. She was convinced by her mother-in-law's case who for years had neglected the issue and then regretted it. She is eligible based on marriage, but the waiting time is uncertain since the government keeps moving the goalposts. There are various advantages to being a citizen. It's not just about health insurance, a guaranteed job and pension, and the family allowance. You can count on statutory salary indexation. The state foresaw even financial assistance for Kuwaiti divorcees which is not thrilling but sufficient to get by. I wonder if she'll complete the process once she's been accepted, as the government now enforces the condition of renouncing one's original citizenship and requires a proof of that, which could be a deal breaker.

Her husband is extremely dedicated to his job, unlike his Kuwaiti colleagues, which leaves them with little time to go out together. Instead, they prioritise spending time with their children, trying to relish this fleeting phase of their childhood. They are not close with his father's side of the family but have created a sizeable circle of trusted American and half-American friends. Corrina says that when her mother-in-law moved from the States to Kuwait, she was thrown into the deep end: to a traditional,

Arab family who could not speak one sentence in English except for her husband. Whenever she could hear a person speaking her mother tongue, whether in a grocery shop or in the street, she would immediately walk over and strike up a conversation. This way, she gained a group of American girlfriends who over time formed a sister-like bond. Finding their kin turned into a peculiar kind of sport, and over time the group expanded further with half-American-half-Kuwaiti children. This is with whom Corrie mainly socialises.

Together with my daughter, I've attended a few birthday parties hosted by Corrie's gang and I have noticed how the two generations of American women operate on the same wavelength. They took care of every guest, made sure that everyone felt at ease, and if the hostess of the party was busy, then her friends or friends' mothers would step in. They would chat up and show around people from outside their group, inviting everyone to take part in the games and fun, and ensuring that everyone had what they needed. I found this to be a beautiful example of kindness and generosity.

Whenever Michelle goes on a holiday, she leaves a void that can't be filled. We miss our dictator who schedules our meetings and makes sure everyone comes prepared and on time. She is bolder, more familiar with the immigrant-mother way of life than the rest of us. When an uncomfortable situation arises, she is the first one to stand up. During one of our gatherings, Kaitlyn spreads a mat on the ground for her son to crawl on and invites other mums to sit on it. As we do so, two Bedouin women in black abayas, one older and one younger, arrive with their children and without a word, they make themselves comfortable on the mat. One of the children starts playing with the toys, and the older woman asks if we have water: '*fi mai*?' After a moment, a man carrying bags of food joins them. We feel uncomfortable in this situation but none of us knows what to do. Michelle steps in and politely explains to the women that they need to move or get up from the baby's mat and we will move. For a minute, the ladies pretend not to understand but in the end, they grudgingly take their belongings and move to another spot.

Michelle talks about all kinds of subjects, from fingernail care to Emmanuel Macron and Syrian refugees, and every time she has something interesting to say. We exchange observations about life here, numbers of trusted paediatricians, and the locations of our favourite shops. Together we laugh at the popular local phrase '*inshaallah*'[63], which, depending on the situation, could mean 'yes', 'no', 'maybe', or 'in your dreams!'. Shall we meet tomorrow? *Inshaallah*. Can you fix this washing machine? *Inshaallah*. When can I pick up the documents? Next week, *inshaallah*. Am I okay, doctor? You'll be fine, *inshallah*.

There are times when Michelle doesn't answer her phone, reply to messages or contact any of her friends for weeks. It looks like she is busy with her everyday life. We always pick up where we left off. When we see each other, she is cheerful and smiling.

Joanna is a slender, tall Polish woman with short blond hair and a mischievous smile that reveals her cute uneven teeth. She is a professional teacher who has worked in many countries before coming to Kuwait. She arrives a few months after I settled there. Every time we meet, she seems drained. As an instructor in the English Preparatory Program at the American College of the Middle East, which is a large private college, she works shifts from 8 a.m. to 5 p.m. or from 11 a.m. to 8 p.m. and teaches about 18 hours of classes a week. Each hour of class typically requires four to five more hours of preparation, correction of exams, and

---

63 Inshaallah – Arabic: God allowing.

marking essays as the groups are huge. When she is not in class, she is required to stay in her office and be at the managers' disposal. Here, working hours are longer than those at most universities in the West, and there are often extra responsibilities on top of the programme. But this is something Joanna does not gripe about – after all, also her salary is higher than in many European countries after tax. The most burdensome and overwhelming aspect of her job is the lack of discipline among the students. When we first met, she was very keen on improving her students' skills and motivating them, but each time we discuss this subject, I hear less and less emotion in Joanna's voice.

'I have no idea why they even show up to class. They don't carry coursebooks, don't complete assigned readings. They are not active during class. Instead, they are busy on their phones or chatting,' she says.

'You could ask them to leave,' I remember this being common practice in many universities.

'Actually, I can't. The management does not allow it. I cannot even ban mobile phones.'

'Don't they care even a little?'

'They only want a piece of paper at the end of the year which says that they passed,' she explains. 'And we cannot fail anyone. We need to give good grades. That's what the pressure from the top is about. If the grade average in your class is low, that's your fault. Management tells us to grade on a curve so that the weakest students could pass, too.'

'Even private universities in the UK inflate grades, don't they?' I draw a comparison.

'Listen,' Joanna says forcefully, 'here you get a grade for nothing. You get a diploma for registering. Because the end game of the college is to get four years' worth of fees out of our student's mum and dad, not to expel him or her at the first hurdle. And because of that, the students can carry on with impunity.' After a moment of silence, she adds: 'At the beginning, I had great ambitions. Normal expectations. Now I am happy when the students in class have a piece of paper and a pen,' Joanna laughs at herself, at the naivety of which she has now been cured, as she assures.

Another matter that keeps coming up during our discussions is the treatment of staff by the college administration. Joanna's strategy is to keep her head down and avoid getting in anybody's way. Others, however, complain about the lack of support from superiors, contradicting and inconsistent instructions, work overload.

'They keep changing our rota back and forth,' confirms Joanna. 'They increase and decrease the size of groups, come up with additional evaluations, change the criteria for grading. They force lecturers to write reports which they don't even collect. There are various absurd projects which are not in our contracts but have suddenly become mandatory. The management keeps us busy with trivialities, killing our enthusiasm.'

Joanna's advice for new hires, who arrive often as staff turnover is high, is to keep any initiatives and suggestions to themselves, and under no circumstances to utter a word of criticism of the management or procedures, because people who do are put in their place. Some are even laid off. People in charge know exactly what is going on and they like it this way. They want to keep the gold mine running at full capacity.

High turnover of lecturers, instructors, and teachers has been a problem in private educational institutions. Firstly, most expatriate teachers assume a certain timeframe for their stay in Kuwait. Secondly, if they are not satisfied with the working conditions, they are prepared to quickly change jobs. This is one of the reasons why headteachers are not in a rush to let go of bad teachers: they are valuable in the sense that they are unlikely to quit on their own accord. Add to that, Arab parents of pupils in private schools and nurseries expect their children to be taught by Western teachers which in their mind equals a certain appearance, putting looks before merit. School owners want to meet those expectations. As there is a limited number of professionals from the West willing to stay in Kuwait for longer periods of time, whenever one gets dismissed from a school or college, another school is already lined up to take them on – a sort of recycling of skill taking place among schools.

When someone complains to Joanna about the ill-treatment and doesn't understand why it is happening, she directs them to a blog set up by a disgruntled former employee of the college, saying, 'If you want, you can read about it.' After four and a half years of work in that place, Joanna lost her passion for teaching. 'No, I don't want to work here anymore,' she shakes her head. Before the end of the school year, she is handing in her notice to quit. And she starts counting down the days until departure. Once she is back in Poland, she is going to do translations for a company with which she has previously worked.

～

Then, Michelle tells me she is leaving Kuwait. She is getting a divorce. She caught her husband cheating and it wasn't the first time, either. Once, an Arab woman came to her building and waited in the lobby to catch her leaving and let her know that she was having a relationship with Damien. Michelle felt shocked and humiliated. She reveals her marriage has been rocky for quite some time – a thing she had been keeping to herself.

The relationship between the two has always puzzled me. On the surface, he seems like a good father who cares about his children, spends a fortune on toys and outings. He is a good host, loud and entertaining, who welcomes his guests with a booming *'bonsoir, mon cheri!'*. However, the interaction between him and Michelle is very odd. When they pick on each other, you don't know if they are joking or if they hate each other. Watching them have these duels can be hugely entertaining. She would let him score as many points as he likes but she would always have the final say. The two personalities are very different, and the gap is hard to cover. She is smart, frank, sophisticated – he is simple, almost average. He was previously married and Michelle had given him his second chance.

Her divorce was a trauma. The man became a vengeful psychopath, taking every opportunity to humiliate and abuse her. He emptied their joint accounts and threatened he was going to take the children away from her. She was left alone in a foreign and strange place.

In a country such as Kuwait, according to the law, the man has absolute power over his wife and children. The mother cannot take the children and leave without his permission; she cannot even sign for a child's medical procedure. The law allows a father to block the children from leaving the country: it is a simple application and can be done over the phone, if you know the right person. For the wife to remove it, she has to go to court, pay the fees, wait for months, and she might not even obtain the legal order if she doesn't have *wasta*. Many non-Kuwaitis married to Kuwaitis have had their underaged children taken away from them with the use of this procedure. They would hear, 'If you want to leave, leave, but the children are staying with me.'

I wouldn't absolve Damien of responsibility. He made a series of mistakes and ultimately hurt his wife, his children, himself. He destroyed his family. But the other side of the coin is Kuwaiti society which empowered and fostered what he already was and enabled what he wished could be normal. This boorish Western man found himself in a setting where men are above women by law and by social norms. Woman is a property. She belongs to her father who could marry her off at any age. She belongs to her brother who has to keep an eye on her, make sure she wears appropriate clothes and give her orders. She is property of the husband and cannot leave the house without his permission. Simple things like a haircut or attending a wedding could require permission from the husband, otherwise, according to the Islamic law, they can discipline their wives by beating. While not all husbands follow these laws, they do exist. Damien was spending time with Kuwaitis who didn't help at home or raise their children as they claimed these were the mother's duties. He was drawn to the idea that some Kuwaitis could earn money without doing any work and they would still spend most of their time outside their house. He saw men in Kuwait who had several wives and girlfriends. He liked to joke about it but you could tell he was yearning for it. He would say to his Kuwaiti friends: 'You are so lucky that Allah allows you to have multiple wives. Polygamy is the natural way for men.'

Several Arab and Kuwaiti girls went out with him knowing that he had a family; some would tell him: not a problem, you can have a second wife. This balding, average, simple-minded man past his prime was a catch for many young and attractive women. Marrying a European meant they could go and live in Europe, which they wanted. Their children would be Europeans by birth. They would be secure with this man who had a stable income, and he would never be as abusive as the average local, they thought.

One of Damien's French workmates converted to Islam nominally and married another – younger – Arab wife, in secret. When his first wife found out, she divorced him but he didn't seem to care.[64] He told others that he felt happy with this new girl and she had almost no demands: she didn't expect him to help with any house chores, and even if he cheated it was not a big deal. After all, he was the man and the provider.

---

64 In all fifty Muslim-majority countries where the constitution declares Islam as the state religion, a man can marry up to four women without permission from or even notifying his previous wife or wives. (Tunisia is an exception. This rule does not apply in Turkey, either, as it is a secular state.)

This sentence stuck in Damien's psyche. At parties, while many people were sitting at the table, he would look at Michelle and say to her: 'This is the hand that provides, you must kiss this hand'. This was something the Moroccan wife often did to her old French husband in public. Whether that would continue once she got her French passport might be a different matter. It is quite common for Arab girls from poorer countries to marry older Europeans and divorce them after they get naturalised. Many women assimilate into their new culture but there are also many who, as they mature, grow more religious and conservative as they miss their societies and cultures, or they don't feel welcome. They may then seek men from their own backgrounds to reconcile with their native culture. Still, many more women, once they realise that they could live on equal footing with men and be treated as full partners, would never go back.

The last weeks before Michelle and Damien separated were painful to even witness – something you don't wish on your worst enemy. The man was disoriented, upset, and treated her like an adversary. He realised that he had ruined their marriage to the point where there was nothing to salvage, and he took it out on her. She told me that once they went out for a meal and he asked her to sit at a different table, telling her in front of the children that he was not going to pay for her food. She had to endure that without protest because she was terrified that he could stop the children from leaving with her. He took it as an opportunity to provoke frequent arguments, yell at her, call her names. She was left without money as all their savings were in his name. It was her parents who sent her some money and paid for her and the children's tickets out of Kuwait.

During her worst moments, Michelle was doing her best to stay rational and resilient. Despite the trauma, tears, and sleepless nights, she was able to pull herself together. It was as if she decided that this relationship was done and the most important thing was to get the children out of this country. Self-pity, flagellation, blaming herself or others was not her thing. She made sure the children went to school as usual, saw their mum dressed nicely and made-up, and witnessed as little of the fighting as possible. She applied for schools for them in France and used every spare minute to plan for the next step. She even arranged for psychological counselling to ensure she would function well once back in her homeland; she was anxious to go back to work. Once in France, she got a lawyer who sued Damien for custody of the children and the money he took. Surprisingly, she was not vengeful, despite all that he did and said and his attempts to turn the children against her. She made sure to make him a part of their lives so that the children could continue seeing him. Since the man was doing his utmost to avoid any expenses related to his children, she even paid for one of his tickets to come and visit them.

Whenever she discusses what happened to her, Michelle says that she is lucky to have smart, beautiful kids who give her life meaning. She has met someone new and is in love again.

After they divorced, Damien left Kuwait and moved to a new post in another Middle Eastern country, where he is trying to live his one-thousand-and-one-night's dream, surrounded by desperate women who see him as a way to a good passport.

Explorers of a new world:
Searching for work, not for happiness

When the question about what life is like in Kuwait comes up, many times the reply resounds: Kuwait is what you make of it. You just need the right attitude and mindset, they say.

One of the most cheerful and friendly people I have met here claims that you can live quite a pleasant life in Kuwait if you are able to respect the existing rules. For a contrasting example, he mentions his former neighbour, a Briton, who used to say about Kuwait: 'They owe us [the British] everything. They should pray to us. I don't care about their laws or restrictions.' He didn't last long; he left after four months.

The reality of immigrant life is more complex. Not one of my Western friends without ties to Kuwait by marriage or blood plan to stay here permanently. They follow a model of working and accumulating capital for a few years before returning to their homelands to build a better life there. It is much easier to endure any discomfort knowing it is temporary. In contrast, immigrants from the East (Asia) often work and live on the verge of poverty as long as they can, and use all their earnings to support their families back home.

Some people enjoy the ease of life in Kuwait, such as having a driver take their children to and from school, and a maid who can handle grocery shopping with the help of the driver. That's Vicky's routine. When she comes home from work, the children are already there, and the fridge is full. It is easy for Europeans to get used to the Gulf lifestyle. Vicki is British; she has two sons under 7 and lectures English literature at one of the private universities. Her husband is employed by the retail giant

AlShaya. They are, however, slowly getting bored with Kuwait and considering a move to Qatar, which is smaller than Kuwait but where 'at least you can have a drink'.

Others stick to their plan. Ulla moved here from Denmark with her husband and their baby when he got a job offer from KDD – Kuwait Danish Dairies. During the two years they lasted, they chose to forgo extravagances to save money: coffee brought from home in a thermal mug instead of Starbucks, playground in the park instead of a family entertainment centre. They insulated themselves from the local politics as much as they could. They built up their savings, taking advantage of the tax-free economy and the lack of social commitments. After returning to Denmark, they were able to buy their dream house: a farmhouse with a big piece of land. Ulla was also pleased that she could return to her old job.

Michelle was one of the people who told me that for families with children, life is easier here than in their home countries. Childcare is cheaper and easily available. A friend living in England went with his wife to the cinema and after the film ended, they ran back home so that they didn't have to pay the sitter for another hour of work. In Kuwait such a problem does not exist – the working hours of nannies are not fixed and there are no demands for a bonus if you're late coming home. Besides, there are plenty of amenities for parents with children: playgrounds at supermarkets and restaurants, baby feeding rooms, changing tables in toilets (also men's), and the more and more popular toilets for parent and child. There is a multitude of nurseries and kindergartens, from Arabic to Canadian, 'Montessori' being a popular programme term. In addition, one can pick from after-school clubs, meet-ups, festivals, summer camps and extracurricular activities: sports, arts, crafts, computer skills, or cooking classes – some free of charge, like Storytime in Amricani Cultural Center. It's true that Kuwait is a place where it is easier to have children but this applies only to small children: once they have grown enough to have to go to school, their education will entail considerable expenditure.

Some people praise Kuwait for a relaxed way of life. 'I love the sense of calm,' one of my friends says. 'People aren't chasing anywhere. They like to chat, joke, they smile at each other. Obviously not on the road… They can somehow enjoy life more. Living here has taught me to slow down.' The concept of rat race, so tangible in European and American cities, is completely foreign to Kuwaitis. The working migrants, however, are usually made to toil for long hours.

According to Kaitlyn, making friends is crucial for survival in this world. To strike up friendships and acquaintances in a new place, we do things that might not be in our nature, like chatting up complete strangers. You also need to get out of the house. 'If during the day I stay cooped up inside, I miss my home [in the States], but when I go out, it is like I was home, you know, it's normal,' Kaitlyn told me. I notice how much effort she has put into furnishing their flat. It doesn't look like a typical, impersonal place you rent. She has shipped in many things, including furniture, and hung family pictures on the walls. I think it works. To feel at home, you have to make that home. If you approach the issue as a temporary situation, one that is not worth investing time or money in, if you intend to wait it out, you might not find happiness.

Alexandra,
the multinational corporation,
and the great actor

Alexandra, her Welsh husband, and their daughter moved here from London, tempted by a lucrative job offer he received. They rent a beautiful apartment with a private pool and access to the beach, and after a couple of years spent here, they both bought brand new expensive cars. In London, Alex left a dynamic career in a huge financial auditing firm, and now her biggest worry is that she might become unemployable since she is not practising, and that she is losing her skills. Even here, she keeps up her habit of starting the day with a press review: she checks online editions of the Wall Street Journal, Washington Post, the New York Times – mainly news on politics and the economy. She hasn't come across any suitable job offers in Kuwait and for a while even considered commuting to neighbouring Dubai. That's why she is excited to get an interview invitation to the Kuwaiti division of one of the Big Four and hopes to relaunch her career. A week after the interview the phone rings: she got the job.

Although she is dissatisfied with the contract she negotiated, the department manager convinces her to agree by painting a rosy future for her with the firm, including a promotion after six months, if Alex proves herself, a great team, attending important client meetings, business trips abroad. For Alex, it is very important to continue working in her profession. She concedes and soon starts working.

The firm deals with some of the most important companies in the world and also represents international firms. Its headquarters is located in an imposing skyscraper in the city centre which boasts a lavish reception area manned by smartly dressed young women. On her first day, she meets the chairman – one of the extremely rich and influential old Kuwaitis, whose fortune is estimated to be over a billion dollars. He warmly welcomes her to the company and invites her and her husband to have dinner at his palace. During the visit, the palace, along with an army of servants, leaves a lasting impression on them. There are Rolls-Royces, Ferraris, and Bentleys parked like Toyotas in the front yard. Alex spends an amazing evening. The chairman is extremely kind; he tells her that she should consider him her dad and gives her his phone number.

As Alex settles into her new role, she quickly realizes that things are not as glamorous as she initially thought. The offices where work is done are shabby and overcrowded. The sight of old carpeting, scratched walls, worn out furniture repels. Only the conference room, where guests are occasionally received, is an exception.

With each passing day, Alex becomes increasingly puzzled by the company's inefficient and disorganized operations. She is thrown into the deep end, coming in to a desk strewn with papers with an almost yearly backlog. Why did they not fill the vacancy earlier? The mystery of the century. Throughout her first weeks, she works twelve hours a day. She does not receive induction to the department or her role – she has to learn on her own while finishing major tasks worth millions of dollars, some of them beyond her contracted duties. Instructions and input from her superior are limited to changing formatting on the documents she has prepared. Alex gets the impression that her boss, whenever possible, follows the 'let George do it' philosophy and also evades responsibility for any mistakes. Wanting to play it safe, Alex often fills in the "CC" line in her emails, keeping the rest of the team updated, when she consults her boss on important matters. He gets upset about it.

Her co-workers are a small United Nations. There are some Indians, Arabs, Europeans from different countries, and very few Kuwaitis. There is nothing in common between the workers but rather they are divided into tribes competing for power.

It seems that only the secretary has a good relationship with the senior manager. She doesn't take her job seriously, she's often absent, misplaces documents, and whenever someone tries to point it out to the manager, he cuts them off mid-sentence. The woman is in no hurry to book airplane tickets and hotel for herself and Alex for a business trip, and on the day preceding the trip, she calls in sick. When Alex sends her messages asking about the travel arrangements, she replies, 'Book for me as well.'

During the following months, the promises of VIP client meetings, getting to know the sister-team from Dubai headquarters, and promotion all fail to materialise. In addition to that, Alex begins to notice other worrying things. In documents prepared by her boss and some team members, she discovers fictitious numbers. There are new documents appearing in client folders but they date far back. She would have noticed these papers before if they had been there! Moreover, the company has a policy of informing each client which staff members are directly working on their accounts, and Alex sees her name on letters for clients she has neither heard of nor dealt with their cases. She also comes across several exaggerated estimations of a specific company's assets, submitted to banks as guarantees for loans, as well as portfolios prepared for shareholders that include misinformation and made-up figures.

Alex does not agree to take part in the company's dubious practices; she refuses to sign papers over which she has serious concerns. She also asks that her name not be used without her consent. This is considered an insult by the management. Over time, Alex notices that their attitude towards her is hostile and filled with animosity. She has the impression that whenever something goes wrong in the department, something is missing or hasn't been done, she is the one to take the blame. She believes the CEO and his sidekicks are ganging up against her. Realising the extent of the irregularities, she calls the Kuwaiti chairman of the company requesting to meet with him urgently. During the long talk they have, she explains that she loves this country, and she is glad to be working for this company, and that she regrets to have to tell him there are many illicit and dubious things taking place there. Figures in official reports submitted to client companies are cooked. The chairman seems shocked and distressed. When he asks for details, she clarifies that many clients don't submit sufficient data to be audited and neglect to provide official copies and required documents for checking. She reveals than all the managers are involved, not just the senior workers. If these matters were disclosed, such a scandal would affect not only the company and the chairman's reputation but also the country as a whole. The man listens, tries to appease her despite his obvious distress, and promises to take action. He insists she shouldn't tell anyone about it and provide him with any proof she has. 'Stay calm and pretend that nothing happened and let me deal with this crisis.'

After that, Alex's manager becomes increasingly hostile towards her in a blatant way. As time passes and no corrective steps are taken, she contacts the chairman again. This time, he is indifferent and doesn't even let her speak. He tells her that he trusts the managers and suggests that she can leave if she doesn't like the work. 'He knew what was going on all along. He just wanted to know how much I knew. He was backstabbing me with a smile, while pretending that I'm crazy. And my work colleagues… He hired people who don't care about this country or anyone beside themselves, and he made sure there is nothing that unites them. Also, they have no one to whom they could disclose the secrets.'

In this country, journalism or the justice system cannot touch the big fish. Alex gets frightened as she is warned by several important people that she could get hurt, sued, or deported. Being a whistle-blower is often a suicide mission.

After exhausting all the solutions she could think of, Alex gives up and, after nearly one year in the job, she resigns. Before that, though, she reaches out to one of the senior figures in the parent company with a carefully worded email. As she leaves the firm, she feels drained, harassed, and defeated. Over time, she makes her peace with it but admits, 'It was an experience that opened my eyes. It changed my perspective on the world.' Then she adds, 'For such a scam to work, can't be a one man show. It needs to be a group operation, starting right from the top. Everyone knows what's going on and they're all playing their part'

CHAPTER 7

When in Rome

A couple of years after moving to Kuwait, I meet a young European girl who has a stall selling homemade cupcakes and cookies at an American school festival. She is wearing a long skirt and tunic top and a light-coloured hijab; she is friendly but reserved and quiet. Later on, I find out that Carola is German, married to a Kuwaiti Bedouin, and has been here for six years. She is content enough with her way of life that she champions it; she has even invited over a friend from her homeland and is searching for a local husband for her. I wonder about her reasons, and she eagerly agrees to share her life story with me.

'What made you fall for your husband?' I ask her.

'He liked me for who I was. And he made an effort. He showed that he respects me. We first met online, that was in April, and then he came to Germany. We were married in October. We didn't want a long-distance relationship.' Carola tells me that she met her husband virtually through a mutual friend. They wrote to each other and talked over the phone, despite the man's limited English. After a while, the man came to see her parents and asked their permission to move in together with her, she tells me. Soon after that, they got married.

'Do you like your life in Kuwait?'

'Overall, I enjoy my life here. First of all, you have peace with the way you live. I don't have people attacking me for my faith. In Germany, you are judged for the way you live and categorised.

In Kuwait, you can be who you want without being judged for it. Even before I became a Muslim, I was accepted here,' she says. 'And I feel like in many European countries the sentiment is: 'be anything but don't be a Muslim''

'So Islam was for you.'

'I watched on German TV as they were interviewing a guy on the street and then criticising him; the man was wearing a *dishdasha* and looked like all the men you see in Kuwait,' Carola recalls. 'And I wondered: are they all as bad as they are being portrayed or maybe was the report a bunch of lies? The man just said 'find your faith and find your god' but of course people see it in a negative way if you look like a typical Arab. So I started researching the topic. I wanted go to the source and find out if it's just a few misguided believers or if it's the religion that's flawed.'

Carola came to the conclusion it was the people who were fallible, not the religion, and eventually converted. 'But that was after I got married. Before that I used to tell my husband: 'you have your faith, and I have mine, so let me be'. My husband never insisted on me converting.' She pauses for a moment. 'Of course, people are not perfect and I have seen in Kuwait plenty of things that are not Islamic. And sure, there are people who will talk nonsense to you or insult you because they don't know any better. I try to ignore that.'

'Do you have a good relationship with your mother-in-law?'

'My mum-in-law has been supportive of us from the beginning. We have had some misunderstandings because of the language barrier but now it's all good.'

'Do you speak Arabic?'

'I speak enough to have a conversation. My husband's family only speaks Arabic, so I practically learned by ear.'

'What else do you appreciate about living here?'

'I've met the most amazing people here in Kuwait: my friends. Some people are friendly but they will never let you into their house, some treat you like a sister. And although it gets unbearably hot here in the summer and things melt in the car, I prefer it over the cold, grey and rainy weather. You just need to have an alternative for when it's too hot to go outside. If you're not super poor, you can enjoy your life here if you choose to do so. There was a time when I felt homesick, and everything seemed horrible but then I learned to accept my new life.'

'Another thing that I like is that men don't come near me. You get respect, you don't get touched. I didn't pay attention to it before I moved here but after you learn how it can be done differently, you appreciate it.'

'Do you meet up with friends?'

'I go out with my female friends. When everyone is busy, I go by myself, visit a mall I haven't been to or a new cafe. Since I've had my kids, I don't know the word boredom.'

'Do you ask your husband's permission to go out?'

'In Islam, you should always ask permission to go anywhere, which is what I do. But there are different types of husbands. Some don't even know where their wives are, some would allow you to meet only certain people. Because in the end, they are responsible for their wives and children. Husbands who don't allow their wives anything – it's their mistake. How do I explain it? Everyone has a different struggle. Some husbands are rarely home but they give money; some come home but they don't give money; and some don't do either. You cannot envy anyone because you don't know the whole package. That's why I'm contented and I don't compare myself to others.'

'After a few years of marriage, you can apply for Kuwaiti citizenship. Will you?'

'I've spent so many hours thinking about it! I would lose my German citizenship, and my kids would lose their German passports.[65] So maybe I'll do it when I'm done having children. The advantage of having a Kuwaiti citizenship is that if something happens to your husband, you have more security. But in the end, it is God that has given us security, not citizenship.'

'Do you go to the mosque?'

'Occasionally, I attend lectures for English speakers at the Grand Mosque.[66] To listen, to learn how to wash before prayer. I converted officially there. I've always felt welcome there.'

'Can you be a Muslim and not wear a hijab?'

'Of course. When I first became a Muslim, I wasn't ready to wear a hijab. When I lived with my husband's family, I would put on an abaya when we went out, just until we were out of the area, so that the neighbours wouldn't talk. Because it wasn't just about me, it was about the whole family. And that was okay because I did it to avoid problems.'

'You seem to be so down to earth, as if you had it all figured out. Is this your personality or do you feel it's more your upbringing?'

'My parents raised me in an Islamic way without realising it. Don't steal, don't kill, don't lie. Don't do to others how you wouldn't wish to be treated.'

After this conversation, I found myself with even more thoughts and questions. Carola's statements, logical at first, appeared to me riddled with contradictions the more I thought about them. Why did she choose Islam? A Muslim's life is filled with rules, conditions; even Allah's love is conditional. You must do certain things and refrain from doing many others if you want to be saved from eternal punishment. How could she claim that this country, or any Muslim country, is safe for women? Should I invite her for a walk around the city to count how many men would harass us?

---

65 Kuwait's Nationality Law does not permit dual citizenship. Theoretically, a person acquiring another country's citizenship automatically loses their Kuwaiti one. Children holding dual citizenship are given two years after reaching adulthood to decide which one they wish to keep.

66 The Grand Mosque is a Sunni mosque.

Is it perhaps that in Islam, a woman puts herself on the sidelines, living in her own little bubble unperturbed by the problems of the great big world? 'Islam protects the woman from external influence so that she can preserve her idealism,' I once read. The author (he or she) of this sentence seems to assume that every woman can and wants to find fulfilment in the role of a wife and a mother, confined to her house and dependent on her husband. Could that be Carola's motivation?

Finally, in order to accept Islam and its teachings, must you accept or turn a blind eye to certain principles? Islam instructs followers to take the words of the Quran as an absolute, but has the average Muslim even read at least the most important of its passages? Do they understand sharia? The history of Islam? The conquests, slavery in Islam?

I personally know a few European women who have converted to Islam. Some of them did it out of convenience, to avoid conflict with their husband and his family and taking into consideration the fact that Muslim women have more rights than non-Muslim ones. It was a conscious trade-off. Others say that indeed they believe in the teachings of Islam. None of them, however, has been able to dispel my doubts or answer my questions concerning this religion.

I had heard from several people about a Polish woman named Monika who was said to be a true, devout Muslim. She is committed to the hijab, does not wear make-up, prays, keeps reading Islamic sources, and also worked as a volunteer for one of the Islamic charities. Her friend, Mirka, described her as wise and well-read. She is the one answering questions of other converts and assuring them that they have chosen the right religion.

Despite my relentless efforts, Monika kept trying to avoid talking to me. I promised her that I intended to be objective and highlighted that it would be a good opportunity to explain her religion to a wider audience. She wanted to know beforehand where this interview would be published and asked for a list of questions in advance. 'I want to ask about your motives for converting to Islam, about women's rights – you'd probably expect that. About what has drawn you to Islam, what you like most or perhaps if there is something you are not convinced about. What was your biggest discovery. Whether you have read the Quran. About the community (…). The rest would surely come up during the talk,' I wrote to her. She finally agreed and we scheduled a date and time to talk online. When the time came, I discovered she had blocked me and I couldn't write to her or call her.

'Girls from Poland who have converted, don't want to talk about it,' Mirka told me to justify her friend's behaviour. 'Did you know that they are being persecuted in the Polish community? There is a lot of prejudice and ignorance. They don't feel well in that company.'

A few minutes later she admits: 'I am leaning toward Islam myself. But I haven't decided, yet.'

'Oh yeah?' I show my surprise.

'Yes. Many things work for me. For example, prayer: you can pray wherever and whenever you feel like it. Unlike in Catholic faith. I am a very spiritual person and that's what I was looking for,' she adds.

'Islam has so many rules, many more than Christianity.'

'I only draw from the most important source, the Quran. The rest – the hadith and so on – does not interest me. The Quran contains really beautiful passages.'

'What about those passages which are not so beautiful? About killing infidels, banning adoption, cutting off hands?' I ask about the obvious.

'Really? I don't know any of those. I am reading the Quran very slowly. A couple of pages at a time. I don't have time to read every day. I will tell you once I've reached them. All in all, Islam makes a lot of sense to me.'

'How about seeking your husband's permission to go out?'

'That's complete rubbish! It really upsets me when people mindlessly repeat some tales they've heard.'

'There are women who ask their husband every time they want to leave the house. A couple of my friends do,' I reply but I don't add that for one of them it is an endless source of marital fights. When I suggest to my Muslim friends, Kuwaiti and non-Kuwaiti, that we grab a coffee together outside and chat without being constantly interrupted by our children, they often reply: 'I will ask my husband.' Perhaps they simply don't want to go out with me, and not because of the Quranic verse that says: 'Stay in your houses and do not show yourselves off'. There are also several sayings of Mohammad that declare clearly that a woman must not leave her house without her husband's permission.

'What about the fact that according to the Quran a son should inherit twice as much as his sister? Have you heard about that?' I ask Mirka.

'It makes sense to me. It is the man that provides for the family so he should get more.'

'You assume we live in a world where women don't work. What about if a man is survived by one daughter? Then his relatives, including his cousins, would get half of all the inheritance.'

'Listen, I really don't want to talk about it anymore. I need to rest,' she is clearly annoyed. I admit, she warned me that she was tired but I pursued the subject anyway. Well, this is not the first time that someone has ended a conversation about religion with me in this way.

Convinced beyond doubt, yet unsure why

I decide to write to Eliška. She definitely understands the religion to which she has converted. Moreover, she studied Abrahamic religions at university so she would also have a better idea about how the three monotheistic creeds compare to one another.

I met her through our children's playgroup and we had many friendly, albeit brief, chats. She comes across as an outgoing, joyful person. She and her Egyptian husband have made their home in Kuwait. From what I could see, she leads a comfortable life. Her children play with expensive toys, ride in luxury strollers, and are dressed in designer clothing, and she is always elegantly, yet conservatively dressed. She frequently posts photos from her family's holidays in exclusive destinations on her Facebook feed. As far as I know, she does not work outside the home.

Eliška agrees to talk to me. She starts by pointing out that it's been a while since she last reflected on the teachings of the Quran and that she prefers to discuss specific examples.

I am curious why she chose Islam.

'It had to be a monotheistic religion. You can be Jewish only by birth,' she laughs, 'and in Christianity I didn't like the idea of the Holy Trinity. Above that, Islam is very logical.' Indeed, when we talk, she has a well-thought-out answer to my every query or issue I touch upon. Everything has an explanation.

I ask her how its possible, in her opinion, that there is one book, the Quran, which is reportedly the literal word of Allah, yet it gives rise to many different interpretations, leading to conflicts and violence among Muslims. Even within the same sect and the same family, individuals still interpret it to their own liking.

'In every religion you get people who explain things according to their own minds. Even the Islamophobes, or the terrorists, they take something out of context and they twist it to suit their agenda. You need to take the Quran in its complexity, study the text and the historical context, and understand the underlying values of Islam. Even modern Islamic scholars have their own agendas. For example, the Saudis claim women shouldn't drive a car because it is *haram* in Islam but actually it's their culture, not Islam. In the time of the Prophet, peace be upon Him, women were riding camels and were active in politics. Terrorists also twist the text and use it for their purpose.'

'Then why couldn't these words be made very clear? Is the Quran a miracle because it is logical and clear to all humans or is it nuclear physics and each person must do a PhD in Arabic language, another one in sharia, and a third one in hadith to understand this universal religion?'

'I think the words are very clear. You need to read entire passages, the verses that follow. Read the explanation. There are many verses that talk about violence but you have to know their context. It was wartime between Muslims and the inhabitants of Mecca, who were killing the Muslims for no reason.'

'You have read the historical account, right? If you consider how quickly Islam was spreading…'

'Which age do you mean exactly? Because it depends. You cannot judge religion by the acts of the people. People make mistakes. But take Indonesia, one of the biggest Muslim countries. Islam didn't come there through violence but with business. Even the [holy] texts say you shouldn't spread religion by force or under pressure. One of the most important Islamic laws says that no church should be turned into a mosque.'[67]

'How about Hagia Sophia and the countless churches that

____

67 As with many of the responses Eliška gave me, this is a loose interpretation of a Quranic verse (Quran 22:40). It contradicts the reality on the ground.

were confiscated and turned into mosques all over the world from Spain to Greece to India?'

'Are you sure? I must check that...'

'What you said about Islam in Indonesia is also incorrect. It was not the choice of the people, but the influence of local rulers, who adopted and enforced Islam among the population. For more than 700 years after it reached that country, most Indonesians didn't embrace Islam.'

'I'm don't know history that well. This is what I was taught.'

'Going back, I am trying to understand… The Quran itself says it is the unchanging word of Allah so it should work in any context, at any time.'

'Not in any context. At any time, yes. You cannot just take a verse; you need to first know what it means. In Quran, things that are *halal* are very clear and things that are *haram* are clear, and then there are some things in between. It is important to use logic. I was going with the logic, that's why I converted. Although there is also another part to do with the heart. … In case of the terrorists, for example, their motives are more political, not religious. Look at the Palestinians. Someone took their land, occupies them. There are many factors: injustice, lack of education, poverty.'

'Sure, but why don't they say they're doing it in the name of their country instead of religion? It's like they were given a window of opportunity.' I later wondered if Eliška ever asked herself why other occupied people or oppressed minorities worldwide, such as Cypriots, Armenians, or Tibetans, have never resorted to terrorism against their occupiers.

'Listen, I had a lot of problems with Islam myself,' she makes a slight pivot in the discussion, 'like with *fikh*[68] – why can a man

---

68 Fikh – the human understanding of Islam's divine rules and laws; a set of legal opinions that interpret the practical application of Islamic law (sharia), derived from basic Islamic texts: the Quran and Sunnah.

have four wives or why does a woman have to wear hijab. It so happened that I went to Cairo to attend an Arabic language course; all the girls in my class were Muslims from different countries. (My mum is a Christian and my dad is an atheist.) I had a lot of questions which I managed to clarify and then I converted.'

'So in the end you accepted…'

'I didn't accept anything at face value. I studied each question until it made sense. Like the four wives – there is a very clear *ayah*[69] that says: you will never be fair with four wives so just take one. At the time of the Prophet, peace be upon him, people had many wives and Islam limited it to four with the intention of limiting it in the future to only one. It was to fix the society step by step.'

'Before Islam, many Arabs had only one spouse. And not just the ones who were Christians. The Prophet himself, his companions, their children, the caliphs, the influential imams – they all had multiple wives, so how were they limiting polygamy? To this day millions of Muslims have several wives based on the example of their prophet.'

'We can be here all night discussing this… And actually, the four wives law is not something I like.'

'How about the inheritance? Woman gets half of what the man does.'

'Yes, until now I keep thinking about this. In the old times, men used to take care of the family and provide maintenance but in our times it's different. This is something on my list I really need to read more about.' Eliška has two daughters, so I understand why this matter particularly concerns her.

'This is my issue: times are changing, and Islam is not evolving. Other religions are.'

'Yes but they are evolving to what the people want them to be. If you change something according to the people – it won't

---

69 Ayah is a verse of Quran.

be time-transcendent any more. I believe Islam gives you a lot of space, actually. For example, you can still be a good Muslim if you don't wear a hijab.'

'There are so many people that would disagree with you. This is your intuition, your truth.'

'This is what I mean. Once you start to explain the religion according to a scholar or people… Honestly, some of the scholars are ridiculous in what they say. I always prefer to see the actual text of the Quran and hadith. And not all the hadith are true. …I went through this stage, I was doubting and I had to clarify many issues.'

I decide to ask her about a specific verse, as she suggested at the beginning of our conversation: 'Do you know this verse that says: you have to abstain from sex apart from your wife and whatever your right hand…'

'*Ma malakat aymanuhum*,' Eliška interjects. She even knows the Arabic term.

'…possesses.'

'Sure I know it. In the old times they used to have these maids at home, right?'

'They had slaves, it's not about house maids.'

'Well, slaves. In Islam right now they don't have slaves and that was the reformation brought by the religion. Islam encouraged people to let their slaves free. You could say that Muslim society was one of the first in the world that got rid of slavery.'

'They had slaves in Saudi Arabia until very recently. Many Muslim countries practiced slavery until recent times.'

'Really? If this exists, it is something exceptional and minor. Let's say we have 1 billion of Muslims and in the Muslim society from the 8th century they abolished…'

'Nooo,' I protest, 'I'm talking a few decades back. I can tell you exactly when slavery was abolished in Yemen and Saudi Arabia. In 1962. And in Mauritania in 1981. And these are Muslim religious countries.'[70]

'Yes, but does it mean the people in them are religious? Saudi Arabia for example is a Muslim country but their people don't really behave in the Islamic way. Egypt – is it a Muslim country? They don't allow *hijabi* women in swimming pools in the really posh places. They threw me out of a hotel pool because I was wearing a burkini. Imagine this: I went to complain to the manager and he was so rude. He told me it's not hygienic or Islamic, and I should make up my mind about who I was. And this man called himself a Muslim. See, you cannot judge by the label "Muslim". Whether it's people or countries.'

'Does it sometimes cross your mind that you might be in the minority and that your understanding is inaccurate? Maybe their understanding is the main and the right one?' I resisted the urge to point out that she had just declared hundreds of millions of Muslims as infidels, much like ISIS does.

'But who am I to judge?' Eliška continues. 'I am trying to do my best. And Islam is the religion of the middle way. And I have my own guidance. For example the killing of innocent people is against Islam. There are things that are clear and things that are not clear…'

'Non-believers are not innocent people. It's in the Quran. The Quran says so.'

'No, sorry, if someone is a non-believer it doesn't give you the right to kill him.'

'*Kafirs* are not innocent.'

'*Kafir* is not a non-believer. It is somebody who knew the truth but refused it. But how can we know that this happened to him? No way. … I mean, we could go on for hours. But if you have certain ayahs in mind, send me a question and I will be happy to give you an answer.' Then she goes on, 'It is different if

---

70 Mauritania was the last country to abolish slavery, and it wasn't criminalized there until 2007. In practice, slavery still exists in that place, and it was resurrected in Syria and Iraq under ISIS in 2015.

150

you convert, you have to go through all the questions and study for yourself. I think the natives are not used to questioning the things that don't match. They just accept them. But Islam is not like that because the first word in the Quran is "read".[71] So we are supposed to ask questions and study.'

I later contact Eliška again to finish the conversation on a positive note. I felt bad because at one point she asked me why I hated Muslims so much. I don't know how she inferred that from my inquiries. So this time, I ask her what she likes most about Islam.

She replies, 'Its values: it tells you to care for the needy, orphans, old people, be fair and don't lie, do good deeds. And I like that all the things I consider detrimental to a happy life, like alcohol, drugs, and gambling, are forbidden. I really love that it's a simple and logical religion to me. I love that you are supposed to educate yourself and read and ask questions. And most of all, that there is nobody between me and God. It is a direct relation through prayer and asking for forgiveness.'

What are the millions of imams doing then, I thought.

I wonder if she believes what she is repeating.

---

71 Eliška refers to verse 96:1 of the Quran, which is believed to have been revealed as the very first verse but was placed towards the end of the book. It begins with the word 'iqra', which has several meanings: read, but also recite or repeat. The latter meaning is the most accurate in this case, according to influential Muslim scholars, as at the time there was no written word to be read.

The Quran contains another verse that says: 'O you who believe, do not ask about things which, if clarified, would harm you' (5:101).

CHAPTER 8

Some are more equal than others

You have been created to rule and they were created to serve.
Mohammad al-Jawahiri, Iraqi poet

The best way to find yourself is to lose yourself in the service of others.
Mahatma Gandhi

Choosing to work hard is the key to being successful.
Jeff Bezos

The practice of domestic servitude is deep-rooted and well-established in the Middle East and Africa. It goes back for many centuries and has taken on various shapes and forms over the ages. Geography has played a significant role in shaping the norms and culture of this old and vast part of the world. The most famous Arab traveller Ibn Battuta documented the prevalence of slavery and domestic servitude in the area in the 14th century. He describes how he bought several girls and boys to serve him and received others as gifts, some of whom he sold or kept during his long journey.

Until the Second World War, slave markets were widespread in the region. Many Kuwaitis, Omanis, Saudis alive today are descendants of slaves brought to this area as recently as the 1930s and 40s. After the abolition of slavery in the late 1950s, the culture of domestic servitude emerged, with children from impoverished families taking on jobs that were previously performed by slaves in the houses of the affluent. In countries like Egypt, Iraq, Saudi Arabia, Syria, Morocco, poor peasants would send their young children to work and live in houses of rich people in the cities as well as get employed in other menial jobs. This resulted from a combination of factors including the high birth rate in rural areas, reduced infant mortality due to medical advancements, the ease of travel, and the vast difference in wealth between the city and the countryside within the same country. Parents would visit their children every month and collect their salaries They sacrificed one or two children so that the rest could live a better life.

In Kuwait, the late sociologist Khaldun Al-Naqeeb wrote about the mentality of the master and the maid (*almazeb wa alseby*) as a pattern that could explain various social phenomena in the Gulf region. For centuries, the elites had maids in addition to slaves. The servants were usually young children who started as live-in maids or errand boys; often, they themselves were children of people who worked for others. As they grew up, some would remain dependant on their boss. They could leave whenever they wanted on paper but not in reality. Some would manage to break free and move up the social ladder, harbouring deep animosity or gratitude toward their former bosses and the system, while others would fall off the wagon and remain trapped in poverty.

Throughout the ages, two different yet interconnected groups have co-existed: generations of servants, and families that have been landlords, merchants, or senior administrators. Psychologically, the relationship between the two groups fluctuates between admiration to hatred. However, being a domestic worker in a rich household might be the first step on the social mobility ladder. Many of the young people are exposed to a more affluent, more diverse environment there, allowing them to grow and gain new opportunities.

One of the richest and most successful businessmen in Kuwait described in a newspaper interview how he started out as a domestic worker. After his father died, his young uncle and his mother found themselves alone with several children to care for. Despite taking up different small jobs, the mother struggled to pay the rent and put food on the table. She asked one of her relatives to find work for her eldest son, who was not even 12. The man took him to the merchants market to see if anyone needed an errand boy, and a well-known merchant liked the boy and hired him. He moved to the house of this wealthy man and became his shadow, doing whatever needed to be done, tending to the business with him and travelling with him. The man even paid for some maths and accounting lessons so the boy could be even more helpful. After more than ten years, the merchant told him it was time to start his own business and gave him a small shop, rent-free, and merchandise to sell. The wealthy man continued to support him and teach him the secrets of the trade. The boy's business expanded, and he eventually became one of the richest people in the country. His wealth surpassed that of his former boss's family. However, not all domestic workers were as fortunate and many were abused and exploited.

After the oil boom, the middle class expanded throughout the region. As their finances improved, women started pursuing higher education and taking up jobs, which led to a demand for workers to maintain households and care for the elderly and children. In the 1970s, domestic workers and drivers came from impoverished societies within the region. Persons belonging to the untouchable caste in India or young people from poor, underdeveloped Arab communities would come to work in the houses in the Gulf. Most of them had never lived in homes with electricity or running water. Over time, these workers got introduced to the benefits of modern civilization. Many of them have succeeded in gaining important knowledge as well as in saving enough money to start their businesses upon returning to their homelands. It is common to meet someone in India or Sri Lanka who would tell you that their father or mother worked in Kuwait or Saudi Arabia, and when they came back, they bought a small farm or established a business.

Having a live-in maid is now the norm for families in the Gulf. Elderly people usually stay with their children and it is them and live-in nurses or caretakers who look after them. Kuwait has just one nursing home with very few residents. When building a house, locals plan it to have enough space for their parents as well as their children, and ensure they have a large hall that can host large groups of people. Family gatherings in Kuwait are often more than 40-guests strong. Given that houses of more affluent families can be as large as residential buildings in Europe and can accommodate over ten people, it is often necessary to employ more than one worker to keep them clean and well-maintained.

Handmaids: Shaping destiny

In many cases, domestic workers are underprivileged individuals driven by a profound desire to reshape their destinies through diligence and self-reliance. These individuals have willingly chosen to step forward, take risks, and leave their homelands behind instead of settling for a life of idle impoverishment. Working in demanding and modest occupations serves as their initial step on the ladder of social mobility.

Angeline was the first live-in domestic helper who worked for me. When I met her for the first time, I was taken by her pleasant character. To be able to work in Kuwait, she had to borrow money, get a passport, put up funds for medical assessment, vaccinations, and training as well as pay the agency on her side. Altogether, she invested 15-20 thousand Philippine pesos ($350-450). During the three-day training, she learned basic phrases in Arabic, how to prepare a couple of dishes, such as Caesar salad and beef soup, how to make the bed, arrange cutlery and serve at the table, how to efficiently clean the house. Most girls on the course didn't know how to use a vacuum cleaner, and Angeline remembers how the instructors would yell at and ridicule them in order to prepare them for the treatment they might experience once on-site. 'They wanted the domestic helpers to be compliant,' she told me. The duration of the contract is 2 years.

Currently, the majority of house workers in Kuwait are from India and the Philippines; there are also some Sri Lankans, Bangladeshis, Indonesians, Ethiopians. The minimum salary of a Filipino woman living with her host family is 120 dinars a month ($390 or 21,000 Philippine peso). The employer also pays a one-off agency fee of around $3,000 and for plane tickets. They keep this entire income to themselves and shouldn't have to spend a penny from it as in addition to accommodation, maids and nannies should be provided with food, clothes, footwear, as well as basic sanitary products. Many employers give their helpers extra money: bonuses, Christmas gifts, gifts for their children abroad.

Leaving her three children behind was probably the hardest thing for Angeline to do but they were also one of the reasons she had to go and earn money. People from poorer countries and regions tend to have larger families than those from wealthier states, and that applies to the Philippines. Children are their pension fund and their only insurance, the principal source of income and support when they are old or sick. The more children someone has the better chances he or she would survive. Being optimistic and thinking that the children would be able to succeed is part of their culture. There is always the notion that God loves children, thus he will take care of them and their parents.

The girl herself comes from a big family. When her parents met, they had already had previous relationships and a couple of children each. She and her brother were raised by their father, who was also taking care of Angeline's children while she was away working. Her mother and older half-sisters (from another father) would pick on her whenever they could find a reason. The mother is wheelchair-bound due to advanced diabetes that led to the amputation of her legs.

Angeline had Skype on her mobile phone and constant access to the internet but even with the modern technology she couldn't talk to her children as much as she or they would have liked. Meanwhile, her father moved from Manila to the province where there was no internet connection, and the time difference and the emotions that came with every conversation made it even more challenging. Angeline would show me photos of her family, her husband, and from her wedding which had taken place just before she left for Kuwait.

Filipino workers, both women and men, are known in the region for their love of children and their ease at taking care of them, and Angeline adhered to that reputation. She was kind and patient, treating my children as I imagined she would treat her own. Since there is a strong tradition of music, storytelling, and other forms of entertainment, she would use that with the children, and they loved it. She was also hard-working, honest, and I admired her resilience when staying away from family all that time.

I would worry whenever Angeline went out without company. Women coming in to work originate from a different culture than the local one, often from small villages; they have an unsuspecting nature and do not realise the potential dangers. Many cases are known where taxi drivers or men chatting women up in the street were able to easily seduce them with empty promises, offers of marriage. In Kuwait, a country with a very low rate of petty crime, kidnappings and disappearances of Asian females do occur. There is no shortage of sex-starved men, and the desert has been a witness to many crimes. Over time, Angeline made friends with girls who worked for one of my friends. They would go out together at the weekends after listening to a litany of cautionary advice from us. They used a trusted Filipino taxi driver. When I asked if she had fun, she would say: 'Yes! We were eating junk food and taking selfies.'

Then one day, when I returned home from a business meeting, Angeline began telling me incoherently about some pills she had taken. After asking several questions, I finally understood what had happened. Angeline had attempted suicide: she had swallowed two or three blister packs of paracetamol in a moment of desperation and shame. A few weeks earlier, at her husband's request, she had sent him nude, hoping it could help prevent infidelity.

Angeline would typically send her entire salary to her father for the children's upkeep. She also gave her husband money to complete a vocational course so that he could work abroad, too, and preferably join her in Kuwait. It turned out that he squandered the sum on gambling and drugs. When she refused to give him more money, he began blackmailing her. He set up a Facebook profile with the nude pictures and electronically invited Angeline's friends and family to view them. When the platform blocked one profile, he would create another one and another. She found out about this from a friend and was devastated.

I rushed her to the hospital, where the two of us endured a long, stressful night in the ER. The only thing that made the prolonged wait and the barrage of questions from doctors and police bearable was the group of Filipino nurses who gathered around us. They did their utmost to keep Angeline's spirits up, many sharing their personal stories of failed love and how they coped with similar experiences.

The blackmail case was reported to the police in the Philippines by Angeline's father, but there was another problem: her husband could take the children away from their grandfather and disappear. These concerns prompted the decision that Angeline's dad would move with the children from Manila to the province and hide. However, he needed a lot of money to execute this plan. Many people rallied to help her, and she was able to send all the funds needed to save her children.

Since Angeline started making 'big bucks' abroad, her mother and sisters became much kinder toward her. They were hoping for a piece of the pie. They were considering borrowing a lump sum from her with no intention of paying it back. It didn't occur to them that Angeline was not saving anything. She was sending all her earnings to her dad: for the children's living expenses, his medical bill after an accident at work, a flock of ducks for his farm. This is a common scenario: migrant workers plan to save up but their relatives keep extending their hands, grabbing what they can, eating up their hard-earned money.

In the end, despite wanting to stay longer, Angeline went back home to solve her family problems. She was planning to limit her husband's parental rights away so that she wouldn't have to worry about him taking off with the children. For some time, she kept in touch with me through Facebook messenger. Her material stance did not significantly improve compared to before she had left her home country. She was only able to earn a small income by selling homemade food and sweets, hence, she planned to return to the Middle East for another contract. Then, ten months after leaving Kuwait, she revealed to me that she had a new partner and was expecting a baby.

Angeline's story serves as just one example of the challenges faced by domestic workers who seek employment abroad. Tragically, countless women run away from exploitation and abuse in their home countries only to face them here. However, it is important to acknowledge that thousands of girls who initially came to Gulf countries to work as domestic helpers ended up marrying local men and later being naturalized. Countless other women have found success and stability in their work. One such success story is that of a sweet, young Sri Lankan girl who worked for my neighbour.

Chandani's father had three daughters and a plan: each one of them would spend a few years working for a family in the Gulf, putting half of her salary aside and spending the other half. For the saved money they hoped to buy a farm with a house, tractor, cows and goats. With such assets the daughters would have more freedom to choose their husbands.

When Chandani first arrives, she claims to be 18 years old, although judging by her looks, high levels of energy, and innocently joyful disposition, one might suspect a more tender age. Hailing from a poor peasant family, she is treated with kindness by her employer, who acts as a stern but protective mother figure: you could tell that there is love between the two, and at the same time, boundaries and limits. Throughout her time there, the girl never spends money on herself, instead sending her entire salary as well as any bonuses and gifts she receives back home. If she keeps a few dinars to herself, the boss becomes suspicious and upset, complaining endlessly: 'Why is she keeping money? What does she need it for?', insisting that she take the girl to the market and buy whatever she needs. Chandani is provided with all the food she could want, clothes, a fully furnished room with a TV, phone, and internet. She is a hard-working person keen on learning and doing her job.

A few months after Chandani and her sisters start working, their father purchases the land with a mortgage, and every month their salaries go towards the instalment. She and her sisters take every opportunity to work overtime, and although the initial plan was based on ten years of work to pay for the mortgage and the equipment, by Chandani's fourth year they have surpassed it. She shows me pictures of her new house, the farm, and the livestock. A few months after she leaves for home, she sends her former employer pictures from her wedding. They show the girl beaming with happiness.

CHAPTER 9

The forbidden garden

During some festivities at the Italian embassy, I meet a photographer who has been living here for many years. He's definitely in his sixties, although you wouldn't be able to tell by his jet-black dyed hair. I am standing in a circle of people and we talk about various matters while the photographer acts as a mentor for the group. At some point, he says to the women in the group: 'You girls are lucky; you've married for love. Kuwaiti girls can only dream of that. In this part of the world, they say that they don't marry the ones they love, and they don't love the ones they are married to.'

Arranged marriage is the norm in Muslim countries, and forced marriage is still common. Technically, there is no alternative way to meet a member of the opposite sex, let alone find a life partner. One-on-one interactions before marriage are socially unacceptable, and the person who chooses to go on a date risks a far-reaching scandal. Rendezvous may not be a crime by law, and even if that was the case, laws could be evaded. Kuwaitis are not afraid of laws. The more severe threat is the prospect of bringing dishonour upon yourself and your family in the eyes of society. The retribution from the girl's family is the biggest worry.

If two young people of opposite sexes are riding in a car and come across a checkpoint or get stopped by the police for some reason, they will be asked: 'What are you to each other?' and if they are not married, which can be determined by the addresses written on their IDs, the couple will be taken to the station. There, the police will fingerprint and check if they are wanted for any crimes, and if they are not, their parents must come and sign a release paper to get them out. This could result in the girl getting killed if the family is tribal or conservative. In moderate homes, it's guaranteed the young person would be in big trouble. A similar situation might occur if an unmarried couple is spotted together or if someone takes a picture of them – this can cause a serious issue for them and their families. Society considers dating a dishonourable act and a major sin, especially for females.

Sexuality is a taboo subject. It is not discussed at home, nor is it taught at school or touched upon in public media. As a topic, it is non-existent, as if it has been wiped out, erased; it is absent. In biology classes, the reproduction of humans has been drastically censored or completely omitted, and the reproduction of animals is either not covered or limited to a few general sentences. No pictures are included. Youth are being deterred from expressing their sexuality through harsh laws and religious doctrine. They are stifled by visions of torture: divine punishment for masturbation, flirting, lustful looks, and extramarital sex equals eternal hellfire. They grow up convinced that intercourse is a necessary evil whose only goal is procreation. This warped perception of self and human sexual instinct is a major cause of all kinds of psychological and emotional distress, suffering, and disorders. Girls grow up convinced that sex is something shameful and painful. All they are told is that under no circumstances should they let anyone touch them: 'You must remain a virgin until marriage; if anything untoward happened, we are all doomed.'

From the time that schools were established, Kuwaiti girls and boys have always attended classes in separate buildings. At universities, most lectures are given twice to keep females and males apart. Universities were the last institutions to be segregated by gender in accordance with a law passed by the parliament with the support of the government in 1996.

This segregation has led to the opposite sex becoming foreign creatures and has also reinforced the taboo around relations between a man and a woman.

'They don't talk about these things at school. They just assume you know,' a thirty-year-old single man told me. 'I'm yet to have a talk with my dad about sex. I learned everything on my own. He's yet to talk to me. When I was 18, I was traveling abroad alone for the first time. I was about to leave the house with my bags in my hands and I said, "Bye dad, I'm going". And he said, "Ahmed." "Yeah?" "Condoms. Be careful of STDs." That was it. That was the only sex talk I had with my dad. He didn't even say "condom;" he said "rubber," in Arabic *matat*. Rubber can mean anything, you know, tyres are made of rubber.'

Sexual problems are a serious issue in the Middle East. Studies investigating the prevalence of sexual problems in different parts of the world showed that significantly more women in the Middle East reported a lack of interest in sex (43.4%), sex not being pleasurable (31%), and experiencing pain during sex (21%) compared to Northern Europe (25.6%, 17.1%, and 9% respectively). The same applied to Middle Eastern men, who also reported higher rates of sexual problems, including a lack of interest in sex (21.6%), sex not being pleasurable (14.3%), and experiencing pain during sex (10.2%) in comparison to men in Northern Europe (12.5%, 7.7%, and 2.9%).[72]

It is hard to determine the generalizability of these numbers as the people who are willing to participate in such studies might not accurately represent the general population.

$\sim$

---

72 Edward O. Laumann and others (2005). Sexual problems among women and men aged 40-80 y: prevalence and correlates identified in the Global Study of Sexual Attitudes and Behaviors. International Journal of Impotence Research 17, p. 39-57.

In public swimming pools and aquaparks, there are scheduled days only for women with children and others only for men. In cinemas, each auditorium is divided into two parts: couples, children, and women sit in the family part, whereas men coming alone or with other males have their own seating area. For thirty-five years, cinemas were banned in Saudi Arabia and the two-parts rule used to apply in restaurants – now, it is slowly changing.

Hairdressing, cosmetic, massage services for women can only be rendered by women, and for men – solely by men. Touching a person of the opposite gender in return for payment is considered prostitution and is punishable by law. Such a beauty salon would quickly lose its licence and the staff would find themselves behind bars. If you are a guy and not happy about getting a pedicure done by another guy, you're on your own.

Even the scantily clad bodies of models on lingerie packaging in shops have to be covered with big black stickers. And imagine this: there is a job in Kuwait which involves flipping through pages of Western magazines and painting over all cleavages and thighs of women in the pictures with a black marker so that these periodicals can be offered for sale.

There are men in these parts of the world, locals and foreigners, who have no idea what a woman looks like underneath her clothes. There have been instances where a man would wait sitting on a park bench until a woman dressed in tight or skimpy clothes comes walking by and masturbate while looking at her. Many women who had been jogging along the beach reported being followed by men in cars driving suspiciously slowly.

It's surprising how quickly Westerners adjust to these rules, no matter how draconian or illogical they might be. Would they accept them in their homelands if they were ever forced to? The few people who do not comply with them are thrown out of Kuwait within the first weeks. Those who wish to stay have no choice but to adapt.

Who puts two hearts together

'The one who puts two hearts together, may God make him live long,' rings out an old Kuwaiti sea song. Reality is not as romantic as that. In these parts of the world, marriage is treated as a business contract. Options are considered: a cost and benefit formula. It's common for young people, especially girls, to be forced into marriages with people they don't know or have never seen.

A complex and powerful caste system dominates all aspects of life in the Gulf states. It can be seen clearly when it comes to marriage. Kuwaiti society is divided into many categories and subcategories, with each group enjoying a specific social status. At the top are the royal family and a limited number of wealthy, well-connected families who claim noble origins. They assert to have settled in Kuwait from the Arabian desert prior to others. Members of these families dominate the government and economy, and they rarely marry outside their group. Furthermore, each of these families has less successful and significantly poorer branches with which they avoid intermarrying to protect their status.

Ordinarily, a Sunni would not marry a Shia and vice versa. This applies to Kuwait as well as the rest of the Arab world. Exceptions sometimes occur, but even then, the bride and groom are of equal social standing: the rich marry the rich, and the poor marry the poor. Arabs and other ethnicities usually do not intermarry. Then, tribal and city folk rarely intermarry. Within the different tribes and branches, there are groups of higher and lower social standing, with families seen as equal often intermarrying. It is generally not acceptable for a man of what is considered a lower origin to propose to a woman of higher origin.

In 2020, this small country was shaken by the news of a horrific homicide. The victim was a pregnant Kuwaiti woman in her thirties, Fatemah Ali. Being a member of a strong tribe, she married a man who didn't belong to a tribe or reputable family. By society's standards, he was of lower social status. Although the bride's father had approved the marriage, her tribe was offended, and her brothers were ashamed that she married someone she loved from a lower caste. After getting married, the couple stayed away from her family. They had one child, and she was pregnant with their second child when her older brother came to her house more than two years after her marriage. He shot her in the head and left her to die. She was taken to the hospital in a critical condition and was admitted to the ICU. The police arrested the shooter, but her younger brother stormed the ICU of the main hospital in Kuwait, Mubarak hospital, and shot her several times. She was pronounced dead. The victim's husband said that he had gone to the police multiple times, seeking protection from her brothers, who had been openly threatening them. Many people consider the actions of the brothers an honourable act.[73]

Unlike the West, marriage here is not a personal matter. Two entire families, the bride's and the groom's, are involved in the process, and parents have the biggest say. The bachelor's mother is the one who can spot an attractive future wife for their son at a female gathering. During parties and weddings, she closely observes young girls who are all dolled-up and without the cover of abaya or hijab, assessing the length of their hair, the flow of their moves when dancing, their beauty and grace. The girls are obviously aware of that, hence, they try to impress the company as much as they can. Later on, there is a chat during which the matron evaluates the girl's intelligence and eloquence,

---

73 BBC News (10 Sep 2020). Jarimat Salwaa: Kuaytiun yutliq alnaar ealaa 'ukhtih alhamil washaqiqiha al'asghar yaqtuluha… [Crime in Salwa: A Kuwaiti shot his pregnant sister and his younger brother killed her…] (in Arabic).

and outside of the party hall – a discreet research into her family history: where the maiden comes from, where she lives, what her parents and siblings do etc. etc. A similar process occurs on the other side.

The next step is a meeting between the mothers. There are no taboo topics during such conversations: both sides need to know ahead of time if the family of the prospective spouse is of good provenance, if they are financially compatible, if there are any hereditary illnesses. Do they enjoy a great reputation in this small-as-a-thimble country? Perhaps the future groom or bride boasts genealogy in the line of the Prophet?[74] It is customary to ask about the education and professions of each family member, although these have usually already been confirmed by other sources. Infertility on either side is a deal breaker. Fabrications and exaggerations are normal and tolerated. When someone says: 'She has a talent for painting, and her family has a summer house at Loch Ness,' it probably means that the girl has taken one painting lesson and that her second-degree cousin once spent a weekend in a B&B near Loch Lomond. This is why caring parents do a CIA-style background check which rectifies the information they obtained so far as well as provides different bits of gossip about embarrassing episodes from the other family's life. There is always a discussion about the dowry: 'Five thousand? That's very little!' and how expensive a gift the groom will give to the bride. It is not uncommon for proposals to fall through because the parties could not agree on these issues.

In tribal communities, the groom and bride are not allowed to see each other until the wedding day. The man has to depend on his mother's description of the bride, while the girl has to rely on information from her brothers. It is very common that the two would later be devastated as they would find the other

---

74 This is a serious matter, however easy to fabricate. Such people are called syed or sayyida, which means noble.

person completely unacceptable. Thus, many prefer to marry their first-degree cousins as they can at least roughly tell how they might look. Marrying a cousin has the added advantage that all assets are kept in the family, a practice as old as Adam and more prevalent than one might think.

Among moderately liberal and city people, the bride- and groom-to-be may see each other once in the presence of their mothers. When both sides are satisfied, the deal is struck. The young man, accompanied by a delegation consisting of the most representative male members of his clan, goes to propose to the girl's family only once he is certain that he is going to be accepted.

That's the thing. It's not only one person that comes under scrutiny but the whole family. Any misconduct committed by one family member, particularly a woman, usually carries severe consequences, for instance, if one of the maidens spent a night outside her home, and there was a hint of suspicion that she wasn't at a female friend's at the time, it would cast a dark shadow over the family's reputation. Her sisters would be perceived in the same light as the supposed 'tramp', and the prospect of spinsterhood would likely await them. Her parents would be ostracised, and her brothers would be viewed as dishonourable. This is why parents are reluctant to report girls running away from home to the police. They cannot risk such information being leaked.

A candidate for a wife should be chaste, religious, obedient, homey, industrious. There cannot be any doubt that she is a virgin. Fussy grooms have special wishes, for instance regarding skin tone, hair length; some prefer the girl not to have a driving licence. Someone might ask if the potential wife works, and if so, whether she has any contact with men in her workplace.

For men, the right social status is a key consideration, and that includes family name and wealth, a respectable job, suitable income, and most importantly, citizenship. Age and looks are of little importance.

More and more young people are rejecting the idea of arranged marriages. They yearn to experience a feeling, emotions, excitement. In the past, some would use the services of a matchmaker, a wise and experienced person capable of assessing the compatibility between two individuals. Nowadays, traditional matchmaking simply doesn't work. Women became financially independent; both females and males travel, are more open-minded, and desire romantic love but at the same time, they have unrealistic expectations. Statistical evidence from recent years is brutal: fewer people are getting married, and almost half of all marriages end in divorce, with this number on the rise.

The marriage deadline

Michelle took me to a Kuwaiti wedding. It was the first time attending one for both of us.

The invitation said to arrive at 7 p.m. We were there at 7:30 p.m. and found the place deserted. The guests began arriving slowly after eight, and the bride didn't show up until ten thirty. The women's party was in a big hotel, while the men were in a different venue. At the entrance, the staff took our phones and asked if we had any cameras, a common practice to prevent guests from taking pictures of the women and girls.

There was no food, only water and juice. They told us there would be no music either until the bride arrived but they put it on after a while. It was so loud that we had to scream to each other and my ears began to hurt after five minutes. Some women started dancing, although I wouldn't call it dancing: they were moving with small steps on the red carpet, lifting their arms up and screwing in air light bulbs. You don't sweat from dancing like that. Michelle and I weren't brave enough to join them. We sat there for three long hours looking at other ladies.

Some of the women looked stunning, with amazing hair, nails, dresses like from the runway. Some of the hairdos were not moving at all. And they all had the same nose. The faces of the women sitting near me at the table looked like they were from the same mould. I think they must have got a group discount from the surgeon. Only a few older women were wearing hijabs, while many of the young girls were nearly naked in strapless, super-short dresses. Some women were dressed like Disney princesses or *haute-couture* models; some looked outlandish – like from the Fifth Element or Cirque du Soleil. Conservative Arab women are said to make up for the daily monotony of black at wedding parties. With the music and the red carpet, it could have been a real fashion show or a film screening at the cinema; only popcorn was missing. A woman next to me was watching everyone so intently that her eyes almost popped out.

Finally, the bride arrived. Her dress was so huge that three women had to be helping her: they walked beside her and held the sides of the dress so that the girl wouldn't fall down. Then, she sat on a stage-like platform where she stayed throughout the rest of the night. Rows of chairs were set around it, higher and higher like in a theatre, so that everybody could see her well. When I looked at her, I felt sorry for her. There was more dress than person. Then, the groom joined the party; at that point, all the girls and women had changed into conservative attire. When the newlywed couple were feeding each other wedding cake, they struggled to bend down to their plates on the small table prepared for them. The groom stayed for some time so that pictures could be taken, and the freshly wedded departed together.

I remember hearing from someone before that such a wedding is not a pleasant experience for the bride, kind of like torture. My heart went out to her. When she was coming into the hall, her body was shaking and tears were running down her cheeks. I found out she was only nineteen. The groom was the same age.

Apparently, most local weddings are very similar. The bride enters the scene late, the speakers play at full blast, and it is best to come with a slightly filled stomach as food is served after the groom leaves, which is around midnight. However, conservative families do not play music. Some guests come to be seen, and some – to see. Oftentimes, the bride is a young girl who, up until this moment, was tied to her mother's apron strings. What does life have in store for such a young couple?

For newlywed Arab couples from the Gulf, both sides are in for a bitter disappointment. Growing up under the glass cover of conservative religious teachings and tribal customs, without any experience of interaction with the opposite sex, they enter the relationship with a ton of misconceptions and irrational expectations. Neither of them knows how to treat the other half or how to talk with each other. On top of that, they grew up in households with poor maids doing the smallest chores for them. The girl has never made a bed in her life. The boy hasn't prepared one cup of coffee on his own – unless he's had a Nespresso machine. He expects sex like in a porn film; she wants to be treated like a princess. If she hears from her husband at the very start: 'Don't expect me to be staying home in the evenings. I'm going to my *dewaniya*,' that's not too bad as that's communicating.

A girl who doesn't get married before her 25th birthday is treated like goods on the verge of their expiration date. Candidates who learn about the unappetizing age of the maiden hold off proposing, even if they themselves are much older. The family falls into despair. Cases of young women who opt for a marriage with an incompatible man to escape spinsterhood, gossip, and the full-of-pity looks of relatives, as well as discrimination by law, are a common pattern.

In the Muslim world, there is a striking imbalance of status between the sexes. Marriages with a big age gap between partners are plentiful. When seeing such a couple, one might mistake the young woman for being out shopping with her father or grandfather, but a moment later, a small child in her arms calls out to the man: 'papa,' and all doubts of the casual observer are dispelled.

A certain woman got divorced. She wasn't happy in her marriage; another man was making passes at her and she was convinced he was going to ask her to marry. Finding out about her divorce, however, he retreated. Now in her thirties, she is alone and lonely. She is probably not going to find a husband. She feels sorry for herself, wanting a man, a family, and being close with another person after she gets back to her parents' home from work. She can feel that she is in the prime of her life but there is no one she could impress with her passion, no one to share it with. She confides some of her feelings to her friends and cries.

Another woman received an invitation to the wedding of a much younger protégé from work. She is single and past forty. She is standing in her office, showing the decorative card to a colleague. Suddenly, she is overcome by a familiar feeling of soul-wrenching grief. 'What about me?' the words escape from her mouth. She sits down, tears running down her cheeks. 'How can I go to this girl's wedding and be happy for her when I have nothing? I have never been with a man. I have never even touched a man. And even when I die, I will live in heaven as a single. And this is fair?'

Eva: The pragmatic bride

Although Eva comes from Slovakia, not the Middle East, hers was also a set-up marriage. It all began when she met an old friend from her hometown with her Kuwaiti husband. Eva felt envious. The man was treating her friend in a pleasant, respectful manner, and more importantly, they were living lavishly, staying in 5-star hotels and dinning at the finest restaurants. Their children were adorable. Eva liked the man and was very impressed by him. He also liked Eva and offered to find her a good husband. The crux of the story is that Eva agreed to marry a man she barely knew because, as she put it, someone came to her with a serious proposition, and that was all that mattered to her at the time. The men she had been meeting in Slovakia were all strange, irresponsible, selfish, and/or penniless.

'Every man I went out with would talk about himself and how he wants a career first, how he wants to make more money, buy a nice place or a new car. I thought that even if I found someone I liked, he might never propose, or he would be one of those guys who don't want children. Many men prefer pets over kids – they can get rid of them and don't need to pay alimony,' she tells me. 'In my country, you can only afford to have one child, not more. A friend of mine has been working at a district council office for fifteen years and she makes $500 after tax. She has two teenage sons. They live in a small flat and can't afford to travel for a holiday. And there he is, Mustafa, telling me so earnestly that he is looking for a steady relationship, that he wants a family, that we would see how it goes and maybe there would be children, and my eyes lit up. Now we have two beautiful boys. I would like one more, a girl.'

'Then you'd better get to work,' I reply.

'You know, it's difficult without a guy. My husband has been away for two years now. He had to go back Egypt and I'm not sure when – if he'll be back.' Eva's husband is not a Kuwaiti but an Egyptian who has been working here for many years.

'Did he not want you to relocate with him?' I ask, curious.

'I told him there's no way I'm not going to live there. I'm not moving from here to that lawless, miserable country.'

'Ouch. How do you see each other then?'

'We go to visit him,' Eva answers, as if it was the most obvious thing in the world.

'Don't you feel lonely sometimes? Alone with the kids, everything on your shoulders?'

'I don't have time to think about it. Before I had my children, there were times I felt lonely. My husband was coming late from work, sometimes at 10 p.m. And now? I wish I could sit down and read a book in the evening, but I have no time. I like reading, watching TV shows for women. For example, about wedding dresses because I've never had one myself...'

'You haven't?'

'Well, no,' Eva replies with a hint of regret. 'We got married in Lebanon, in a Muslim court. A dingy one. That was when I came on holiday here for the second time.'

'So you were in love then, since you came for the second time?'

'No, absolutely not. I didn't want to go. But he convinced me.'

'And he convinced you to get married, did he?' I venture a guess.

'A friend of mine suggested that if anything happened, getting a divorce was equally easy, even in absentia. He wouldn't even have to come to the court. I took my chances. He was thirteen years older, but he was quite handsome, except then I found out he already had a family and grown-up children. They are still here, in Kuwait. They are keeping an eye on me.'

I nod. A few of my friends in their forties and fifties are still looking for 'the one' life partner. To some extent, I understand Eva.

Then, I ask my last question.

'But all in all, are you happy?'

'Especially now, that my husband is not here.'

Mustafa is one of those men who don't shake hands with women because it is prohibited for a Muslim to touch a person of the opposite sex. He made a big scene when Eva shook the hand that her friend's husband extended to her. Another time, he saw a photo of Eva on Facebook without the hijab and made a fuss over it. Despite that, at the embassy event she took me to, I saw Eva without the scarf, smiling and dancing, life of the party. She looked like any other Western girl her age. However, when you see her wrapped up in hijab, you would think she is an old woman.

According to Eva, the hijab matters when you live in Kuwait. She shares an experience she had shortly after moving there. 'I was riding in a car with a friend one evening. We were both wearing hijabs and abayas. We noticed a man driving behind us; he was following us. When we reached the house, my friend phoned her husband to come out and get us as we were slightly scared. Her husband confronted the man, and they got into a fight. Unfortunately, a policeman – a secret police – was passing by and saw us. He told us to go to the police station to give our statements. And that policeman in the station explained to us that if anything serious happened, it would have been that other man's fault because we were dressed the way we were. He mentioned that the same applies to sexual assault: if a woman is dressed in an Islamic way, the fault lies with the man. I've found that even at a playground, when any conflict occurs, such as the kids fighting, and I am dressed in a hijab and abaya, the other person is intimidated.'

I also receive a valuable piece of advice: I should formally convert to Islam and keep the certificate in a safe place as proof. This would give me more rights compared to remaining a Christian, should things go awry in my marriage. 'You have to have that piece of paper,' Eva emphasises, and gives an example of her friend Nina. 'Nina married a Kuwaiti Bedouin. It was a modern marriage: they drunk vodka together. One time, they had a fight, and he drove his car while drunk and crashed. He died on the spot. They had two children, around 12 and 8 years old. The man's family took the children away from her. They obtained a court order which stated that the children should be raised in an Islamic environment, and that their mother was not a Muslim and thus couldn't be trusted to raise them as good Muslims. Recently, after three years of court battles, she was able to regain custody of one of the children because at the age of 14, children can be summoned to court to decide with whom they want to live. At the beginning of her fight for custody, the lawyer had told her: "If only you wore hijab, we would have found some witnesses to testify that you are a Muslim. You could have got the paper for it." I have that paper,' Eva adds at once. 'My husband doesn't know, or else he would have asked me to pray with him…'

It's difficult to say how tall Eva is at first glance: when she puts on her platform shoes for special occasions, she seems to tower over other women. She also gains a sexy sway to her step. The first thing you notice from a distance, after her fair-skinned face framed by a dark scarf, is her ample bosom, accentuated by blouses buttoned up to the top. Her headscarf, embellished with shiny crystals, is always tightly, expertly wrapped. Big eyes gaze from underneath dark eyeliner and mascara-coated eyelashes. 'I keep my make-up minimal,' Eva claims that she doesn't have time for a full makeup routine every morning. With her beautiful, rosy complexion, shapely nose, and blue eyes, it's easy to imagine there to be voluminous blond locks under her headscarf. But in reality, her hair is dyed a colour that depends on her mood. All these elements combined create an image of a half-matron, half-wildcat.

She says she's lived in Kuwait for so long that she remembers when the small but elegant city-centre and Salmiya malls were the go-to shopping destinations before the Avenues and 360 Mall existed. She seems to have many friends and to be well informed about who, what, when, and how. At parties where Europeans gather, she greets numerous people and chats with everyone.

There are people who feel they owe Eva a debt of gratitude for her friendly attitude and help. Natalia, who came to Kuwait almost a year ago, says: 'Thanks to Eva, my first year here was bearable. I've met some wonderful people through her, and after that it got much easier. About a month or two after my arrival, she invited me to her birthday. She introduced me to Hanna who has lived here for over twenty years. A very kind-hearted woman. I didn't have a car then and she offered to drive me to work,' Natalia recollects. 'Apart from that, Eva told me about various interesting places, shops and so on. I also met through her people who weren't the best but that doesn't matter.'

As I get to know Eva better, something about the picture of a good wife in a hijab does not seem to add up.

Once, I ask her out of curiosity: 'Have you noticed your hair getting weaker because they're not getting any sun?'

'No, actually, I think they're thicker. Besides, when we go for example to the desert, I take off my headscarf,' she replies.

I can't help but wonder about this desert trips and who she goes with, but I don't ask any further.

In addition to that, she makes a point of mentioning staying out at parties until 6 a.m., or she complains about being hangover, saying: 'My head is pounding after last night. I can't even look at whisky right now.'

Another time, during a girls' gathering, she mentions casually that she is late because she gave a male friend a ride to the airport.

'Are you sure you're safe driving some strange guys around?' someone asks with concern.

'He's a friend, a good friend. He helps me out, too. When I need to change my car engine oil, I ask him to do it. If I went myself, they would charge a woman, an expat on top of that, at least sixty dinars. But when he goes, they charge fifteen. Now one of my tables got broken, so I'm going to ask him, too. You know, a favour for a favour.'

'Aren't you worried that he might want something more than getting a ride to the airport?'

'Well, he might,' Eva laughs. 'He says that when I get divorced, he's going to marry me. But you see, he's twenty something, and me…' she doesn't finish but she's still smiling. I cannot tell if she's slightly embarrassed or amused.

'Listen, don't they ever stop your car when you're with male company?'

'I've never had any problems. See the way I dress: hijab, all covered up. Even when I was riding back from the desert one night, but I was all wrapped up because it was cold, my hands covered, too, I was dozing off on the passenger seat, and there was a checkpoint on the way, they didn't ask to see my papers. And it was three o'clock in the morning! I asked my friend who was driving: "They didn't want my ID?" And he said: "You're sitting all wrapped up, with a headscarf on, they have to assume you're my wife."'

She also matched a newcomer to Kuwait with one of her local acquaintances, she tells us. A friend asked her to take care of the young woman and show her around the city. After a while, Eva introduced her to Abdullah. As proof of her achievement, she shows us a video message from the man in question. In it, he says: 'Hi. I hope you are fine. I want to say thank you for last night. I have to tell you this: you make my life better. You're like a star, like the sun, you make everything brighter. It was a great time. Thank you.'

The chase: Dating the Gulf way

With all the religious and cultural constraints, young Kuwaiti men and women have developed their own methods for romance. Firstly, there's flirting in cars. At traffic lights, young men may chat up girls through open windows, trying to get a phone number. Or they chase after girls in cars, shouting marriage proposals, hoping they will stop or turn into a side street for a conversation. There is a stretch of Second Ring Road the locals call Love Street for precisely this reason. Young Kuwaitis drive up and down the streets in their freshly polished cars blasting loud music, searching for amusement, thrills, and sometimes, a relationship.

Appearance counts, from the brand of the car to clothing, hairstyles, sunglasses. Ironically, a big number of the cars taking part in the love race are rentals.

Street-flirting has its own code of conduct, with girls using a set of manifold looks to express their stance without words. A lengthy gaze, an overdone smile, brushing the hair away from the face signal interest, while a squint, a filthy glare, or a dramatic up-and-down once-over before stepping on the accelerator equals rejection. If the boy gestures for the girl to open her window and give him the number while on the road, it might mean that he is just collecting numbers and his intentions are not 'earnest'. A suggestion that they both turn into a car park or side street to talk is a sign that he is really interested.

Any way is good as long as it's quick and incognito, away from the watchful eyes of strict adults.

After all that I have witnessed, I am inclined to believe various stories, among them an anecdote about two women in the United States who called a police station to report a car that had been following them for twenty minutes after they had left a restaurant. The police stopped the suspect, a foreigner, who admitted he only wanted to get the women's phone numbers to ask them out. He didn't see anything wrong with his behaviour. 'That's what we always do in Kuwait,' he explained.

Another popular flirting method for young Kuwaitis is the 'hunt' in a shopping mall. They notice each other while sitting at different tables in a café or walking around shops, exchanging subtle looks and smiles to establish mutual interest. It takes a split of a second for a note with a phone number to exchange hands, or a boy might whisper his number to a girl riding an escalator in front of him. They might sit at a safe distance and whisper sweet nothings to each other. Apparently, there was also a phone app that allowed registered users to see who was nearby and contact them, but it was blocked in Kuwait shortly after being published.

Dating without a chaperone is socially unacceptable in Kuwait, and couples who want to disregard this rule have to be cautious and creative. (Wearing a niqab can come in handy, too.) 'I've had a few serious relationships. Being with someone requires a lot of sneaking,' Fahad shares his experience. 'I always knew when my dad was asleep or away from home, so I knew when to bring the girl over. Going on dates? I didn't care, I just went out. If the police stopped me, I would say: "she's my cousin" or something like that. I've been stopped multiple times by the police. If you're under 21, they have the right to take you to the station and then they call the parents. And after that, it's the parents' job to deal with you.'

Girls don't like trysts in public places, he also explains. 'Going out for a coffee is for single Arabs the most difficult thing to do. It's almost like you're getting married.' For a single girl, appearing in male company at a place where she could be spotted by someone, a friend or an aunt or brother, is a significant risk. It can arouse gossip, tarnish her reputation, and invite harsh punishment from her parents. Therefore, she wouldn't agree to meet just any man or someone who hasn't proven his intentions are serious. In Kuwait, where families are sizeable and society is small, even one pair of unauthorised eyes is enough for a scandal to erupt. The boy is also playing with fire. If he is unlucky, he could end up beaten up (or worse) by the girl's brother or cousin. For these reasons, many people are more inclined to meet in a private apartment or a hotel room rather than in open view.

Stolen glances and whispers in coffee shops are child's play compared to never-ending pursuits at breakneck speed, as seen through Fahad's eyes.

'You get in a car and then chase girls for hours. You and ten other cars will be chasing this one car with ladies, at full speed, risking your lives, all to get a phone number.'

'And you don't even know what they look like,' I want to confirm if I understood correctly.

'You haven't seen her clearly, obviously. You just saw hair. Because this is how it is in Kuwait. You see flowing locks in a car and you think, "Oh, long hair, on it, man!" And you and your friend drive behind that car for what seems like an eternity, fantasising about the girls until they finally park. And when they do, it's not really all that, sometimes. The girls turn out to be dumb. Or they don't know how to speak.'

'And once you have the number, what then?'

'Well, according to the rulebook, you're supposed to talk to them on the phone for weeks,' Fahad replies. 'From midnight until 4 a.m., 5 a.m., 6 a.m. – a minimum of six hours every day. And Kuwaiti girls don't really have much to say, so you're just breathing on the phone with the other person,' he demonstrates with a loud inhale and exhale, 'and waiting. I could never do it, the six hours. Maximum thirty minutes, maybe an hour. And they're like, "What? You don't want to talk to me?" Girls are complicated creatures. At the end of the day, it's about proving that you really want them, that you're giving them the attention. That you're chasing them.'

Fahad continues, 'Sometimes my cousin sleeps over at my place. He's constantly on the phone with these girls, talking sweet thing like "I miss you. I love you. Do you love me? Yes? Me too." I ask him, "Have you even seen this girl?" He says, "No, I hooked her up on Instagram." I think young Arabs are just missing affection, emotional connection. They aren't getting it from their parents, so they try to find it elsewhere. On the phone, that's the easiest place: I love you, you love me, so much love in the air.'

CHAPTER 10

Corruption: Never enough

Some of us, immigrants, come to Kuwait to make money, with delusion that this country is the goose that laid the golden egg. We don't delve into local issues. We see our situation as transient, preferring to mind our own business and not to step beyond our front yard. Some people cast a question into the void: 'Why is Kuwait not reaching its full potential? It could be such a magnificent country!' I've known so many who came and went without batting an eyelid.

This really is hardly surprising. We are often not brave enough to get involved in the politics of our homelands, let alone a foreign country. We are too busy with the mundane to think about changing the world.

There are also people who don't want to know. They have chosen ignorance as their strategy for a happy life. The director of one of Kuwaiti museums is a friendly American woman and an expert in her field; whenever she gives a talk, whether it's to a big or small group, she would praise the generous prince Nasser al-Sabah for allowing the museum to exhibit some of his private collection and procuring such magnificent artefacts with his private money. It seems that she has never asked herself where this money came from or how he acquired treasures of other nations that were never for sale. When you hear how she speaks about him, you would think she is a teenager who has just met her favourite pop singer.

Corruption in Kuwait is generally obvious and visible rather than disguised – in contrast to the West. One group rules the country and enjoys the lion's share of its income. The prime minister, the emir, the ministers of defence, foreign affairs, and interior must be from Al-Sabah clan, while the speaker of the parliament, ministers of commerce, finance, and oil are mostly from the few elite families. While there appear to be several competing factions, they all ultimately belong to the same group. They are the ones that decide what gets covered by the media and what is deemed irrelevant. They have a consensus on prolonging their grip on power.

I once gently touched on the subject of the political situation in Kuwait during a conversation with an elderly Kuwaiti lady. It was during the rule of the previous emir, Sabah al-Ahmad. I was asking her why there weren't many investments in the country's infrastructure or its people, why more immigrants were being brought in, and why laws were becoming increasingly complex and illogical. I was shocked by her boldness and directness. Speaking slowly and with emphasis, she said: 'It's not that the emir doesn't know what's going on. He knows very well and wants it this way. In their [the ruling group's] minds, what we have is a gift from them, their charity.'

She went on to tell me that when Emir Sabah al-Ahmad assumed power, he raised his annual allowance from 25 million to 150 million dollars and took 10 years' payment upfront as a bonus. A question crossed my mind at that time whether people ever feel that they have enough money, and on what one could possibly spend these kind of sums. Soon, a very concrete answer came when I stumbled upon photos and videos from the wedding of the emir's grandson, Sheikh Fahad Nasser Sabah al-Sabah, which had taken place in April 2015 and shaken up social media. The food and serving staff were brought in from France, and the flowers from Holland. One of the bespoke dresses worn by the bride was custom-made by a Chanel designer. Wedding guests were treated to performances by major Arab stars such as Myriam Fares and Mohammed Abdu. Fireworks were set off from the metal construction of the tent, and the most distinguished guests received diamond rings as gifts. How much did the celebration cost? Probably even the newlyweds would not have been able to say exactly, but estimates put the total at 70-80 million dinars. That is almost a quarter of a billion dollars spent in one night.

Sometime before that, the wedding of Emir Jaber's grand-daughter and Emir Saad's grandson took place, and no expense was spared in that instance as well. Crystal chandeliers were hung along the street leading to the bride's home. Although official sources did not provide any details about it, in case of both weddings, photos and videos taken by the guests were leaked and circulated among Kuwaitis.

Kuwait's small size and tight-knit community mean that local events attract significant attention, and information spreads quickly. Instances of greed and corruption might be more visible than elsewhere in the world. This absolutely does not mean that Western countries are more ethical. As I once heard on the radio, 'We are part of a worldwide system of greed.'

One businessman I interviewed for this book couldn't get over a conversation he had with a minor sheikh whom he had been friends with for a long time. The sheikh, who was in his forties, was spending tens of thousands of dollars every night on drugs, prostitutes, and parties. When the businessman suggested that he should be more careful with his money, especially since he had children and a wife, the sheikh looked at him and said, 'What money? With every morning, I have stolen another half a million dinars without even moving a finger.' The sheikh was selling residency permits and renting properties to the government at gouged prices, securing tenders and contracts which he then resold to small contractors for a profit. Of course, he had people doing the work for him; he would just watch as messages arrived indicating that another lump sum had been deposited into his account.

When you drive by the city centre, an extraordinary building straight out of Star Wars looms in the city skyline: a short cuboid propped on two gigantic legs, with a glazed stripe from top to bottom along each leg – the forty-story high twin towers. One day, shortly after moving to Kuwait, I wanted to take a closer look at it and see what might be inside. The guard said that the building had been rented out to the Ministry of Endowment and Islamic Affairs for two years, however, they had not properly moved in yet.

Isn't it ironic that an institution which calls for humility and charity is housed in a brand-new, luxurious high-rise? In fact, this is only one of several buildings in the city that they occupy. It's interesting to note that the tenant has been paying for two years from the state budget for offices which are nearly empty. Their main headquarters is a massive complex that is larger than most other ministries or the Kuwaiti parliament itself.

Another way of syphoning public funds into private pockets, popular also in the 'civilised' West, is through government tenders. In the area where I lived in Kuwait, there was a small piece of land designated for a public park, playground, and ball courts. Construction on it was ongoing the entire time, with a new contract being awarded every year. Even now, I wouldn't bet that it has been completed. Was the contractor waiting for the next instalment of funds? Or perhaps they were planning to delay the project long enough to charge for the same work again?

In Kuwait, companies have a habit of charging multiple times for doing and redoing the same job. It is well-known who these companies belong to, despite attempts to disguise the ownership under an unknown individual. In reality, a share of the profits is always turned over to the powerful people who are the true owner. These companies consistently win tenders, leaving little chance for fair competition.

~

In Kuwait, I experienced one of the most puzzling and shocking events of my life.

It all begins with a mundane visit to my German friends in Amwaj Tower. As I make my way down the hallway, I am met with chaos: the path is blocked by cardboard boxes, oversized children's toys, and bikes wrapped in plastic. My friend's neighbours are moving but the moving company they hired failed to show up, leaving them in a mad rush.

I've met these neighbours. The man is a senior manager at one of the largest property developers in the Middle East, and of Jordanian nationality. The company has branches in various countries and he frequently travels between them. My friends used to see him and his wife now and then, but lately, he hasn't been home for months. He is in Dubai and not coming back to Kuwait, and Ola has been left to pack up their entire life and organise the move by herself. According to my friends, the couple and their children are currently headed to Lebanon, the wife's country of origin. From there, they plan to eventually move to Switzerland. It's just that at the moment, they are having trouble with the transport company, and apart from that, they are unsure if they will manage to sell their Ferrari, Land Rover, and Harley Davidson motorbike standing in the underground garage before leaving. 'Now Ola has to pack everything on her own,' my friend says, 'including this huge TV. It has all these gadgets, and it's voice-operated. They have two of them.'

Just days before this incident, the headline news in the country reported on a huge scam involving several major property developers. These companies had defrauded people by taking hundreds of millions of dollars for the construction of houses and chalets that were never built, on plots of land they never had. Most of the front men, who were non-Kuwaitis, had fled with millions of dollars, among them Alaa Alayan, my best friend's neighbour. His wife and children left Kuwait unhindered, and they are all happily living their lives, evading the full extent of the repercussions for their fraudulent deeds. Except for a few cases, the public did not get to know the names of the real perpetrators.

Fast forward several years, and thousands of victims are still battling in court to recover their lost funds but ending up with nothing. Among those who lost money in this scheme was a dear friend of my husband who had invested all his savings, in addition to a loan he had taken out, to buy several properties, hoping the revenue would serve as his pension. Convicting sentences were given to minor non-citizens, most of them in absentia. These men were used as pawns by powerful Kuwaitis to steal from their own people.

~

Such a hoax is a trifle compared to the $4.5 billion embezzled from Malaysia's national development fund, 1MDB. Dozens of important people and institutions have been involved in this financial scandal, such as the American bank, Goldman Sachs, as well as a Kuwaiti sheikh, Sabah Jaber Mubarak al-Sabah, the son of the prime minister at the time. It has been one of the biggest embezzlement and money-laundering operations in the world so far.

The main suspect, the alleged brain and facilitator behind the scheme, Low Teak Jho, established contact with that sheikh at the beginning of 2016, after the U.S. State Department started investigating him in response to complaints from banks in the US and other countries. In Kuwait, not only did he gain further business partners and money-juggling channels but also a temporary shelter from law enforcement. He was granted a visa to Kuwait despite being on the Interpol wanted list.

Jho Low had been involved with Kuwaiti financiers before that. According to the press, in 2006 he helped the Islamic bank Kuwait Finance House invest in Malaysia, and then in 2012, he bought shares in Electrum Group simultaneously with the Kuwait Investment Authority.

The matter began to unravel for Sheikh Sabah when a Chinese bank in Kuwait filed complaints that his account had received several wire transfers between 2017 and 2019. The investigation found that a payment of over 1 billion dollars, labelled a consultancy fee, was deposited into the sheikh's company account, which he then moved through various other accounts, some offshore. A portion of the money was transferred further to Jho Low and Malaysian officials. With his cut, the sheikh bought a yacht, a private airplane, cars, jewellery. His personal secretary admitted to receiving around $50 million.[75]

Sheikh Sabah was arrested in July 2020 and subsequently released on bail. In March 2023, a Kuwaiti court sentenced him and four others on money laundering charges related to the 1MDB scandal. Both the sheikh and his business partner were given 10 years of prison, while a Kuwaiti lawyer received a seven-year sentence. The court also ordered confiscation of the money deposited in their bank accounts.

While the 1MDB turmoil held the world's gaze, another affair emerged in Kuwait, concerning Sheikh Sabah's brother. In September 2020, a video recording was leaked of the secret service interrogating Sheikh Hamid Jaber Mubarak al-Sabah, which had taken place in 2018.[76] Fragments of the recording show a relaxed

75 Manshoor (12 Apr 2023). Qisat alsunduq al-Malizii min alhabat 'iilaa alquba [The story of the Malaysian Fund from the beginning to the end]. (in Arabic).
76 Fragments of the recording appeared among others on Twitter on 1st September 2020 via handle @janobalsourra1.

atmosphere of the interrogation, with everyone sitting comfortably on the sofas, officers offering the sheikh tea and coffee, saying that he has nothing to worry about, and the sheikh making some joking remarks and promising a promotion to the commanding officer of the secret services.

During this conversation, the sheikh touches on the subject of surveillance of citizens. He brags about having a network of employees whose job is to hack into Twitter and telephone accounts, including access to sent messages. The captain of the secret services in turn says that he commands a unit which controls the social media: 'We can make a story trend or we can kill it.' He claims that in case of unfavourable news, he is able to divert public attention by making another event trend.[77]

In response to this scandal, the government applied its usual method of dealing with such things. Official commentaries claimed 'manipulation of the recordings', taking things out of context, and emphasised the need to pay attention to the reliability of such information. The officers responsible for leaking the videos were arrested.

While searching for information about the involvement of Kuwaiti elites in the 1MDB case, I came across an article about another, much older financial scandal. In 1986, the Kuwait Investment Office – the predecessor and current London office of the Kuwait Investment Authority – bought majority shares in the Spanish company Torras, which collapsed six years later. As a result, the KIO incurred a loss of 5 billion dollars. At least a portion of that sum found its way into the hands of people who had left Kuwait during the war with Iraq, including the upkeep of the ruling family 'in exile'. Additionally, after the war, the Kuwaiti government purchased 20 billion dollars of bad debt owed by its citizens in Kuwaiti banks. It was revealed that '90% of the

---

77 Material sourced from videos published on Twitter by @janobalsourra1. Press coverage is not available.

money was owed by perhaps 1,000 wealthy Kuwaitis', including the ruling al-Sabah family.[78]

In July 2020, the local press announced that some of the money from the COVID-19 Containment Contributions Fund, which was donated by private institutions and citizens, was directed toward the purchase of weapons, ammunition, and bulletproof clothing. The Ministry of Interior allocated $5.2 million from the collected sum of $178 million to 'ensuring the safety of citizens and residents'.

A fish rots from the head down. The ruling elite sets the standard for the rest of society to follow. The entire system encourages various forms of shady activities: pretend work, illegal apartment rentals, selling work visas, acting as a fake sponsor, buying black-market alcohol, one-night rendezvous in hotel rooms, or pretending to be Muslim. With one caveat: people who are not part of the ruling class will sooner or later be held accountable for their misdeeds. This can happen instantly or later, when leverage is needed to pressure that person or discredit them if they dare to criticise the authorities. On the other hand, people who refuse to conform are troublesome. For example, the financial auditor, Alexandra, quit her job after nearly a year at a prestigious firm. When her boss realised that she was not going to play by their rules, he started bullying her until she left. It was her fault, she could not fit into the company working culture. In a setting where everyone steals and cheats, one honest person poses a problem.

---

78 Los Angeles Times (10 Feb 1993). $5-Billion Loss Riles Even Oil-Rich Kuwaitis: Scandal: Parliament's probe of public funds poses the most serious challenge ever to the ruling family's power.

The Lucrative Business of Immigration

Every foreigner who wished to live and work in Kuwait, except for citizens of the Gulf states, needs to have a Kuwaiti sponsor. Companies receive a quote from the government specifying the number of foreign workers they can bring into the country. It is common for two neighbouring businesses of similar size to receive vastly different licenses, with one being permitted to bring in 1200 workers while the other is only allowed 12.

Many, if not most, of the super-rich people sponsor tens of thousands of foreign workers. It is one of the most lucrative businesses in the country.

There are two prominent women in the country who formally own large service companies and hence have the right to bring in workers from abroad on working visas. The immigration office swiftly issues them tens of thousands of visas and renews them every year. On paper, these workers are contracted to work in the companies owned by the women but in reality, the visas are sold to people in their home countries, allowing them to come to Kuwait and search for work on their own, with promises of protection and help. However, upon arrival, they are told that they have to fend for themselves and be cautious as in case of any violation, the sponsor would claim that the worker left the sponsor's employment without permission, leading to the cancellation of their residency and subsequent deportation. Most people who arrive in Kuwait using these visas know someone in the country, whether a friend or relative, who would help them find work. Many end up working on construction sites e.g. as guards or taking any odd jobs that nobody else wants for less money. Every year or two, they have to pay the sponsor for renewal of the visa, or they decide to stay on illegally.

In October 2016, the Kuwait Times reported the arrest of a man who had forged 35 working visas, selling each one for 550 KD ($1700).[79] The price of a black-market visa can be significantly higher, depending on how strict the criteria are for a particular nationality. In June 2020, a Bangladeshi MP and businessman Mohammed Shahid Islam was arrested in Kuwait on charges of human trafficking, bribery, and money laundering. Together with his accomplices, which included high-ranking Kuwaiti officials, he is said to have brought more than 20,000 Bangladeshi workers to Kuwait in exchange for over $163 m. The Bangladeshis paid between $4600 and $6000 each to come and work in Kuwait.[80]

Working visas for Syrians are the most difficult to acquire and are therefore the most expensive on the black market. Before the pandemic, they were offered for $6000 to $8000 each, while price rose to as high as $15,000 after COVID-19.[81]

After the COVID-19 pandemic broke out, the Kuwaiti government implemented new policies restricting or cutting working visas for specific groups. Many people were denied a visa renewal but nevertheless chose to stay and continue working, despite being paid even lower salaries than before due to their visa status.

79 Kuwait Times (20 Oct 2016). Egyptian mandoub arrested for issuing work permits; Illegal plastic surgeries.
80 Gulf News (26 Jun 2020). Kuwait sends Bangladesh MP Shahid Islam to jail.; U.S. Department of State, 2022 Trafficking in Persons Report: Kuwait.
81 Arab Times Online (14 Aug 2022). Visa trade flourishing once again in Kuwait – KD 1,500 to KD 5,000 for work visa.

The boundaries of justice

A charming article in the October 2016 issue of Vogue Arabia takes readers on a tour of 'secret' Paris with Fajer Fahad, a Kuwaiti fashionista in her twenties. The girl poses in front of her favourite modest and down-to-earth spots, including a little florist's shop, a bakery, and a café. The authors touch upon Fajer's swift journey to join Hollywood's celebrity circle but do not reveal her family name, how and why she found herself away from her homeland, or why she chooses not to return. The source of her affluence is also undisclosed.

The story of al-Rajaan family is definitely one worth telling. Fajer's father, Fahad al-Rajaan, served as the chairman of Kuwait's Public Institution for Social Security (PIFFS) for thirty years. This institution is one of the largest sovereign wealth funds in the Middle East, tasked with controlling and investing public pension money. It is a major shareholder in numerous European and American corporations, with current assets estimated at over $134 billion. For years, top CEOs were queuing to meet with al-Rajaan, who had been appointed to this post by his brother-in-law, Emir Jaber al-Sabah.

The story started in 1970s, when an attractive girl from a poor Bedouin family caught the eye of Crown Prince Jaber. He added her to his many wives. Unlike such other marriages, this one lasted for a long few years. They had several children, which tightened their relationship to the degree that when he became the emir, he promoted her family to the ranks of the country's elite. The woman's brother, Fahad al-Rajaan, in particular, benefited greatly from this patronage. During al-Rajaan's three decades as head of PIFSS, many board members, journalists, and MPs were accusing him of corruption, money laundry, and embezzlement. They pointed time and again to his lavish lifestyle and his countless properties both in Kuwait and abroad, which didn't fit with his background or his salary. Calls for a full audit of PIFFS assets and an independent committee to oversee its investments went unheeded, despite several consecutive ministers of finance being questioned by MPs on allegations of corruption and gross misconduct in PIFFS, and some being impeached and forced to tender their resignations. Still, nothing rattled Rajjan, as he remained the institution's czar from 1984 to 2012. An independent audit of how he was managing the billions never took place.

A columnist wrote in 2008 that several American presidents had come and gone, several British PMs had come and gone, several Saudi kings had come and gone, several Kuwaiti emirs had come and gone, the country had been invaded, occupied and liberated, and several ministers of finance had come and gone, all that while Fahad al-Rajaan was still in power controlling tens of billions of dollars and thousands of employees.

Six years after the death of his former brother-in-law, al-Rajaan was finally charged by the general prosecutor with laundering and embezzling billions of dollars and causing further billions in losses for the fund. But before the court hearings, al-Rajaan requested permission to travel to Mecca for pilgrimage, which was granted. From there, he escaped to London with his wife and children.

Kuwaiti authorities later revealed that before leaving, al-Rajaan had sold 156 properties in Kuwait worth hundreds of millions and what was left were 56. These are the ones that were registered under his name. In 2022, the Ministry of Justice auctioned off 42 of these remaining properties, including a seaside plot that sold for 6.6 million dinars ($22 m) and a house that sold for 3.4 million dinars. They found that he had bank accounts, properties, and companies in Switzerland, Lebanon, Singapore, Lichtenstein, the Bahamas, and the British Virgin Islands. The general prosecutor also recovered assets and cash totalling $100 million from Bahrain. In 2019, the British court froze assets worth $847 million in the UK, while Swiss authorities froze 82 million Swiss francs. To this day, it remains unclear how much money was laundered and stolen, how much was transferred into secret accounts or assets in other people's names, how much was lost due to poor decisions, and who was involved. Reading the sentences of Kuwaiti courts it appears that evidence provided was limited to specific cases and instances.

In 2016, the Kuwaiti court convicted him in absentia of money laundering and embezzlement and sentenced him to 10 years in prison.[82,83] Three years later, he and his wife were sentenced to life imprisonment, again in absentia, in a sham trial aimed at appeasing the outraged Kuwaitis. But did al-Rajaan truly care? He lived a lavish life. His children don't have to worry about their financial future. They were said to be living in Knightsbridge, one of London's most exclusive neighbourhoods, until al-Rajaan's death in 2022. Meanwhile, Fajer could take her pick between apartments in Paris, Dubai, and a house in LA's luxurious Holmby Hills area (which she reportedly bought in 2018 for $8.7 million). Only in the memories of his fellow countrymen will al-Rajaan remain the man who stole their pensions. One can only imagine what they must be thinking and feeling when they look at the glamorous photos of Fajer al-Rajaan in Vogue Arabia.

~

The concept of justice and the reality of institutionalized corruption are inextricably linked. Societies want to see justice served, with equal treatment under the law and accountability for those who break it, regardless of their wealth, status, or connections.

---

82 Kuwait Times (15 Nov 2015). Arrest warrant out for Rajaan.
83 Finews (22 Jul 2020). Swiss Banks Accused in Kuwaiti Pension Scandal.

Unfortunately, all too often we are met with painful disappointment. Justice is often elusive, and legal systems are imperfect.

Despite the officials repeating that the 'Kuwaiti judicial system is fair, independent, and impartial', Kuwaiti laws remain complex, vague, and contradictory, and punishments are severe. This way the code of law can be used selectively to punish some and let others scot-free for a similar deed.

Most lawyers in Kuwait are Egyptian. The country's judiciary system was established by Egyptian legal advisors. The legal systems of these two countries have many similarities as they both combine the principles of British common law, French civil law, Egyptian law, and Islamic law. From the beginning, Kuwaitis have been a relatively small nation where many people are related, acquainted, or otherwise linked, therefore judges from outside were thought to be more impartial when ruling between citizens. It is common for all the Gulf states to hire foreign judges. Thus, Egyptians often decide the fate of Kuwaitis in legal cases.

It is common for people to sue each other in civil law cases, even over seemingly trivial matters. Then, there are also divorces and custody hearings, as well as criminal cases. Many of the family issues end up in criminal courts as it is common for divorced couples to accuse each other of various crimes, including kidnapping, if one of the parents keeps the children beyond the designated visiting time. A significant number of cases are prosecuted by the state.

In 2018, a total of 707 judges issued 1,262,000 sentences. Of these, 310 judges delivered 1.2 million sentences in the first instance: it was calculated that each judge ruled on around 50 cases every week. Judges presiding over violations (minor crimes) ruled on average on 250 cases per day. There were 312 court of appeal judges who issued rulings in 50,000 cases. The higher court of appeal with 85 judges examined 16 500 cases that year: they delivered sentences in 12,000 of them while 5,000 remained without a sentence. There was also a backlog of 28,000 cases in the Kuwaiti judicial system.[84]

This means that during the year, each adult citizen is involved in several legal proceedings held against him or her. More, if you are active in politics or business; some bloggers have hundreds. Among the 1.2 million cases, there are also some lawsuits against foreigners but these are not frequent. There aren't many people who would take a maid or other poor immigrant to trial – usually if there is any problem, they simply get deported; they cannot afford court anyway.

In a single morning, a judge might adjourn dozens of proceedings. Sides or their legal representatives often have to appear before a judge every other week, wait their turn as no specific time is scheduled, and on occasion, the judge will be very late or won't show up at all. Some lawsuits take many years to finish. In many instances, defendants in debt claim cases, even regarding small amounts such as thirty dinars for a speeding ticket, or political cases are barred from leaving the country until the trial concludes or the debt is paid by being placed on the so called no-fly list. Being a plaintiff or defendant in a legal case is often a traumatic experience.

A major scandal shook this small Arab state when an Iranian businessman Fouad Salehi, who had lived all his life in Kuwait, was arrested for money laundering and during interrogations police found numerous text messages between him and more than 20 senior Kuwaiti judges, as well as videos of them in compromising situations. The content of these exchanges was leaked to the public.

Nine senior judges were referred to court on allegations of corruption; the court sentence and accompanying materials were leaked and published online. The Iranian man's admission and the text messages between him and these judges revealed that he

---

84 AlJarida (14 May 2019). Milyun wa 262 alf qadiat fasal biha 707 qudaat fi 2018! [707 judges ruled in one million and 262 thousand cases in 2018!]. (in Arabic).

had bribed them, as well as several workers of the Justice Ministry, with cars, yachts, alcohol, and cash money in exchange for sentences against various people. Salehi acted as the intermediary in bribery deals which involved state officials, known lawyers, and court clerks, among others. He used to arrange parties and procure prostitutes for the judges. In one of the deals, a judge sentenced a man to 5 years imprisonment in exchange for $150,000. The investigation revealed that Salehi and his network had carried out their illegal operations for five years.[85] This was the first ever instance in Kuwait's history that the immunity of judges was revoked and they could be prosecuted.

It is important to note that many of the judges involved were not prosecuted. Moreover, the general attorney issued an order banning any publication or discussion concerning the case.

It is common knowledge that corruption in the judiciary is rampant. Who wins in a court trial of an average person against another average person? Is it the side who has the truth? Or perhaps the one who presents more convincing evidence? The person who has a better lawyer? That side wins who was meant to win.

From some of more obvious examples, a Shiite rarely wins a case where the opposing side is Sunni, a foreigner rarely wins against a citizen, and a win by a regular person against a member of the ruling family or their associates is a dream. Some lawyers are known to charge exorbitant fees due to their perceived connections with senior judges, leading clients to assume that hiring them guarantees a win in their cases. Often, bribes are given by both sides of an important lawsuit.

Family courts are known to be particularly corrupt. In many instances, judges bluntly invite one of the sides to tip the scales in their favour. If the side of a trial is a woman whom the judge finds attractive, the price for ruling in her favour, such as granting

---

85 MEMO Middle East Monitor (29 Dec 2021). Kuwait jails 6 judges over money laundering.

her custody of her children, might be sex. She might be called into the judge's office and hear the proposition directly or receive it in a more or less disguised form through her lawyer. Women who feel like they've been backed into a corner agree to such conditions. This is what the locals say – there are no official data or press articles on the subject – but why would any woman lie about it? In Bahrain, a women's rights activist, Ghada Jamsheer, spoke publicly about the fact that judges seek sexual favours from women involved in legal trials. Due to her activism advocating women's rights and fight against corruption, Jamsheer was put on trial many times by the state, spent several months in prison, and was under constant surveillance by the secret police. The local media were banned from publishing any information about her.[86] Bahraini women now have a codified family law for Sunnis thanks to her efforts.[87]

86 Human Rights Watch (01 Jun 2005). Bahrain: Courts Try to Silence Women's Rights Activist.
87 During the reform, the Shiites did not agree to the changes in their family law proposed by the government.

Players and pawns

In one of his talks, the late Christopher Hitchens eloquently describes how the previous Iraqi regime was notorious for purging its loyalists, including those who were friends with the leader and staunch supporters of the ruling party, as much as the enemies or the ordinary people. Loyalty and connections could prove to be a double-edged sword in this part of the world. People in power tend to be paranoid and keep everyone terrified. In his book 'Republic of Fear', the Iraqi scholar Kanan Makiya described how no one was truly safe in a totalitarian state.

Hamid Al-Jibbouri, one of the most prominent Iraqi politicians and an old friend of Saddam Hussein, said in a documentary broadcast by Al-Jazeera that even he was spied on by the secret police while serving as a minister. He recounted how an important Iraqi Army general, known for his loyalty to Saddam, was summoned to meet with the president. In the palace, he was arrested and taken to a room where he was shown a video of his wife and daughter being raped by secret police. After that, he was taken to meet with Saddam, who acted as if nothing had happened. Al-Jibbouri revealed that he kept a loaded Kalashnikov under his bed. If they came to take him or rape his wife, he would have killed them, himself, and his wife. The Syrian and Libyan regimes are known to use similar tactics, and people who are close to the leaders don't know what could happen to them or when. There is no 'why'. Uncertainty creates fear, and fear is useful for the ones in power. The idea that you don't know what could happen, the fact that people in power don't require a reason to inflict harm, and that there is no way to resist the authority creates a submissive, anxious society.

Gulf state rulers are not as cruel or as irrational as the Iraqis or Libyan or Iranian or Syrian regime but still, they are known for being intolerant of defiance and threats to their power. Also, people in power in these countries tend to be divided and in-fighting can also lead to further repression of political opponents and instability. In recent decades, many senior officials in Kuwaiti, including senior sheikhs who were serving as ministers, have been impeached, humiliated, charged with criminal activities, and defamed. They were simply purged, and some ended up in jail or forced to spend their lives in courts trying to clear their names and unfreeze their bank accounts. In many cases, all this was done on the orders of their uncles, siblings, brothers, who used the legal system, parliament, media outlets as weapons. In most cases, no one knew the reason behind the downfall, not even the devastated men.

The story of Salman al-Sabah might be a good example of this phenomenon. Born in Kuwait in 1939 to a minor branch of al-Sabah family, he studied law in Egypt and New York, and served on various posts before being appointed as the minister of justice in 1976. He held that position until his impeachment by the parliament in 1985. The impeaching members of parliament presented secret documents and a copy of a wire transfer as evidence that he had embezzled several million dollars, while the media carried out an intensive character assassination campaign. This crusade against him was orchestrated by more powerful people who may have seen Salman as a threat, disliked him, or perhaps wanted him to serve as an example of what they could do to anyone who dares to challenge them. After his resignation, rumours started spreading that Sheikh Salman and his family were not members of al-Sabah clan but distant relatives who had taken on the name many decades ago. In February 2022, the Amiri Diwan issued an edict revoking the status of sheikhs from Salman al-Sabah, his brothers, and cousins. The 43 people on the list were stripped of all privileges associated with the title, including special treatment, a generous monthly allowance, a diplomatic passport. It became illegal to refer to them as sheikhs or treat them as such.

At the beginning of 2019, The Kuwaiti newspaper Al-Rai reported on an ongoing investigation by the interior ministry into the citizenship of an army general. Initial information suggested that the general's father obtained Kuwaiti citizenship through forged documents. The report also highlighted that the general was a member of the investigation committee formed by the Minister of Defence, Sheikh Nasser al-Sabah. He was in charge of looking into corruption in the army between 2015-2017, specifically focusing on military contracts for the purchase of Caracal and Eurofighter aircrafts, signed under the previous defence minister, Khaled al-Sabah. Based on information published on Twitter accounts of individuals connected with the press, it was suggested that the accused was Major General K.M.S., Assistant Army Chief of Staff in the Kuwaiti Army, who had participated in the defence of Kuwait during the 1990 invasion and its liberation in 1991.[88] The investigation was opened during the time when Sheikh Nasser al-Sabah was in open conflict with Khaled al-Sabah, then Minister of Interior, responsible for charging the general with forging his citizenship.[89] Many people speculated that the Minister of Interior was attempting to punish the general for following orders. If the Minister of Interior had succeeded, he would have stripped the general, his siblings, and all their children and grandchildren of their citizenship, rendering them Bidoon like many others who were subjected to this procedure. However, there are no reports or mentions in the media of what happened later. Major general K.M.S. disappeared from public view.

88 Ayman Saleh (19 Feb 2019). Aitiham dabit kabir bitazwir aljinsiat alkuaytiat yuthir aljadal fi albalad alkhaliji [Accusations against senior officer of forging his Kuwaiti citizenship stir controversy in the Gulf country]. Erem News (in Arabic).
89 Gulf News (17 Nov 2019). Kuwait Defence Minister Shaikh Nasser takes aim at outgoing premier Jaber.

These stories are just a few of many that illustrate how people in positions of power have no regard for those beneath them, using or discarding them as they see fit. There is a willingness to use power and influence to satisfy personal desires or agendas. Ideas such as friendship, loyalty, and even blood ties hold little value or meaning for the powerful.

CHAPTER 11

The curse that keeps on giving

For decades, economists have categorised the oil-rich Gulf countries as rentier states and warned about the unsustainability of their economic model. According to the established definition, a rentier state derives a significant portion of national revenue from external rent, and only a small segment of the population is engaged in its generation, while the majority reap the fruit of it, with revenues being accrued mainly by the government.[90] 'Rent' in this context is understood as an unearned income or windfall, as it is derived from a resource which is a gift of nature rather than a product of the state or society's labour or effort.

Many economists have argued that the oil wealth of these rentier states hinders democracy, creativity, economic development. It is also believed to play a major role in fostering authoritarian regimes and impeding the social progress within these societies. However, these theorists seem to have neglected testing their premise by drawing comparisons with other countries in the region which have similar conditions except for the factor of oil. Most of the Middle Eastern states which cannot be described as rentier states suffer from lack of democracy, limited social progress as well as weak economies. Is Sudan, a vast country abundant in natural resources, more liberal and progressive than Oman or the Emirates? Are Egypt, Jordan, or Syria more

---

90 Hazem Beblawi (1987). The Rentier State in the Arab World. Arab Studies Quarterly, Vol. 9, No. 4 (Fall 1987), pp. 383-398.

advanced than Kuwait or Bahrain? Is Yemen doing much better than Saudi Arabia economically, politically, freedom-wise? Facts on the ground and recent studies demonstrate that the 'resource curse' view is false.[91] Various writers argue that without oil, Gulf States would not be prosperous democracies but rather impoverished dictatorships.[92] The phenomenon we witness here requires a deeper understanding.

Before the discovery of oil in the region, local lords and tribes were fighting over fertile lands, ports, and oases, not over empty stretches of desert. Democratic tradition didn't exist in this part of the world for many centuries, and for over a thousand years there were no borders between the different nations and countries. It was the British and the French who drew the current maps of the region and decided which territories belonged to the Emirates, which to Kuwait, Saudi Arabia, Egypt, Sudan, Syria, Lebanon, and others. European and American engineers extracted the oil, built refineries, pipelines, storages, industrial complexes, ports, airports, streets, hospitals. Initially, they gave a small portion of proceeds to the local governors whom they had helped install in power. Later, these countries gained independence, set up their own oil companies, took control of the established industry and started selling the oil themselves.

Nowadays, thousands of Kuwaitis and foreigners are hired in the oil industry, however, it is still the big Western companies that handle most of the major works, receiving a fraction of the revenue generated. Kuwaiti workers, who are often paid exuberant amounts of money, play a small part in the production process.

---

91 See Stephen Haber & Victor Menaldo (2011). Do Natural Resources Fuel Authoritarianism? A Reappraisal of the Resource Curse. American Political Science Review 105(1), pp. 1-26.; Michael Herb (2005). No Representation Without Taxation? Rents, Development, and Democracy. Comparative Politics 37(3), pp. 297-316.
92 David Waldner & Benjamin B. Smith (2013). Rentier States and State Transformations. Oxford Handbook on Transformations of the State, 2014, Forthcoming.

Since the production of oil began in the Middle East in late 1930s, the most common notion has been that oil is a non-renewable, finite commodity. Countless experts and politicians have declared that Kuwait, Saudi Arabia, the Emirates, Iraq, Libya need to diversify their sources of income, as oil reserves would be depleted in the near future, and prices would fluctuate as demand for oil shifts. The reality is that over the past eighty years, these countries have enjoyed the benefits of petrodollars without the need for the majority of the population to participate in the creation of the wealth. Governments have been employing millions of citizens in jobs that are not needed and do not significantly add to the national output. The oil revenue has facilitated the development of some of the best airports, modern infrastructure, schools, malls, magnificent houses with swimming pools. Whether it is Oman, Saudi Arabia, Qatar, or Bahrain, people there don't pay income tax. These states import the majority of goods, from planes to needles. It seems unlikely for this status quo to change anytime soon.

In 1972, the Kuwaiti minister of oil warned the parliament that oil production would start to decline in the following years and the country's oil reserves would run out by 2026. However, in 2023, it was estimated that Kuwait still has another good 100 years to go with the current level of production.

In 1969, Kuwait's daily oil production stood at 2.6 million barrels, rising to almost 3.5 million barrels two years later. Since 2004, the daily production has not fallen below 2.5 million barrels, with the CEO of Kuwait Petroleum stating in September 2022 that they were producing over 2.8 million barrels per day, out of which around 1.9 million barrels were sold as crude oil and 760,000 barrels were refined locally and exported at a higher price. Oil extraction costs in the Gulf states remain relatively low at $2-3 per barrel, while the sales prices at times surpassed $145 per barrel. Despite challenges such as fluctuating global prices and environmental concerns, Gulf states have been benefiting greatly from oil exports, which significantly boosted their economic growth and geopolitical influence.

Kuwait has established sovereign funds to invest the surplus oil revenues abroad with the aim to preserve them for future generations and to support the country's economic development and growth. The main fund, Kuwait Investment Authority (KIA), set up in 1953 as Kuwait Investment Office, is one of the oldest and wealthiest sovereign funds in the world. It is estimated to be worth $700 billion. Over the years, the Kuwaiti government has acquired shares in most of the big international corporations that in addition to lucrative dividends give them power and influence over Western countries. In addition to KIA, the Kuwaiti government owns entities such as Kuwait Investment Company, Kuwait Fund for Arab Economic Development, Kuwait Investment Projects Company, the Future Generations Fund, as well as sovereign wealth funds under Kuwait Petroleum Corporation and the Public Institution for Social Security, among others. In several separate years, the dividends from these funds brought the country more money than oil exports. Several members of parliament complained publicly that no one knew the value of assets held in these funds, not even the minister of finance. The same could be said about the reporting of oil extraction in Kuwait, with many figures being based on foreign estimations and sales going underreported.

Currently, all the Gulf states have similar funds worth hundreds of millions of dollars. So far, the wealth flowing into the region has been unending, proving many economic forecasts to be false.

Landlords: The books are ours

There is an Egyptian film much-loved by Kuwaiti intellectuals as they believe it accurately portrays how the ones in power perceive and treat people and laws. It tells the story of a small village mayor whose marriage is going through a rough patch. He cannot have children and is unhappy. He falls for a beautiful poor peasant, but she is already married. He summons the village imam and asks him what to do. The imam says: 'Don't worry. The books are ours. We divorce her from her husband and we marry her to you. She doesn't even need to know.'

Petroleum is not the only source of income and power for the ruling class. Another one is land. Public lands can be registered as someone's private property. Sheikhs and merchants have amassed fortunes by selling vast pieces of public land which they had taken for free.

When one of the group is set to be made rich, a more or less attractive piece of land is carved out from public lands and signed over. Then, the new owner can easily sell the land obtained for free to the government or to a developer. Alternatively, the landlord can take a bank loan and build on the land, and one of the ministries will rent the building from him at a high price before it is even finished. The land can also be divided into smaller plots and sold on for millions of dinars. A plot of land of a minimum size of 400m2, which is typical for family housing, in the capital governorate costs roughly $1,200,000, while in the most prestigious areas the price reaches more than twice that amount. Many current residential areas had once been empty lands signed over to sheiks. Furthermore, on many occasions, a sudden owner appears to claim ownership of some empty land that has been designated for a public road or buildings. The government would compensate this person with a substantial sum of money to give up what they should have never possessed.

State-owned land has also been leased to connected people. Many of the malls in Kuwait have been constructed on public land given to specific individuals for a minimal annual rent. The famous Avenues Mall, one of the largest in the Middle East, was built on land originally intended for social housing. Similarly, the Marina Mall and Marina Waves hotel, which occupy prime locations by the sea, stand on public land granted to a private entity.

In 1950s, before Kuwait became independent, around two-thirds of its lands were assigned to the Kuwait Oil Company, while the rest was mainly government property. After that, many sheikhs claimed their share. They continue doing so. As a result, the lands available for the general population became limited. To address the housing needs of the most disadvantaged citizens, the government established a social housing program under the Ministry of Labour and Social Welfare. At the beginning of the programme in the 1950s and 1960, individuals were required to prove that they did not own a property to be eligible. They waited a year or two before being provided with a small house on a plot of land. Over time, the only way for most Kuwaitis to acquire a home has become through this programme, which expanded, leading to the establishment of a Ministry of Housing and a housing bank to accommodate the increasing demand.

Each married couple who does not own a property can apply for a house from the government through the Public Authority for Housing Welfare (PAHW). When their turn comes up, they have the option to either purchase a house at a reduced price or acquire a plot of land and get a low-interest loan. Many people prefer the land since it allows them to build a house according to their own design and standards. For the duration of their waiting period, which can often span 18 years and more, registered married couples receive a renting allowance of 500 dollars a month.

Nowadays, the housing programme is crippled. There are thousands of couples waiting. According to a report from the PAHW in 2021, there were 91,794 families registered on the housing welfare list, an increase from 87,828 in 2020.[93] The land and houses provided through the PAHW are located far away from the city. For instance, to reach the Sabah Al-Ahmad area, which was established a few years ago, one needs to drive an hour through the desert. After that, an area closer to the city was established and designated for those who had been waiting for more than 20 years. The plots closer to the capital cannot be sold on or rented out for the period of 10 years. This social programme has also been marred by corruption, as with every new project contractors, subcontractors, and officials would be charged with embezzlement and fraud.

Studying Kuwait from bird's eye view, one will see that only about 5-6% of the country's surface has been built on. After subtracting farms, oil fields and military bases, what is left is desert, accounting roughly for 70-75% of the country's area. Nearly 92 thousand families are waiting for a piece of it. Many accuse the officials of colluding with the big landlords and developers to keep prices beyond the capabilities of the average family.

The scarcity of available land has in a major way contributed to land prices in Kuwait being among the highest in the world. There are very few properties on the market, and their prices are beyond the means of most people. The subject of a housing crisis is regularly brought up in parliament, and like with many other issues, little action is taken. The government continues its politic of limiting the release of land to the public while paying out renting allowances to thousands on the waiting list.

---

93 Times Kuwait (11 Sep 2022). Kuwait among the most difficult country in the world to own a home: Markaz.; Arab Times (21 Feb 2020). Govt allocates KD 336 mln for residential projects.

Meanwhile, various other lands have been transferred into private hands. People are well aware of this. They would point out different locations and say: 'Do you know that mall, that hospital, that residential area? That used to be public land.' They swallow the thought of these practices like big, bitter pills. They feel personally affected and believe that something was taken from them; they were robbed of their property. What are they to do? – the books are in the hands of those in power and they can do as they please.

The price tag of education

If you have children in Kuwait and you want to ensure they get a quality education, then you are in for a rough ride. The public school system, available to citizens, was once excellent. Since the 1990s, it has been slowly but systematically dismantled. Several merchant families have established their own private schools and turned them into cash cows. Currently, there is very little science or English taught at public schools. Children study from outdated coursebooks, some with information and pictures from the 1980s and 90s, and the primary focus is on Arabic language and Islamic texts. Kuwait's educational system is one of the areas where numerous voices have been calling for reform. But how can you bring about meaningful outcomes in a state where ministers change as quickly as the images in a kaleidoscope?

For Kuwaitis, enrolling their children in the private, expensive schools has become the primary way to provide them with good education. Places are limited and people compete for them. Expatriates, on the other hand, have no other option but to pay for schools: the choices range from these posh English or bilingual schools which follow British or American curricula to more affordable schools following Pakistani or Indian programmes.

For many Kuwaitis and European expatriates, tuition eats up the lion's share of their earnings. School fees for two semesters in a reputable private kindergarten average $6,000, while primary and high school tuition is $10,000-15,000.

One of my friends, Ahmad, is a professor at Kuwait University. He earns an annual salary of around $100,000, and his wife Samar, who is an engineer, makes approximately $50,000. They allocate more than $50,000 each year towards school tuition for their four children and another couple of thousands for uniforms, notebooks, and transportation. Due to Kuwaiti banks not providing mortgages and the prices of homes starting at a million dollars, they cannot afford to buy a house. They have been renting for many years, which costs them $40,000 annually. Given their long working hours, Ahmad and Samar employ two live-in maids from the Philippines to assist with household chores and help care for their children. This leads to an additional expense of around $20,000 a year. Ahmad has been driving the same American jeep for over 12 years. When I once asked him if he was planning to get a new car, he told me that he couldn't afford to repair his jeep properly, let alone think of buying a new one. Although people who meet him abroad may think he is wealthy because of his expensive watch and elegant clothes, in reality, Ahmad is sinking in debt. Nonetheless, when he travels, it has to be business class and a four- or five-star hotel.

Kuwait University is the one and only public university in the country. For years, the government has been suffocating it, cutting its budget, and undermining its independence, while giving free land and grants to the rich merchant families to establish private colleges and universities. The government also covers full tuition for thousands of students in these institutions. These private universities do not teach subjects much needed in the country, such as medicine, nursing, hard sciences. Instead, they focus on business and social sciences, which don't require advanced facilities or highly skilled professors and researchers. Even then, real teaching is lacking, as students are awarded undeserved grades and diplomas, and no one could be failed. The management doesn't want to risk losing the fees that come with each student. Students in these private diploma mills openly announce their expectations to the lecturers and tutors from the start: 'But I paid money. Do you mean I have to do the work as well?' Meanwhile, various reports indicate that Kuwait scores very low in the categories of the labour market, innovation, and graduates' skillset, and that the skills of the nationals are ill-suited to private sector needs.[94,95]

Kuwait Airways is another example of how the ones in power create wealth for themselves at the expense of their country. It used to be one of the world's top airlines. However, incompetent managers were installed who drove the talented and dedicated individuals away to other airlines or to retirement. Furthermore, attacks were launched against Kuwait Airways through members of parliament and media. Next, its budget was slashed and its operations frozen. While the flagship carrier, which had been profitable and had provided many people with decent jobs and good salaries, was being dismantled, private airlines subsidised by the public treasury sprang up. These private airlines are owned by sheikhs and merchants who belong to the same affluent and connected families that control the hospitals and colleges. Unfortunately, these airlines hardly hire local people.

94 Global Competitiveness Report issued annually by World Economic Forum.
95 Report prepared by TIGC (2017): Increasing private sector employment of nationals in the GCC; labour policy options to the rescue. Kuwait.

Healthcare odyssey

The healthcare system in the country is another field riddled with issues such as mismanagement, corruption, and a shortage of professionals, which results in substandard care and has negative consequences for the population.

Lifestyle-related and chronic diseases, such as obesity, diabetes, heart conditions, cancer, and mental disorders, are widespread among Kuwaitis. Studies indicate that almost 40% of Kuwaitis aged 18-69 suffer from diabetes or pre-diabetes[96], while 37% of adult citizens are overweight and another 40% are classified as obese.[97] These health conditions have been on the rise among children. But there are few preventative measures, and dealing with the effects is a significant challenge for the health sector.

Kuwaiti and other GCC citizens receive healthcare services free of charge while residents of other nationalities are required to pay a mandatory public health insurance fee. In addition to this annual cost, patients pay small fees for every service. For decades, these used to be symbolic, starting from $3 for a visit at a policlinic, which also covered basic medication to be prescribed by the doctor. This was a way to ensure that migrant workers received basic medical care at a minimal cost, without burdening their sponsors with excessive additional expenses. In the long run, with the huge numbers of foreigners residing in the country, this scheme became unsustainable. Public health institutions are overwhelmed with foreign patients. For instance, in Sabah hospital,

96 Abdullah Alkandari and others (2018). The prevalence of pre-diabetes and diabetes in the Kuwaiti adult population in 2014. Diabetes Research and Clinical Practice 144, pp. 213-223.
97 Elisabete Weiderpass and others (2019). The Prevalence of Overweight and Obesity in an Adult Kuwaiti Population in 2014. Frontiers in endocrinology 10, 449.

218

the largest and best-equipped governmental maternity hospital, natives constitute less than 30% of patients.

What is also surprising in this wealthy country is that public clinics suffer from a lack of new technologies, chronic shortages of equipment and much needed medications. But when queues at governmental facilities are long, a portion of patients end up taking appointments at private hospitals, where diagnostics tests and treatment are costly.

The owners of private hospitals and big clinics belong to the privileged group who had been given permissions to establish them. Most of these private hospitals are built on public lands rented to affluent businessmen at low annual fees. Since the key private companies in the country are largely owned by members of same group as the hospitals, money from health insurance policies taken out by these companies ultimately returns to the purse out of which it came.

Another significant issue is the lack of trust in the medical staff within the domestic hospitals and clinics.[98,99] These facilities often have a workforce comprised of less-qualified doctors and nurses, with a significant number of them being recruited from Egypt and India in an attempt to address the shortage of personnel. Many of these medical professionals have received inadequate training and education from subpar schools. The minimum requirements are set at a low level, and the Ministry of Health exam is a mere formality with a passing grade at 60%.

In many instances, to be able to hire them, the ministry granted medical staff permissions despite them not holding the necessary licences, registering them as 'under training'.[100] Unfortunately, there is hardly any training or evaluation afterward, and

---

98 Bader Alhendi, Saleh Al-Saifi & Aliaa Khaja (2020). Medical tourism overseas: a challenge to Kuwait's healthcare system. Int J Travel Med Glob Health, 8(1), pp. 22-30.
99 Sarah Ahmed (08 Jan 2015). Lack of Trust in Doctors in Kuwait. Kuwait Times.
100 Kuwait Local (10 Sep 2015). Most of Medical Errors Caused by Unqualified Doctors. After: Arab Times.

instances of malpractice are rife. When one of the health workers commits an error, it is often covered up, and their superior would say that what happened was Allah's will. On some occasions, particularly when the malpractice is difficult to conceal or if the patient who suffered harm was important, the doctor would lose their job and be deported. Foreign doctors tend to flee once they realise they have botched up a surgery or medical procedure. The underlying issue is that highly skilled professionals do not tend to stay long in Kuwait or have better options in the first place, thus requirements had been lowered to fill in the void.

The same principle is applied to teachers. Public schools abound in teachers who often ended up there because they couldn't find other jobs. Only a handful of private schools pay well enough to attract and retain highly skilled Westerner educators, and even this is becoming less common.

Fortunately, when all the local institutions failed to help, there are always the ones abroad. The United States is where the emir of Kuwait goes for his medical check-ups and treatment. Local news report it every time he goes, which is – regularly. Prior rulers would do the same. Senior officials and all the important people do it. They choose the United States, Switzerland, Great Britain, or Germany for medical care. There are many hospitals and doctors in the country, yet, they prefer to get treated abroad and there is a reason for it.

Every year, thousands of the most privileged nationals, sponsored by the public budget, travel to receive treatment abroad. Year 2017 saw a record number of 12,000 people using the scheme.[101] Others pay for treatment abroad from their own pocket. They undergo surgeries and treatments in orthopaedics, internal medicine, oncology, and neurology. Some procedures are simply not performed in Kuwait. The most popular destinations are the United

101 LaingBuisson News [International Medical Travel Journal] (14 May 2019). Politics of treatment abroad for Kuwaitis.

States and Britain for public-sponsored treatment and the Czech Republic and Turkey for self-paid treatment. In the Great Ormond Street Hospital for children in London, there is an entire ward dedicated to patients from Kuwait and Saudi Arabia. Migrants from developed Western countries, based on their personal experience and anecdotal information shared on social media, have formed a similar opinion about the local medical services in Kuwait. They fear misdiagnoses and poorly performed operations.

Five workers for a single position

At the private company where my British friend works as a manager, all the employees are foreigners with the exception of a few Kuwaiti women who were hired due to a law enforcing a quota of nationals in every company. When you enter the room where these women are stationed, you will find that their computers are switched on but they're not actively working on anything. Some of them are busy on their smartphones or painting their nails, others chatting and sipping tea. If you come at a different time, they might be having breakfast, which they seem to do a few times a day. Some chairs are empty; it's not clear if the employee has stepped away for five minutes or left for the rest of the day. According to my friend, the company tried to assign work to these employees, but they either wouldn't do it at all or would do such a bad job that no one would ask them for anything again. In the end, they know they've been hired because of the quota, not because they need to do work. For showing up, they receive around $1000 in salary in addition to the employment support allowance from the state, which amounts to $1500 or more depending on the person's education and marital/family status. This particular company requires the Kuwaiti workers to come in to the office; many companies don't even have space to accommodate them.

The situation in the public sector is even more troubling, as every year thousands of people are hired to fill non-existent posts. Maryam, who works for the department responsible for testing water quality, spends only one day at her work, although she is employed full-time. The workload in her unit could easily be handled by a single person but it has been divided among five employees. Hence, these girls have made an arrangement between themselves to rotate duties throughout the week. On a given day, one of them carries out the tasks, and the rest only comes in early in the morning to fingerprint, returning home or running personal errands after that. Maryam told me that when it is her turn to stay, it takes her two hours to complete the necessary work, and the rest of the day she spends on her phone.

Governmental institutions and state-owned companies are bursting at the seams with excess admin staff. Here are a few examples: the Ministry of Education employs 88,730 female and 17,054 male Kuwaitis (with approximately 400,000 students); the Ministry of Electricity and Water employs 29,913 nationals (compared to 19,689 four years earlier); the Public Authority for the Disabled – 1,813 nationals; the Public Authority for Food and Nutrition – 1,115 nationals (an increase from 287 in 2018), the Direct Investment Promotion Authority – 272 nationals, and the General Authority for Printing and Publishing the Holy Quran – 88 nationals.[102] One might get the impression that some of these central institutions have been established with the sole purpose of supplying positions for the sons and daughters of influential government figures.

According to data from 2019, the public sector of Kuwait employed 311,000 citizens and around 100,000 foreigners. For comparison, there were 74,000 Kuwaitis and around 1,636,000 foreigners working in the private sector at the time. These figures do not include 715,000 registered migrant domestic workers or illegal workers – to realise the total number of foreign workers, one would have to include these numbers, too.[103]

Still, many of the skilled jobs, even within the public sector, such as nurses, medical doctors, IT technicians, are filled by

---

102 Data from Central Statistical Bureau (30 Jun 2022): Employment statistic in government sector (Kuwaiti/non-Kuwaiti).
103 This data comes from ALSHALL Weekly Economic Report, Vol. 29, Issue 32 (11 Aug 2019).

non-Kuwaitis. The departments with the highest numbers of immigrant workers are the Ministry of Public Health and the Ministry of Education as well as the Ministry of Endowment and Islamic Affairs, with over 35,000, 27,000, and 2,800 foreign workers respectively. Among state-owned companies, Kuwait Airways, Kuwait Flower Mills and Bakeries Company and Kuwait Public Transportation Company employ the largest numbers of expatriates, with 4,167, 4,236, and 1,868 employees respectively, constituting 80%, 96%, and 96% of their total workforce.[104]

It is difficult to imagine a Kuwaiti nurse, baker, electrician, mechanic, or a Kuwaiti driver sitting behind the wheel of a city bus, since they are not interested in manual and non-prestigious jobs or even encouraged to do them. On the other hand, it is true that that many professions and jobs, especially in the private sector, have been given over to the immigrants while there is de facto unemployment among the nationals. For Kuwaitis, artificial positions are created within public services because historically the state has taken it upon itself to provide every citizen with employment, which is now enshrined in the law. Each year, the mass of professionally active people increases with thousands of youths joining it, and they outgrow the number of fresh retirees.

Job allocation in Kuwait usually relies on whom one knows, not what one knows. A Kuwaiti who has graduated in Islamic studies might be assigned a post in the Ministry of Health; it is difficult to guess what that job will entail. It is common to find individuals working in fields unrelated to their educational background. There are people with degrees in media studies or political science working in schools and hospitals. Despite this, most new graduates still choose the option of working in the public sector. This is not surprising, considering that the average monthly salary for citizens in the sector is 1,555 dinars.[105] Kuwaitis,

---

104 Data from Central Statistical Bureau (30 Jun 2022): Employment statistic in government sector (Kuwaiti/non-Kuwaiti).

similarly to Emiratis, Qataris or Saudi Arabs, simply don't want to work for private companies. Compared to positions in public services, here duties are more demanding, working hours longer, and salaries lower. There is also less job security: they can be fired more easily. This subject has been covered in a report prepared for the Kuwait Investment Authority in 2017, which adds to the above: 'The skills of GCC nationals are not always adapted to private sector needs.' [106]

In 2001, the government introduced a law that gave citizens working for private companies a wage support allowance. The allowance, called labour support (*da'm al-'amala*), was meant to bridge the salary gap between the private and public sectors, serving as an incentive for both employers and job seekers. Furthermore, as part of the nationalisation policy, private sector companies are legally bound to employ a quota of nationals, which varies for different branches of the economy, regardless of their actual need. These measures resulted in new forms of misconduct and fraud on both sides of the labour market balance, the companies and the jobholders. At its peak, the percentage of ghost employees – hired only on paper – among young Kuwaitis who recently took up jobs reached almost 20%.

When in 2015 public administration institutions installed fingerprinting systems for monitoring employee attendance, it transpired that a proportion of staff who were abroad, or even better – in prison, were still drawing their salaries.[107] Instances were revealed of public authority units paying salaries to people who had been dead for years. This was the case, among others, in the Ministry of Education.[108] In many companies, workers come

---

105 Arab Times (03 Oct 2022). Kuwaitis average pay 1,513; Expats get KD 343.
106 Report prepared by TIGC (2017): Increasing private sector employment of nationals in the GCC; labour policy options to the rescue. Kuwait.
107 Arab Times (02 Nov 2015). Fingerprint attendance system exposes workers – Sheikh Salman launches award for youth excellence, creativity.
108 Kuwait Times (10 Jan 2016). Ministry to receive Jaber Hospital September 2016.

only for a few minutes in the morning and afternoon to clock in and out through electronic fingerprinting. Someone has already come up with a way to bypass this counter-absenteeism technology by placing a copy of the fingerprint onto a silicone prosthetic stamp, which could be passed on to a colleague.

While official reports refer to a total unemployment rate of slightly above 2%, in 2017 a parliamentary study disclosed that disguised unemployment, or underemployment, in the public sector nears 79.4%. A similar number was provided by the Minister of State Muhammad Al-Abdullah, who declared that the public sector employs three times the necessary workforce.[109] This means that over 200 thousand workers are superfluous. Such a finding changes the entire picture.

The beginnings of this predicament go back to 1960s when the government started giving out public posts on a massive scale. In the 1970s, they further pushed average citizens out of the private sector. They implemented a ban on simultaneous employment in both sectors: someone who was running their own business, even a small store or workshop, was not allowed to work for the state, while those on the payroll of any state institution had to forfeit the possibility of setting up private businesses.[110] The intention was to consolidate control over the private market among a select few people and clans. Nowadays, the largest, most prominent private companies in the country are owned and controlled by a very limited number of individuals who tend to come from a few specific families. They are an essential part of the establishment. You might call them the Kuwaiti 'House of Lords'.

Kuwaitis own all companies in the country, big and small, as dictated by the law. A tailor from Pakistan, a photographer in a mini-mall, and a seller of fake handbags in the *souk* have

---

109 AlQabas (05 Aug 2017). 79% min muazafi aldawlati… bitalat mqnae [79% of state employees… constitute hidden unemployment] (in Arabic).
110 Article 26 (also: 25) of Law No. 15 from 1979 regarding the Civil Service.

to have a Kuwaiti sponsor and a Kuwaiti business partner/boss. Obtaining a licence to establish any venture in Kuwait is an extremely challenging and tedious task that could take years. Certain licences are worth hundreds of thousands of dinars precisely because the state wouldn't issue many. To open a shop, one must submit piles of paperwork, provide proof of citizenship, verify non-employment in the government[111], demonstrate sufficient funds in their bank account, and provide fire and safety certificates as well as approval from the city council for the rented space. For instance, it is nearly impossible to obtain permission to establish a property development or construction company. Even if the applicant fulfils all the requirements, the Minister of Trade must authorize it, and the waiting period for approval can extend for years, often ending in rejection. The few affluent families, who are well connected to the power and traditionally have always been part of the government, hold all kinds of business licences. Their members possessed licences even while working for the state also before 2018 when the law prohibited it.

Until recently, small businesses were primarily owned by retired or unemployed Kuwaitis, as well as the small group of nationals employed by private corporations. These individuals would obtain licences for small shops or services, such as a tailor's workshop, which they would then lend or lease to migrant workers for monthly payments. The tailor one of my Kuwaiti friends uses comes from India and manages a team of five or six tailors-seamstresses; the company has been there for years and seems to be very prosperous. However, it doesn't always turn out that way. In many instances, the person leasing the licence incurs debts or stops paying rent for the premises and subsequently flees from Kuwait.

Establishing a successful firm that offers specialised professional services like a doctor's or lawyer's practice, or a marketing

---

111 This law was relaxed in 2018. A person employed in the public sector is allowed to register a private company but not to work in it.

company, requires more than just permits and certificates. A crucial aspect is finding a suitable place. The prestige of the office, which depends on the specific building and its location, plays a significant role in attracting potential clients. However, to secure such a place, one needs connections. Floors for rent within fashionable high-rise towers are not offered to just anyone, and even the rent depends on who the tenant is. This market is strictly controlled. Property agents can dismiss undesired clients, either at the owner's request or based on their own judgement, by quoting exorbitant rental prices or by not returning the calls.

It's true that the average Kuwaiti might be found guilty of lacking ambition, being lazy, or having a corrupt streak. There are, however, numerous factors that enable these tendencies or outright impose them. They are also the reason why Kuwaiti enterprises are not going to become more efficient or competitive in comparison to foreign companies for a long time to come.

CHAPTER 12

Heritage born of sea and desert

Many people tend to think of Kuwait as a new city sprang in a desert with no culture, heritage, or music. A Canadian teacher once told me that Kuwait is a gas station built by the Brits, who imported people to man it. This perception couldn't be further from the truth.

Listening to old sea songs, which date back for centuries, can move even the hardest of hearts. These beautifully written and performed songs, accompanied by traditional dances, served as the laments of mothers, wives, and daughters awaiting the return of their men from voyages. A typical trip lasted four months and ten days, and as the deadline approached, women would start gathering by the shore, waiting for the ships to appear. They danced and sang to the sea, beseeching it to bring their loved ones safely back home. They spoke with the night and the darkness; they implored the sea to fear God and allow the pitiable sailors, who risked their lives to provide for their families, to return safely – a plea that all too often went unanswered.[112]

Song and dance also accompanied the sailors while they prepared the ship and then during their time on board, and even ship builders had their own tunes and dances. On every ship there was a singer, known as *naham*. There could not be sailing or pearl diving without music. It is the music that helped

---

112 Daniel Pearl (14 May 1996). These Songs Bring Tears to Your Eyes, or Worse. The Wall Street Journal Archive.

these people withstand the harsh life. Through the sad melodies, they expressed their longing for their folks and the fear that they might not see them again, should the ship capsize or they fall prey to sharks while diving.

Kuwait had a rich maritime culture, with shipbuilding, pearl diving, and sea shipping serving as its main industries. The people of Kuwait were renowned for their seafaring skills, and the country's strategic location at the crossroads of important trade routes enabled its inhabitants to live in a land that had no fresh water or agriculture.

Traditional Kuwaiti shipbuilders used locally sourced materials, such as palm wood and plaited palm fronds, to construct small, nimble boats known as dhows. These boats were employed for a variety of purposes, including fishing, pearl diving, and transport. A boom, which is a medium-sized deep-sea dhow, is featured in the emblem of Kuwait. Larger ships, such as baghlahs, were also built, using traditional methods and imported timber, and served long-distance trade and transportation. European travellers who visited Kuwait before the discovery of oil would describe its bustling market, brimming with all kinds of goods imported from Iraq, Iran, India and Africa aboard these wooden ships.

Traditional dhows are still being used by fishermen, although now they are manned by foreigners. Rows of these vessels can be seen docked in the small Sharq harbour. Every day at the break of dawn, they bring in fresh catches. Many Kuwaitis visit Souk Sharq, the main fish market, at dawn to buy their fish and seafood.

Souk Sharq, much like the one in Tokyo, should be considered a local tourist attraction: there are fish auctions held here, too – but which tourist would be willing to wake up at 4 o'clock in the morning to watch a group of men shouting amidst plastic baskets filled with fish dripping water onto a tiled floor? Nonetheless, any visitor who gets there will witness a slice of authentic daily life: local species of fish, crab, squid, lobster caught at night in the Gulf, arranged elegantly on the stalls, and the fishermen-sellers with their sleeves rolled-up, cleaning and weighing their goods with deft hands.

This small country boasts a rich culture, rooted in the sea as well as the desert. In its 19th-century heyday, Kuwait thrived as a vibrant hub of culture and trade in the Middle East. Al-Arabi, established in 1958 by the government, was for decades the leading Arabic-language intellectual magazine, hundreds of thousands of copies being read throughout the Arab world. Kuwait University, founded in 1966, was one of the first universities in the Gulf region and many thousands of foreign students studied in it for free. The Sultan Gallery, which opened in 1969, was the first modern art gallery in the region – it held among others an exhibition of Andy Warhol's work, at which the artist himself appeared. This heritage has shaped enduring cultural traditions.

Kuwaiti traditional dance and music are vital elements of the nation's rich culture. Anyone who has listened to Middle Eastern tunes will attest that they differ significantly from their Western counterparts. They aren't based on seven-note scales but on modulation, incorporating microtonal intervals smaller than the semitones found in conventional Western music, producing a distinct effect. Melodic embellishments, such as trills and slides, intricate rhythmic patterns, and improvisation lend Middle Eastern music its unmistakable identity and distinctiveness.

One of the most popular instruments used in Kuwaiti sea music is the oud, a stringed fretless instrument similar to a lute, capable of producing just about any frequency of sound within three octaves. It remains a favoured instrument among Arab musicians from the Gulf, Syria, Egypt, Iraq, Libya. Tickets to concerts of celebrated oud musicians are in high demand and sell out quickly. Alongside the oud, percussion instruments like the daf and tabla add depth and texture to the compositions.

Other instruments commonly found in Kuwaiti music include the qanun – a type of zither, the violin, the accordion.

The lyrics of Kuwait's sea music often told stories of the sea and the challenges and triumphs of life on the water. They depicted the dangers of pearl diving, the thrill of catching a big fish, and the beauty of the sea and its creatures. These songs served not just as entertainment but also as a means of building community and strengthening social bonds as well as preserving cultural traditions. Musicians would pass down songs and melodies from generation to generation, ensuring the continuity of historical legacies.

The region is the birthplace of various popular musical genres, such as sawt (or sout) and fijiri. In sawt, meaning 'voice' in Arabic, poetic, emotive singing is accompanied by the oud and the mirwas drum. Often, the audience would join in the singing. Sawt was established by the Kuwaiti poet, composer, singer and oud player Abdallah al-Faraj (died 1901/1903). It served as the art music of the early urban centres in the Gulf region, beginning in Kuwait and Bahrain.

Fijiri, performed by men from pearl diving communities along the coasts of Bahrain and Kuwait, celebrates the bravery and feats of pearl divers. Fijiri dance is an integral part of the performance and involves a group of men who move in a circle and clap their hands in unison, while singing. Through its lyrics, beat, and movement, the art of fijiri imparts the values of strength, perseverance, and solidarity.

One of the most renowned regional folk dances is the ardha, a traditional sword dance native to Kuwait, Saudi Arabia, and Qatar. In this lively dance, a group of men rhythmically move in sync while brandishing swords or rifles, all to an invigorating musical beat. Originally a pre-battle ritual among Arabian Peninsula tribes aimed to display their strength and boost morale, nowadays the ardha is performed during national and cultural events, and sometimes weddings or graduations.

Similarly to seamen, camel drivers and shepherds had their own song. Hida (or huda) is one of the oldest forms of singing in the region, predating the rise of Islam. It serves as more than just a means of prompting the camel to move faster or gather the herd around the hadi when he sings. This unique tradition entertains both the camel driver and the camel during long journeys across the vast Arabian Peninsula. It originated from the realization of the calming effect singing had on camels, as well as passengers, and evolved into an art. Saudi organisations are actively working towards inscribing it on UNESCO's list.[113]

Social gatherings and weddings used to involve many other dances, or arts as they are called, like the samri, khammari, zaffan, tanbura, or fannanah. The sung poems of the khammari centre around themes of love or flirtation. The lead singer can be male or female. Some arts were typically performed by women, who might have been accompanied by a male music band.

Kuwaiti traditional songs, music, and dances have been an important factor in shaping the country's cultural identity and fostering a sense of national pride and unity. While there was a decline in the creation of traditional folk songs and music after the discovery of oil, recent years have marked a renewed interest, leading to their revival. In cultural spaces of the Gulf region called dars, descendants of pearl divers and pearling crews as well as other enthusiasts cultivate the tradition through practice and performance. Despite the impact of modern Western music and dance styles, folk traditions continue to be celebrated and enjoyed by people of all ages and backgrounds. Alongside them, today's innovative styles blend traditional elements with contemporary influences, as new lyrics are written to timeless folk melodies.

In addition to song and dance, traditional arts such as calligraphy, pottery, and weaving are still practiced today in the region, complemented by a growing interest in contemporary art. Thuraya Al Baqsami, Shurooq Amin, Khalid Al Gharaballi, or

---

113 Ruba Obaid (3 Jun 2020). Arabian camel drivers' songs aim for place on UNESCO heritage list. Arab News.

Ghadah Alkandari represent but a few of the numerous talented contemporary artists from Kuwait, their work reflecting the rich and diverse cultural landscape of the country.

Kuwaiti literature is diverse and explores a broad range of themes and styles, with a wealth of talented poets, novelists, play-wrights contributing to the nation's vibrant literary scene.

Kuwait has long been a pioneer in theatre, film and television in the Gulf region. Theatrical tradition dates back to the 1920s, while the first Kuwaiti feature-length film was produced in 1972 and depicted life in Kuwait before the oil-era. It may be hard to believe but Kuwait has the oldest performing arts industry in the Arabian Peninsula. When Kuwait started expanding beyond the old wall, several public theatres were built. In addition to a clinic, a commercial plaza, and a park, each of the old districts has had and a theatre, however, with the ascension of the Islamic move-ment, fewer and fewer plays were produced. Kuwait had one of the oldest arts colleges in the region. Many famous Arab actors, singers, scenographers got their education and training in Kuwait's Higher Institute of Dramatic Arts (HIDA), established in 1973.

To this day, theatre is cherished in Kuwait, particularly the plays produced in the 1970s and 80s. Filmed recordings of them are regularly broadcast by national TV stations. Many of these plays were daring, addressing issues that are still considered taboo in many countries across the Middle East. They touched upon the relationship between the state and Islam, women's rights, political corruption, homosexuality, and romance.

One play that particularly captivates me is a comedy from 1984. It cleverly portrays how Islamic movements employ religion to gain wealth, fame, and power. This play stages a fascinating dialogue between its main characters, two brothers. The older brother, a wealthy and corrupt businessman, contrasts with his younger sibling, who is frank and funny. In one scene, the younger brother enters, visibly upset, holding a newspaper. He reads aloud a report stating that his brother has donated three million dollars to the Afghan *mujahideen* fighting against the USSR. Tossing aside the newspaper, he asks his brother why he wouldn't help him or his wife, who are in need and being chased by debt collector. He wants to know: 'What is it that connects us to the Afghans? We have different languages, cultures, and even our food and clothing differ from theirs.' The elder brother, with a knowing smile, hints that his donation to the Afghan jihad is a strategic investment that will bring him greater wealth and power. It will make him look good in the eyes of the people and the government, opening doors to numerous public contracts and tenders. In another scene, we see the young brother engaged in a heated argument with his radicalised nephew, who destroyed his uncle's alcohol collection. He defends his drinking as a personal choice and confronts his nephew: 'Who gave you the right to enter my home and destroy my private property? Is this how you thank me for my kindness? I used to take care of you more than your own father.' The nephew asserts that it is his duty as a good Muslim to uphold sharia laws by force.

The play provides thought-provoking insights into societal issues, highlighting the complexities and contradictions within the Kuwaiti context, and offers a satirical lens to examine them.

Kuwaiti TV dramas and soap operas produced over the years have enjoyed wide popularity across the region and beyond. They hold the distinction of being the most-watched in the Gulf, owing it to the diversity of captivating scripts, a cast of compelling actors, as well as the beauty of interior and exterior scenography. These productions resonate with audiences, although some viewers accuse them of predictability, exaggerated reactions of characters, and the overuse of slapping. Certain drama series are praised for their sophisticated content, verging on social issues and politics, often enlivening social discussion. Kuwait's TV drama industry, subsidised to an extent by the government, produces annually a minimum of fifteen serials, continuing to serve as the Gulf region's primary hub for television drama and comedy.

Over the years, the country has produced several accomplished actors and actresses who have made significant contributions to the world of film and television. These artists, while promoting Kuwaiti culture and identity, have pushed boundaries since the 1950s, with actresses performing without the hijab and male actors taking on female roles.

With such artistic vibrancy Kuwait has earned the nickname 'Hollywood al-Khaleej' – the Hollywood of the Gulf. Moreover, the country's contribution to music is equally noteworthy. From the 1950s to the late 1980s, Kuwait boasted the biggest professional music studios in the region. These studios attracted artists from all corners of the Gulf, who flocked to Kuwait to record their music.

If someone perceives Kuwait as a young state lacking culture, language, or cuisine, they would be mistaken. Prior to the stricter laws of the 1980s, theatres staged countless plays, and renowned international musicians were invited to perform concerts. Kuwaitis still love to watch recordings of these plays, listen to old songs; they still read ambitious poetry for which there was never room in schools, and forbidden books. The national identity of Kuwaitis is strong. Most of them still use vocabulary comprehensible only to fellow Kuwaitis (no other Arab nation says *'guwwa'* as hello). References to old poems and quotes from old stage shows are common. They hum traditional songs, which captivate with mastery of the word and deeper messages in their lyrics. There are words and expressions in the Arabic language behind which entire stories lie in wait – sometimes they have to be told in order for the word to be understood. Even insults can sound poetic: *naal ibn alnaal,* meaning 'you slipper, son of a slipper', is strangely enough a highly derogatory expression.[114]

---

114 Other insults popular in Kuwait include: hmar – fool, literally: jackass, donkey; haiwan – brute, beast, literally: animal; zift – sh*t, crap, literally: asphalt.

Many Arabs, including Kuwaitis, have poet's souls. Why indeed should Arabs not be associated with lyrical verses rather than radicalism? They take pride in the fact that in Arabic language every name carries meaning. For instance, Badr signifies the full moon, Thuraya literally means the Pleiades, and Hadeel represents the cooing of a pigeon. Even today, Kuwaitis continue to favour the name Dana for their daughters, which denotes a pearl, but not just any pearl – the largest, flawless, and perfectly shaped one, the most prized. When in the 19th and early 20th century their ancestors were diving for pearls on a single breath, equipped with nothing more than a nose clip, finding such a peal was a sensational event. Its high value allowed the pearler who found it to pay off all debts and secure a decent living for the rest of his life, providing the option to avoid returning to diving if he so wished.

———————

CHAPTER 13

———————

All that shines

In this part of the world it became obvious to me that often appearances are everything. What meets the eye stays in the mind. This concept applies to every tier of society, from the privileged to the poor.

Donald Trump was shocked to discover that the Kuwaiti sheikh's airplane was not only much bigger than Air Force One but much more lavish, too.[115] It was not just Trump who expressed dissatisfaction with Sabah al-Ahmad's airplanes; a prominent Kuwaiti MP, Abdullah Al-Nibari, was brave enough to point out that the Amiri Diwan owned more airplanes than Kuwait Airways. The Amiri Diwan issued a statement claiming that it had just eight airplanes; the MP responded with a written statement that included a detailed list of 27 aircraft owned by the Diwan. The list comprised three Boeing 747-8s, five Airbus A340-500s, two Airbus A300s, three Airbus A320-200s, two Airbus 310s, two Airbus 319s, five Gulfstream G-550s, four Gulfstream G.Vs.[116] These aircraft serve the official and private use of the emir, crown prince, and members of Al-Sabah family, and are maintained by the state. In addition to that, many of Al-Sabah

———————

115 Emily Shugerman (08 Sep 2017). Donald Trump 'jealous of Kuwaiti ruler's plane because it's bigger than his'. The Independent'.

116 AlziadiQ8 (20 Mar 2013). Fidyu: „Al-Nibari": maysir aldiywan al'amiriu eindahum 18 tayaarat walkhutut alkuaytiat maeindahum shay (…) [Video: „Al-Nibari": It's not acceptable that the Amiri Diwan has 18 planes while Kuwait Airways has nothing, and all of their planes are old.] (in Arabic).

own private jets, which are also maintained using funds from the state budget.

Inside the country, the emir, the crown prince, and the prime minister move in a motorcade consisting of hundreds of vehicles that includes ambulances and armoured vehicles. They reside in magnificent palaces adorned with lush parks and staffed by thousands of servants. In these palaces, you can find abundant amenities, from private beaches and artificial lakes to Olympic swimming pools, golf courses, horse stables, botanic gardens, and even cellars housing an exquisite selection of liquors. The Bayan Palace is said to hold one of the rarest and most expensive wine collections. Kuwaiti sheikhs also love to boast about their palaces in Europe and the United States.

Owning massive expensive yachts is another way to display affluence among Kuwaitis, even if they are rarely used. A visit to the Yacht Club or any of the numerous yachts docks in Kuwait reveals how many of these extravagant boats are treated merely as toys. Countless Kuwaiti superyachts stand docked in marinas across the globe, including Marbella, Nice, Monaco, and others. During my time in Nice, I met an Indian man who shared that he had been brought there by a Qatari sheikh to oversee his boat. 'He rarely visits but I am getting a good salary,' he mentioned.

Collecting cars and artefacts is yet another arena in which sheikhs compete to showcase their wealth and influence. Sheikh Nasser Mohammed Al-Sabah, for instance, boasts a vast collection of the rarest and most extravagant cars ever produced. His cousin Nasser Al-Sabah al-Ahmad's collection of artefacts includes exceptional ancient pieces procured over the years from around the world.

Kuwaitis have built thousands of grand mosques and Islamic centres across Europe and North America to display their wealth and influence while acquiring the potential to interfere in domestic affairs of these regions. The Kuwaiti government financed the construction of some of the world's most expensive mosques; it spends millions of dollars on their upkeep. The former emir Jaber Al-Ahmed himself contributed funds and later presided over the official inauguration of the Islamic Cultural Center in New York City, which comprises one of the city's largest mosques along with an Islamic school. Kuwaitis contributed to building the East London Mosque and donated $300,000 to the London Central Mosque Trust and Islamic Cultural Centre. They financed the Al-Noor Mosque in Hamburg, which stands as the biggest in northern Germany. During Ramadan of 2021, the Kuwaiti Embassy distributed 3,000 meals to mosques in Rome.

Kuwait can boast of its charitable contributions to many causes away from home. After the catastrophic earthquake and tsunami in Japan, Kuwait provided a significant aid package worth around $524 million. It donated $5.5 million to support Italy's health services in their fight against COVID-19.

Several research centres and academic institutions in prestigious American and European universities were established with grants from the Kuwaiti emir. For instance, George Washington University received $13 million just between 2005 and 2013, part of which was allocated to create the Middle East and North Africa Research Center, while another part founded the Institute for Middle East Studies.[117] In 2005, the university bestowed an Honorary Doctorate of Law upon Sabah al-Ahmad, then Prime Minister of Kuwait, in recognition for his 'service of humanity,' as reported by Kuwaiti News Agency KUNA.[118]

Durham University accepted a $4 million donation from Sheik Nasser Al-Muhammad Al-Sabah's 'personal funds' in 2012, which was after his resignation as Kuwaiti Prime Minister over

---

117 Mary Ellen Mcintire (29 Apr 2013). Gifts from Kuwait tally $13 million. The GW Hatchet.
118 KUNA (30 Jun 2005). GWU grants Kuwait's PM honorary doctorate for service of humanity.

corruption charges.[119] He had allegedly bribed thirteen (out of fifty) Kuwaiti MPs. According to the member of parliament who disclosed it, these MPs received the bribes in cash and deposited bags of banknotes, which alerted the banks. One MP received $2.3 million, four MPs – between $3.3-5 million, three MPs – $10 million, two MPs – $13 million, one MP – $20 million, one MP – $23 million, and one $32 million.[120] When questioned by the district attorney, many of the MPs refused to disclose the source of the money. One of them stated on record that he had discovered $12 million in cash inside a cupboard belonging to his recently deceased mother, while another one claimed that the money was gifts from sheikhs but he could not recall from whom exactly. Yet another MP stated he had got the funds as a gift from his brother, a football player. Ultimately, the general attorney closed the case due to a lack of applicable laws, and no one was put on trial. Most of these MPs got reelected time and again after the scandal. One of them said in a campaign opening that he takes money from sheikhs and gives it to people in need.

Paying individuals of significance to win them over is a Middle Eastern tradition that goes back for centuries. Mohammad Sabah al-Salim, a nephew of the emir, made headlines when he resigned from his post as deputy prime minister and minister of foreign affairs in 2011, declaring that $200m had been transferred through his ministry without his knowledge. He accused his cousin, the Prime Minister, as well as the Kuwaiti ambassadors to the US, Britain, France, Germany, of corruption and embezzlement. He submitted documents to the general prosecutor which revealed vast sums of money being transferred to the Kuwaiti ambassadors with instructions to distribute them to different individuals. The identities of these individuals, along with the reason

---

119 Andrew Marszal (01 Oct 2012). Durham University's £2.5m Kuwaiti gift 'astonishing', says Conservative MP. The Telegraph.
120 Twitter @R_Aladasani (26 Jan 2016).

for these payments, were not known to the foreign minister. In a press conference, he emphasised that the money belonged to the people of Kuwait and they had the right to know, and he urged the general attorney to shed light on the matter and provide answers.

The general attorney summoned and questioned several of the ambassadors, and records of the questioning were leaked and shared on social media. In his answers, the ambassador to Britain admitted to regularly receiving money from the Kuwaiti Central Bank to be handed out to specific individuals. He acknowledged receiving instructions specifying the amounts and recipients, although he refused to reveal their identities. When asked about the purpose of these payments, he claimed some of them were related to national security, and some were financial aid for people in need. The documents submitted by the foreign minister indicated that some individuals were receiving money on a regular basis, while others were paid from time to time. The amounts and frequencies varied from person to person; some were given thousands, and some hundreds of thousands. Ultimately, the general attorney closed the case, bringing it to a conclusion.

Prince of humanity

In 2014, the United Nations awarded Emir Sabah al-Ahmad al-Sabah the title of 'humanitarian leader', and during the tribute ceremony, the secretary general lauded him as 'a great humanitarian leader of our world'. Since then, this title has been adopted not only by local publicists and sycophants but also by commentators and public figures from around the world, including heads of state. The Emir preferred the more endearing title of 'prince of humanity'.

The Kuwaiti parliament gets dissolved or suspended regularly, often prompted by a gridlock surrounding policy issues and legislation or members of parliament seeking to impeach ministers or the prime minister. In February 2021, the emir suspended parliament for a month amidst tensions surrounding an amnesty bill aimed at pardoning former MPs who had participated in a 2011 protest that ended with the storming of the Parliament. A more recent dissolution of parliament took place in June 2022 and new elections were announced. But the Constitutional Court annulled the new results in March 2023 and restored the previous assembly. Then, a dissolution was announced again in May 2023.

By and large, the same people as before continue to stand for election and win. These individuals are de facto loyal to different factions within the ruling class and their primary role is to help their backers dominate the other factions, while others maintain a pro-government equilibrium among the representatives.

In this country, in many instances, the parliament has proven to be a decoration, a brooch on the lapel of the political system. Instead of enacting laws which could bring about a change towards a more democratic rule, members of parliament have passed legislation that, when implemented, would impose severe punishment on people for expressing their opinions. A striking example is the 2012 vote, where a vast majority approved a law penalizing those who mock or insult Allah, the Prophet Muhammad, or his wives with death or life imprisonment.

The parliament is another trick in the grand show served to the local society and the international audience: 'See, we have democracy, and it is not that good for you.'

Instead, there is another vital function which the National Assembly serves: it is an arena for internal dealings between factions of the powerful people that lends legitimacy to their claims. Through parliamentary questioning, they are able to humiliate or dismiss ministers who defy whomever installed them, or punish a branch of the family that was, for instance, too greedy. This is one of the means they settle their internal scores.

During his impeachment proceedings, Sheikh Mohammad Abdullah Mubarak al-Sabah accused members of parliament who were questioning him of acting on behalf of his cousin and former brother-in-law, Ahmed al-Fahad. He told one of them, Hussain al-Qallaf, that 'it is all because of the London jab. … I heard it was $600,000 from Abu Fahad [a nickname of the cousin].'[121]

Once, I asked a well-connected person who had known the emir of that time about the purpose behind the construction of Jaber Al-Ahmad Causeway. Why did Kuwait spend over $3 billions to build a bridge spanning across the sea to reach a desert? There had already been highways leading to that place. Having driven both through the 48-km causeway and via the highway, I found that both routes took almost the same time. He replied that this project was immensely important. It allowed His Highness to boast about constructing the world's most expensive and

---

121 Transcripts and recordings of the impeachment are widely available in Arabic language.

longest causeway. Moreover, numerous powerful people made huge profits from the project and stood to gain even more through its maintenance. Investments were already planned on that piece of desert. 'Can you imagine how much money will be poured into it? Many will be rich from these ventures,' he said.

Collecting former senior politicians and technocrats from the West as trophy advisors is a hobby of all Gulf governments. They compete to recruit prime ministers, ministers of foreign affairs, ex-presidents, former heads of financial institutions, for their benefit. And it is not obvious if they are being compensated for future work, past services rendered during their time in power, or a combination of both. One of the striking examples is Tony Blair, who approved of the American-British invasion of Iraq in 2003. The Kuwaiti government was the first client of his consulting company, Tony Blair Associates.

When at the end of 2010, 'Kuwait Vision 2035', a development plan prepared by Blair's company was revealed, it garnered attention from both local and international media. However, that was not due to its proposed innovative solutions or its expected efficacy. The authors of the report indicated how Kuwait could become the region's important financial and trade hub by 2035, effectively achieving the much-desired economic diversification away from reliance on oil revenues. They envisioned development of infrastructure, including a new business centre Silk City in the North of the country, a new harbour in Boubyan island, railway, and metro systems. It also addressed improving the investment environment (among others, simplifying administrative procedures), enhancing the education and skills of the young people, and promised cultural changes in the society and political system (clarity, efficacy). The plan turned out to be unrealistic, maladjusted to local conditions and soon after, it was quietly shelved. However, news of the fee to be charged by Tony Blair Associates for the duration of the contract, which was supposed to last several

years, became a global sensation: $43 million.[122] Both the consul-
tancy and its client denied this figure to be accurate.

122 Nabila Ramdani & Tim Shipman (14 Dec 2010). Tony Blair's company 'to make
£27m advising. Kuwait on how to govern itself'. Daily Mail.

The allure of promises:
The art of making others wait

Once you've spent a considerable amount of time in Kuwait or any other Middle Eastern country, you will quickly notice a recurring pattern in the news: government crackdowns, police interventions, parliament suspended, parliament dissolved, jail sentences for political activists, amnesties for political prisoners. And regularly the Bidoon issue would emerge, briefly gaining attention before fading into obscurity without resolution.

Back in 1973, the Minister of Interior Sheikh Saad Al-Sabah, who later became a prime minister and crown prince, pledged to have the statelessness (Bidoon) issue solved within months. Yet, as time passed, the Bidoon community continued to wait without any significant progress. In 1983, the current emir, then serving as the minister of interior, stated that there were two committees working on naturalising Bidoons who worked for the army and police. In another official statement issued in 1986, he assured of the government's utmost efforts to tackle the Bidoon crisis. In 1993, the Minister of Interior Sheikh Ali al-Sabah said that he needed until December to end the Bidoon issue. Similarly, in 1994, Saleh al-Fadalah, the vice speaker of the Kuwaiti parliament, declared the Bidoon issue would be solved within six months.

In 1985, the Kuwaiti emir survived an assassination attempt through a car bomb. During the incident, several bodyguards and police officers responsible for securing the route were injured, and two stateless individuals lost their lives. The emir awarded citizenship to the deceased men, as well as their children and wives; the families also received compensation and a pension. Other stateless working for the police and the national guards, who were part of the motorcade, were promised naturalisation for their dedication to the job. It wasn't until twenty-nine years later, in 2014, that these four individuals and their families were granted citizenship and became Kuwaitis.

When it comes to the art of making promises, few can rival the Kuwaitis in their ability to deceive others.

At first glance, an alluring facade masks the truth – an interplay of people and laws striving for that picture-perfect image. Kuwait paints an image of stability and wealth in the consciousness of the world, promoting itself as a well-functioning, open, tolerant state, and this is the speciality of governmental PR-men. On the other side are international humanitarian organisations writing reports about violations of basic liberties in Kuwait. 'But we have a parliament, we grant university scholarships, we invite guests from abroad, we maintain relations with democratic powers.' In 2016, a military orchestra from Scotland came to perform at His Highness the Emir's invitation. Two young women from the band with whom I spoke during the break in the show expressed delight with the generosity of the hosts and the five-star hotel where they were accommodated. It made me wonder how many of the thirty band members would go out and speak with the locals on the ground to understand the culture and find out what life is really like here – and how many would only remember the lavishness and return home to present a narrow and potentially misleading impression of this land.

Winning people over with wealth, generosity, and grandiose promises trickles down from the top to the average person. In addition to a Porsche parked in front of their house and a Rolex on their wrist, they love to boost their status with some big talk. 'I'll get it done', 'I know a man', 'Don't worry about anything, consider it done'–there are no impossible tasks for a Kuwaiti because they know the right people. Just don't expect a phone call the following week with the announcement, 'done,' as the right person at the city council office has just been transferred to a different department. Or your friend, who volunteered help without being asked, is currently extremely busy and was not able to attend to your matter.

One of the famous proverbs in Kuwait says: 'The reputation of wealth, not the reputation of poverty.' It simply means that individuals who are perceived as rich find it easier to gain respect and obtain what they want. Therefore, keeping up appearances is second nature to the locals.

Upon entering a Kuwaiti house, guests are received in a lavishly decorated room: pictures on walls, curtains with valances, beaded cushions on sofas, vases filled with artificial flowers, crystal chandeliers. Members of the household ordinarily don't use this room. They have the rest of the house for their everyday activities, and it looks much more prosaic.

Kuwaiti women turn their noses at the sight of certain brands. A handbag for $500 is too cheap, too common. Anything with a huge, visible LV logo or the interlocking Cs of Chanel will do. The level of ostentation is well reflected in an Instagram post by a Kuwaiti woman, featuring a picture of a highly coveted Hermès handbag filled with baby nappies: 'My long-awaited Birkin. My favourite diaper bag.' For the same reason, Kuwait offers easy access to A-grade or lesser quality knockoffs. A little bag modelled on Dior, made of leather and neatly finished, costs around $300. There would be only one displayed on the shop's shelf, and the lady in a burqa anxious to buy it will call on her husband, who will then haggle with the seller for a better price.

A Kuwaiti husband phones his (Kuwaiti) wife from an overseas business trip:

'Honey, I'm shopping right now, I wanted to get you a handbag. What kind would you like?'

'Hmm,' the wife ponders, 'I would like something casual, for everyday. Louis Vuitton…'

After he finishes the conversation, the man turns toward his colleague and remarks: 'She says something for everyday and it has to be LV. It looks like she's not getting anything.'

Worldwide, we can find people who live by the maxims 'pawn but splurge' or 'kippers and curtains, fur coats and no knickers,' which translate into the fact that glamorous and rich appearances might not match the reality. In Kuwait, this is not just an occasionally invoked principle – it is a culture. A secretary on a governmental post drives a sports Maserati, for which the replacement of brake pads costs around $700; the lion's share of her salary every month goes toward the car loan.

After their shopping is finished, men and women walk with bunches of bags nonchalantly hanging off their shoulders, wearing pleased, almost proud expressions on their faces. It doesn't matter that they have maxed out all four of their credit cards.

I have two acquaintances who are talented pianists and they both offer private piano lessons to children. I was curious about the percentage of Kuwaiti students they have.

'The majority are expats. Sporadically, Kuwaitis,' Martina says. 'They usually give up after a few lessons.'

Elisa nods in agreement. 'Yes, they don't last long. One of my pupils has just quit because her parents bought her a piano. A digital one. She believes she can teach herself now and doesn't need a tutor,' she chuckles.

'I've had students who wanted to practice on an iPad,' Martina interjects. 'One girl asked me: "If I download this app, can I use my iPad?" The app had twelve keys – one octave.'

'Do you sense a genuine love of music in them?' I'm curious.

'No way! Prestige, it is all about prestige. The parents can brag: "My child plays," and this is what they are after.'

Can one make an impression with their piousness? In the land by the Gulf, anything is possible. The endocrinologist who was treating me, apart from a fine grey suit and a Gucci tie, boasted a greyish-red stain of considerable size on his forehead. Every time I went to my appointment with him, this stain would put me off my stride. I had to ask someone about it.

'Your doctor prays fervently,' a friend clarified for me.

'What do you mean, prays?'

'He has a scab from hitting his forehead on a *turbah*.' [123]

'Oh, the kind of grey soap?'

'Yes. It's not soap.'

'Does he have to hit it so hard? Is his prayer fervent or aggressive?'

'He prays as Allah commanded.'

This mark on the forehead has a name: *zabiba*. Many Muslims in the public arena bear it, for example Mahmoud Ahmadinejad, the former president of Iran, as well as many Egyptian politicians and members of the Muslim Brotherhood. In their case, *zabiba* forms as a result of friction against the floor or prayer mat, as Sunnis refute the validity of using *turbah*. Egyptians even claim that this symbol of Islamic fundamentalism originated from their homeland. It's a recognisable symbol that can be seen from afar, similar to a long beard on an Islamic fundamentalist from Saudi Arabia. It serves as a way to demonstrate affiliation as well as superiority over others, both non-Muslims and less devout Muslims. In some Egyptian schools, a notion is being instilled in children that Muslims who don't pray should be killed.

Regarding piousness for display, men nonchalantly dangling *misbah*[124] beads in one hand while walking in the city or sitting in waiting rooms or cafés, occasionally sliding the beads along the string, are a common view in the Gulf. It reminds me of my fellow countrymen who hang rosaries on the rear-view mirror of their cars.

---

123 Turbah – a piece of hardened soil or clay used by the Shiites for prayer.
124 Misbih(a), tasbih or subha are Muslim prayer beads consisting of 33 or 99 beads, used to help in reciting the 99 attributes of Allah, or repeating one of them the appropriate number of times, as well as in other prayers that involve the repetition of specific phrases.

'An interesting combination,' I remark to my friend, returning to the subject of the endocrinologist with the Gucci tie and scar on his forehead. 'Elegance and piety.'

~

In the local reality, it is not only the clothes that make the man but also a slender, well-groomed body and a beautiful face. Although, not too long ago, a rotund body was associated with high social status and wealth. Today, women in particular strive to look good. They invest in gym memberships and then climb on a stationary bike to pedal a little on the lowest setting while browsing through Instagram accounts of acquaintances. A gym card is in fashion but physical effort – not so much. The preferred option is to take the path of least resistance: why bother with diet and exercise when liposuction and gastric sleeve surgeries are available? Those who opt for them tend to overlook the side effects, which are very common. They may add a nose job, a few shots of botulinum toxin in the right places, and blue contact lenses. The mould has not been broken but instead, reused repeatedly.

Plastic surgery is in high demand here. However, it also carries risks. The wealthiest people seek out the best surgeon in Switzerland, while the less wealthy who aspire to emulate them look around for a deal. In October 2016, three Asian men were arrested in Kuwait for illegally performing cosmetic surgery using falsified qualifications. They acquired clients through an Instagram account. Such fraudulent clinics pop up all over the world and there is never a shortage of clients.

Supermarket shelves are filled with whitening creams since Kuwaitis believe that a lighter skin tone goes hand in hand with good ancestry. After all, this notion could be found in various places around the world. Whenever I went grocery shopping, I would ask the family maid if she needed anything, such as snacks or cosmetics. The girl would ask that I get her nothing other than the allegedly skin-lightening cream Fair & Lovely. It's interesting how this Sri Lankan girl, who came from a small village in the middle of nowhere, was so concerned about the tone of her skin. Meanwhile, astonished locals watch Europeans seized by sunbathing madness.

The Middle East, in turn, has a different obsession: people love to smell incredibly good. They use huge amounts of perfumes regardless of whether they are attending a ball or taking a walk to the park. A friend of mine who is a perfume fanatic once chased after a Kuwaiti woman simply because she smelled so delightful. 'It was such an extraordinary scent, I had to ask her what it was,' she says. 'She named four or five different perfumes and *bakhoor* on top of that. They burn this incense and then lift up their abayas so that the smoke goes into their clothes.'

At times, they apply so much fragrance that the odour of alcohol becomes unbearable, forcing others to move away in order to breathe. Arabs have a particular fondness for heavy oud derived from agar-wood trees, as well as rose oil and musk. They might combine these with their favourite perfumes of Western brands, layering one on top of another. Companies from the Gulf region have mastered the production of oil-based perfumes, which are more potent and long-lasting on the skin.

What type of car you drive holds great importance, too, and typically, the bigger the better. American brands like GMT and Dodge are popular but European cars such as Mercedes and BMW are considered more prestigious. Some models are only available on request, like the Mercedes G63 AMG, which resembles a small tank and carries a price tag equivalent to that of a studio flat in any small, charming European town. The Mercedes showroom in Kuwait receives a limited number of this model each year, all of which have been pre-reserved by potential buyers. To have a chance of purchasing it, a down payment must be made, and the demand is so high that some individuals make a profit by selling their place on the waiting list.

Having a car is important, and not just any cheap car. Kuwaitis consider taking a cab as embarrassing and beneath their dignity. This sentiment may have originated from the fact that taxi services used to be unregulated and highly unreliable: one couldn't be sure if or when the car would arrive, and there were instances where passengers would ride one way and then be left stranded on the outskirts of the city. Moreover, cabs were often in a sordid state and using them was unpleasant. The biggest deterrent, however, were stories of kidnappings and sexual assaults. These were mostly accounts circulating among people rather than press or TV reports, as women don't typically report such cases to the police. Despite improvements in the quality of taxi services, negative connotations persist. If a Kuwaiti is unable to drive due to any reason, they won't do without a chauffeur.

When local residents want to enjoy a cup of coffee, they can chose from places like Burberry Café or Versace Café. I cannot believe that in my old clueless and uninspired life, I did not know about such establishments. The Boulevard complex was originally intended to be a park with greenery, fountains, and playgrounds, but then restaurants, a ballroom, and a shopping mall were added. Later, the Lamborghini Café was launched inside the mall. As I passed by it one Saturday afternoon, I saw a long line of people in front of its door, eagerly waiting for a table.

Even kindergartens have names like Little Doctor (referring to the academic title), Little Genius, Little Einstein, Future Generation Academy, Little Harvard, Future Stars, Bloomingdales Nursery, Superkids, Kuwait Dream Center. These names strike the right chords in the Kuwaiti imagination. Local parents desire that their offspring is taught English by native speakers from the UK or USA, preferably someone with the appropriate accent and appearance. There was a British Muslim woman working in one of the renowned language centres, and because she wore a headscarf, the centre's manager received complaints from students that she wasn't 'British enough'.

Kuwaitis have long appreciated the presentation side of things. Decoration on the cake and a pretty packaging are the basics when it comes to success in the confectionery business. For various occasions such as birthdays, Teacher's Day, the birth of a child, or the end of the school year, locals order sets of wrapped chocolates encased in decorative boxes, chests, or polyresin dishes which have been made in China especially for that purpose, and which often cost more than their content. These containers come in fanciful shapes and colours, for instance, they could look like a treasure chest, a garden with gnomes, a miniature baby pram. Square or round platters with appetizing arrays of chocolates in colourful, shiny wrappers arranged into rows or patterns are particularly popular. In Kuwait, you will find chocolate pralines in Chanel logo wrappers, although it is unlikely that the Chanel headquarters in Paris is aware of this. To celebrate a child's school achievements, or simply the end of the school year, parents traditionally order a beautiful tray of sweets with the child's pictures on each of the little wrappers, which the proud boy or girl joyfully offers to teachers, family, and friends.

Food artistically arranged on a plate, served on elegant china, and accompanied by a matching napkin is more appealing than a plastic-tray meal, even if they offer the same nutritional value. Similarly, gifts handed in a pretty giftbag and colourful tissue paper bring more delight than those packed in plain brown cardboard boxes, whatever their content might be. Have you ever been treated with extra attention at a public authority office just because you had put on a suit jacket instead of a worn-out sweatshirt? Kuwaitis understand that it is human nature to judge a book by its cover. They take appearances to the next level.

There are really three things that matter in this country: your family name, your connections, and the air you project around yourself. They are all part of the theatre of life.

If you belong to one of certain families, people typically assume you are powerful and wealthy. Some will go out of their way to show respect even if you are a third-degree poor cousin of the prominent sheikh, because they don't know for sure. And others might display their resentment, presuming that you have become rich through corrupt means. The intimidating phrase 'Do you know who I am?' gets the message across more often than not.

The significance of one's surname became evident to me one day when I arranged to meet Corrina at the zoo. She had also invited other friends, an American woman and her Kuwaiti husband. In one of the first sentences he uttered after saying hello, he bluntly asked me: 'Is your husband Kuwaiti? What's his family name?'

It appears that in some regards Kuwait is not much different from the village in which I grew up. It is enough to mention someone's name, and everything about that person becomes obvious: if they are *haadar* or *bedu*, whether they come from a Sunni or Shia family, that family's social status, their business connections (petrochemicals, car dealership, construction industry, or perhaps they belong to a tribe associated with bringing in slaves from Africa), whether they originate from Iraq, Iran, or maybe they have Yemeni or Saudi Bedouin roots. Learning someone's last name is like peering into a magic crystal ball, revealing their past and future.

In comparison, within the expatriate community, people are often put in a box based on a simple question: 'What do you do for a living?' or 'What does your husband do?' For many women, being asked about their husband's job right at hello makes them see red. The following question goes: 'Which school do your children go to?'

One of the expat mothers in Kuwait created a Facebook sub-group with the purpose of organising meet-ups of its female members with children in cafés or diners. The administrator posted a supposedly open invitation for all women in the main group to participate. However, over time it became apparent that she would ignore requests to join sent by Arab or Indian women, and the group became an American-British mutual appreciation society. One of the mums whose request to join was met with silence later complained on the bigger forum, writing: 'At gatherings here, cliques are very apparent and if your face doesn't fit, it never will!'

I witnessed a situation at a playground where one mother stopped interacting with another after discovering that her child did not attend the one and only most prestigious private school. Similarly, only select friends are invited to certain children's birthday parties. Neither is the work environment free of discrimination among colleagues. Elisa, who is Romanian, works as a teacher at a large private school. Every year, at the end of the school year, the school's owner throws a dinner party in a restaurant to thank the staff for their work (this gesture would have been charming if attendance wasn't mandatory and workers weren't held accountable for being absent). One year, Elisa arrived at the restaurant and searched the crowd for familiar faces. She approached a table where two British teachers from her department were already sitting and asked, 'Is this place available?' 'For the moment, yes…' she heard in reply. Especially among expatriates, it is plain to see how false the motto of diversity and equality is about which the West brags so loudly. People may not openly admit what they truly think, but eventually, the truth will come to light.

$\sim$

Appearances are a powerful tool in achieving objectives. They have helped Kuwait influence, manipulate, and outsmart big politicians equally with insignificant immigrants who came here for two-year work contracts. But scratch the surface, and an altogether different picture emerges – one that reveals the intricate complexities of Kuwaiti politics and society, a realm of secrets, hidden stories, a depth and diversity.

Kuwait is a country that offers keen observers a magnifying glass through which they can grasp the prevailing realities around the world. What happens here happens everywhere in the world in varying shades and degrees, but it becomes particularly vivid in this small country. If we were to replace the name 'Kuwait' with Sweden, Britain, Switzerland, the American dream, or Canada, we would be confronted with similar images and arrive at similar conclusions.

An open mind and discerning eye can lead to surprising insights. We have the capacity to question, investigate, peel back the layers, and challenge the illusions that adorn the surface, if we are only brave enough to try.

By delving beyond the superficial, we not only embrace the richness and diversity of each individual, attempting to see them for who they truly are without relying on stereotypes or preconceived judgments, but we also gain insight into hidden agendas, schemes, and manipulation techniques, and ultimately develop the ability to guard ourselves against malevolence. We catch a glimpse of the truth that lies beneath.

About the Book

Julia Firley unexpectedly found herself living in the Middle East, interacting with people from diverse cultures, backgrounds, and ethnicities. Their life stories fascinated her and compelled her to document and share them with others.

In her book, Julia presents stories of perpetual expatriates, natives striving to change their world, and the country they inhabit. We witness how some of these people were able to find happiness and serenity despite considerable obstacles and daunting challenges. Yet, others fell prey to deception, paying a high price for their kindness, gullibility, or greed.

The cast of characters includes a German girl escaping her past, a French woman who turned her life around after her husband left her for a less demanding, younger partner, a Slovak who traded herself for grand promises that proved to be lies, a European man who became a polygamist, and an American Southern belle who made a home in this region. We also meet the locals who stood up against radical ideas and censorship, and the intellectuals who resigned themselves to servitude and duplicity. Lastly, we learn how taboo mentality deprives people of their basic needs and rights.

These tales promise to inspire and move readers as they reveal the depth and complexity of human experiences.

Alongside these true stories, the book provides facts and analysis that should provoke cause for concern, because what happened in this small oil-rich state is a pattern recurring in many different countries worldwide.

LIBERTY IN PRINT